CROSSING
THE WAKE

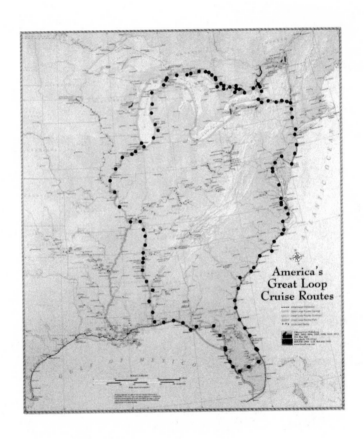

America's
Great Loop
Cruise Routes

CROSSING THE WAKE

one woman's great loop adventure

TANYA BINFORD

MCP Books, Minneapolis

MCP Books
322 First Avenue N, 5th floor
Minneapolis, MN 55401
612.455.2294
www.MCPBooks.com

ISBN-13: 978-1-63505-237-4
LCCN: 2016910902

Distributed by Itasca Books

Cover Design by C. Tramell
Typeset by Lydia Fusco

Printed in the United States of America

I dedicate this book to Yvonne Louise Villa, who died of cancer on November 27, 2012

Disclaimer

Great chefs can make wonderful broths out of a multitude of veggies and beef, or maybe chicken. These stock soups are boiled down and refined, so the resulting taste is intensified. What may start in gallons becomes distilled into tablespoons. Such is the truth of the memoir.

This book chronicles six months of my single-handed Great Loop journey of 5,000 miles in 2014 and has been refined to a couple hundred pages, with numerous drafts and edits to intensify and refine the flavor. What is the Great Loop? It is the circumnavigation of the eastern United States by water and those who attempt this voyage are called Loopers. I have done my best to keep it interesting, without adding extra spices, but allowing the flavor of each story to speak for itself by leaving out the mundane parts. By no means does this book represent my entire journey. Do you really want to know when I learned to pee standing up into a portable urinal because I couldn't leave the helm after my autopilot died?

This is my story, colored by my own lens, including my mistakes, experiences and world view. My memory is not the same as anyone else's. In the parable about the elephant in a room with five blind people, each will describe something different, depending on which part of the elephant they feel. This is my version of doing the Great Loop, the way I experienced it, felt it, and lived it. Every other woman who has done the Great Loop has her own experience—very different, and very real, which is her story. In life there are not two of us with the same story, which is the very thing that makes life interesting.

1

Dreams

Sometimes a path is laid out for us. My own path opened when I went to nursing school where I met a close friend, Vonnie, ten years my senior. She had left California State University in Hayward, where she was pursuing her bachelor's degree in nursing, to come to Chabot Community College for an associate's degree. She'd heard Chabot produced better nurses. She wasn't concerned about the degree; she just wanted to be the best nurse she could be.

We were a small group, less than forty students. Most of us were older, with an average age of thirty, my age at the time. We all had life experiences that we brought to the table. I was divorced with two kids, qualified for Section 8 housing and food stamps. I had a supportive boyfriend, who occasionally brought over groceries, and if I was completely financially strapped, he'd "loan" me money, meaning he'd never ask for it back.

With a five-year waiting list for Section 8 housing, I would never receive a reduction in rent. I wasn't planning on being poor for that long. The food stamp allocation was based upon my qualifying for Section 8 housing, whether I had it or not. I was paying $920 a month for rent, but Section 8 thought I should pay $280, based on my income. Based on the $280, I received $57 a month for me and my two children for food stamps. Hence, I was grateful for my boyfriend dropping by periodically with groceries, or fixing us dinner at his house.

I can do the math a hundred times, and to this day, I don't know how I managed to keep a roof over our heads or food on the table.

The last assignment we had in nursing school was to write down three goals we wanted to accomplish within the next five years. The first two were easy for me: work full-time day shift and buy a house. The third goal was much more difficult. One of my classmates whispered to me, "Tanya, just write anything down; write something that will make the teacher happy." So I wrote, "And go back to school to pursue my bachelor's degree." At the time, I had no idea how powerful it could be to write out my goals, even if I didn't mean it. I hated school; it had always been a struggle for me, and returning to school was the last thing I thought I would ever do.

After graduation, we had to take National Certification exams to become Registered Nurses. Additionally, we had to submit paperwork to the State Board of Nursing for our licenses. The process could take three months from our graduation date. Vonnie and I were in the first graduating class to take the computerized test and received our results in eight weeks.

Two significant things happened when I graduated: first, I was evicted from my house for having a dog, not for lack of paying my rent. The eviction notice came a few months before I graduated, and my landlord agreed to let me stay until graduation. The second significant event was my boyfriend breaking up with me. He threw me a big graduation party and then said he wanted to date his hair stylist. OUCH!

Vonnie and her family made adjustments in their home to accommodate me and my children. We wouldn't be homeless during the waiting period while I took my National

Certification Exam, applied for my nursing license, and found a job. Vonnie and I took our exams together and received our passing scores on the same day. We celebrated our well-deserved achievements!

While living with Vonnie, I went on a date with a handsome sailor. Dave lived in a small coastal town, Benicia, California, which sits on the Carquinez Straights, in the San Francisco Bay area. We had met many years before, when I was married and also lived in Benicia. Dave asked if I wanted to go sailing with him. I jumped at the opportunity and asked Vonnie to take care of my kids.

I arrived in Benicia before the sun came out and met Dave at his dock and we boarded his sailboat. I remember the layout of the boat more than the size, with two benches in the cabin. I can think back, realizing that it must've had a diesel engine because of the pedestal ship's wheel, which we sat behind. There was a safety rail around the front of the boat. Most importantly, I remember how he handled her, as if he and his boat were one. The plan was to sail to Sausalito, have a picnic lunch on the boat, then sail back to Benicia. The sailing was exhilarating. I loved the feel of the wind coming through my hair and the smell of the sea. When I was at the bow, I could feel the salt spray on my face. I'd look back to the stern and see Dave at the helm smiling. We anchored near Sausalito and ate our sandwiches. The wind and weather changed as we were sailed back to Benicia, slowing down our homeward stretch. The sun set behind us and as the evening got cold, Dave wrapped his arms around me to keep me warm. I felt safe and secure on his sailboat, melting into his arms. He had grown up sailing and handled his boat with confidence.

Until that day, the idea of sailing was beyond remote for me. Sailing was a hobby for rich people, or well-to-do professionals like doctors and lawyers, not ordinary people. Dave was not rich. He had grown up sailing, and it came naturally to him. Dave could never imagine his life without a sailboat, even as I could not imagine a life without my kids.

Dave called a few times after our sailing trip. What I recognized was that as much as I could have easily sailed into the sunset with him, I needed to focus on my children and find stability. Had I run into Dave before having children or after my kids were grown, we could have sailed the world together. The memory of our day together has always stayed with me, a small spark, waiting to be ignited.

Six months after my sailing date, I moved to Tucson with my kids so we could be closer to my mom. I put my sailing dreams on hold indefinitely. My kids, Dean and Shayla, were my priority, and I needed Mom's help to navigate the challenging teenage years. At 11 and 13 they were already a handful—latchkey kids lacking supervision when I was working various shifts.

The concept of sailing lingered and blended into the background of everyday life. I'd talk to my patients and ask about their dreams; sometimes I'd share my own. My own dream may have started with meeting a handsome sailor and sailing off into the sunset. Over time, the dream changed to just me sailing off into the sunset. Who was I to expect someone else to share my dream? Maybe I gave up on meeting a special man, or maybe I just decided that I shouldn't rely on other people to live my own dreams. Perhaps I was being practical and realized I wasn't likely to meet a sailor in the Arizona desert.

Over the years, I visited Vonnie in California. I remember her and her husband Bill arguing about what to do in their free time. When he'd say something about going fishing, she'd respond, "If you want to go fishing, GO!" He'd tell her that he wasn't going without her. They spent their days working, and Bill never went fishing.

At age 59, Vonnie died from bone cancer. Her children, grandchildren, mother and paternal grandmother all survived her. When I flew out to California a month before she died, I didn't recognize the frail body in the wheelchair, but her voice boomed forth as strong and clear as ever.

A month later at her funeral Bill said to me, "Once everyone has gone home, I'm going fishing."

I smiled at him and said, "It's about damn time." Whenever I think of Bill, I hope he is out fishing and I imagine Vonnie is smiling.

Vonnie's death hit me hard. It was difficult to hold myself together on any given day, even when I was working. I cried for months, until finally I met a counselor to help me through my grief.

After nursing school, Vonnie and I both moved closer to our parents and we became the best nurses we could be. After moving to Tucson, I did go back to school and became a nurse practitioner. Having achieved my goals after my associate's degree, I needed to set new goals and reevaluate my future. My kids were growing up. By the time I graduated with my master's degree, my daughter was 21 and my son was 19. I was a young grandmother.

I went through school with a vengeance, taking extra classes each semester, going to school in the summer, and doing everything possible to minimize how long I'd have to suffer. I wished I was one of those people who liked school. Nonetheless, my education allowed me to do the work that I love.

For ten years, I worked as a registered nurse in psychiatry. As a psychiatric nurse practitioner in the state of Arizona, I could work in public mental health or have a private practice. I started with both and quickly gave up the private practice, as I was terrible at collecting money. Ironically, my public mental health practice was paying for my bad business decisions in private practice.

Over the years, as I worked hard, I noticed too many of my friends coming down with serious illnesses in their fifties. I also had patients who died young of cancer or heart disease. One of my favorite doctors died the week he was retiring from many years of teaching at the university hospital.

As I approached fifty, I wondered what I might do differently if I died before I reached sixty. If I were lying on my deathbed, would I have regrets? Do any of us know when that day will come? What would I have done differently? How many people have I known who put off their dreams until retirement, then don't live long enough to enjoy their dreams?

I decided to come up with a mid-life plan. When my mother retired early from her job at IBM, she took a year to travel around the world. My sister, a college professor, takes sabbaticals every few years. She has traveled to more countries than I can count, with plans to visit the Arctic and Antarctic during her next sabbatical. I'd have to quit my job to implement my midlife dream.

2

Negotiating Contracts

In 2008, I was negotiating my contract with the CEO of the company where I worked. Jim looked more like a cowboy than a CEO, wearing Wrangler jeans, boots, and hat. Over a few years, I had gone from employee to subcontractor. Yet, we were negotiating my becoming an employee again. Jim wanted to give me the position I had designed that was part-time administrative and part-time clinical, so I would stop looking at alternatives. I said, "You want me to be in a committed relationship with this company?" He said, "Yes, that is what I want."

I told him, "I don't have a good history with commitment, but I'll give you five years."

"What's happening in five years?"

"When I turn fifty, I plan to go sailing for six months. Maybe more."

Cynically, he replied, "Sailing? Where will you be doing that?" To be honest, this was a reasonable question, as we were having this discussion in Benson, Arizona, surrounded by hundreds of miles of desert.

"I don't know yet." I wasn't sure how I'd go about it. I lived in the desert, worked in the desert, and grew up in the desert. I'd been on a few sailboats when I lived near the San Francisco Bay, but I'd never been on the water for more than a day or researched the sailing lifestyle.

For a long, silent moment he looked directly in my eyes. I wondered who would blink first. Finally, he said, "Okay, then.

I'll take the five years, as long as you come back after your sailing trip."

I'd love to say I stayed with that company for five years, but destiny was not so simple. In 2010, the bid for our public mental health geographical service area was given to a "for-profit" company, and my company was virtually demolished, with the exception of a few clinics that were reduced in size. I was spending half my time in administration and the other half seeing patients. The mental health clinic in Nogales, where I had worked for many years was closing completely. Our building was leased to one of the three new mental health agencies.

As the closures happened, my next conversation with our CEO was if I'd be willing to stay with the old company and change clinics. I chose to stay with the patients I had known for many years in Nogales. I loved each of them, and treated them like I would want my own family to be treated.

The new behavioral health authority had a new motto, patients would have a "voice and a choice." It sounded good; however, a small, rural community that once had one clinic for mental health services now had three competing clinics. Our Nogales clinic was divided, some of us staying in the same building with a different name etched across the front door and some employees moving to new clinics. During the months leading up to the change, the stress impacted everyone in our office, from our patients and staff to our clinic director, Maria. As much as we all wanted a smooth, fluid transition, such ideas were impossibly delusional. All of the company switches took place overnight.

On November 30, 2010, early in the afternoon while I was trying to see the last of my patients, an administrator barged into my office to take my computer. Crawling under my desk by my feet to unplug the lines, he seemed oblivious to patient care. The clinic was chaotic. Staff members took home their personal belongings, so they could bring them back the following morning without anything being thrown away. The staff boxed and labeled medical records, sending them to the corporate offices in Benson. At 5 p.m., a cleaning crew tossed anything left behind. There was animosity between some staff who'd stay in the building and those who'd go to different clinics. A few people completely lost their jobs. None of us knew what the future held for us in public mental health. The one goal we had in common was to take care of our patients. This glue would hold us together after the chaos and hopefully repair the hurt feelings.

With the new company, I'd see patients in Nogales, but I'd also be working in Bisbee and Douglas, two other border communities in Arizona. As it was impossible to drive to all three locations, I'd see my patients through videoconferencing, also known as telemedicine. It wasn't ideal, but I could live anywhere with good Internet.

Once again, I found myself negotiating a contract with a new CEO. Having agreed on an hourly rate, I wanted to negotiate the term of the agreement. "One year, to be continued monthly."

Fred, the CEO curtly responded, "Three years, to be continued monthly, with a three-month clause for either party to end the contract."

"How about two years?"

"No. Three years."

"In two years, I want to go sailing."

"Three years."

"Okay, I'll postpone my sailing trip for a year, but I want two weeks off every quarter." We agreed and settled. Over the next month we fine-tuned the contract. I didn't have any history with Fred, and he didn't care about my goals or dreams. He had a business to run, period.

I still didn't know anything about sailing, but was ready to move to Southport, North Carolina. I had found the small coastal town after drawing a line on a map, heading east from Arizona. My grandmother had lived in North Carolina and I loved all the trees. When my grandson was eight, I took him on a trip to North Carolina and the Outer Banks. As much as I loved the many lakes, I wanted to live on the coast. Living in the desert had made me intolerant of cold weather, so I chose one of the southernmost towns, known for sailing. After the announcement of the work changes, I spent my vacations planning my move. I fell instantly in love with the small town. For the first time in my life, I felt this wave of relief come over me that I was home. Southport was far enough south to still be relatively warm in the winter, but not too hot in summer months. It would be a huge change for me. I'd miss my family, friends, and co-workers. Yet, it felt right; this was my chance to live where I wanted to live, without any restrictions.

In July 2010, while spending a month in Southport, I bought my house. Between August and November, I flew to Southport monthly over long weekends to paint. The master bedroom was fuchsia, a very passionate color. The rest of the house was fluorescent yellow. Granted, I paint a little outside the box, so I can't complain too loudly. My color pallet changes like a chameleon with every house I own.

After the change in companies, on the 1st of December, I went to Yuma for training at the new corporate office, then drove to North Carolina and set up my home office. Dean, my grown son, came with me, both of us looking forward to new beginnings. In his early twenties, he had struggled with addictions and bad choices and was ready for a fresh start in life, where his past wouldn't define him or hold him back. Together, we'd learn about boats.

3

Boating

The spring after we arrived in Southport, Dean and I rented a boat. The best way to learn about boats was by being out in one. Dean really wanted a jetboat, a larger version of a jet ski. Every time I'd been on a jet ski it ended with me dragging it to shore. Granted, I'd only been on jet skis a couple of times, but they didn't leave me feeling warm and fuzzy. My good sense failed me, or at least arguing with my son did. We rented the jetboat, with twin engines and seating for four. Our plan was to go up the Cape Fear River to Wrightsville Beach, 25 miles north. Alan, who rented the boats, suggested we stay close to Southport. Dean was determined, though, and asked if it was possible to go to Wrightsville in the boat. Alan agreed it was possible and the plans were made. We had nine hours to make a 50-mile trip in a boat that could easily do 30 mph. It seemed pretty straightforward.

Alan made sure we had life jackets, reviewed basic information about the boat, and sent us on our way. Anyone with half a sense about boats could probably see our plan had disaster written all over it.

We powered up the Cape Fear River, with Dean at the helm, oblivious to any of the dangers of the river. We had looked at a map and knew enough to go through Snow's Cut, just north of Carolina Beach, which connects the Cape Fear River to the Intracoastal Waterway. If we missed Snow's Cut and stayed on the Cape Fear River, we'd end up in Wilmington. North Carolina is known for shallow waters where boats run aground frequently. We didn't know anything about staying in channels, which are dredged so boats don't run aground. Somewhere south of Snow's Cut, we noticed our boat was taking on water, and we were slowly sinking. Dean's plan was to keep the jet boat on plane, riding above the water as much as we could, to keep the water level from rising. We were outside the channel in shallow water and didn't even know it. We aimed straight toward Carolina State Beach Park and pulled into their small marina. As we slowed down, the boat filled quickly with more water. We called Alan, and he agreed to bring us another boat. Later, Alan told Dean that a plug was not replaced in the exhaust manifold during scheduled maintenance.

During our two-hour wait for Alan, we bought a chart book of North Carolina waters and dreamed about all the places we could go if we had a boat. Alan brought a center console fishing boat with an outboard motor to replace the jetboat. By now, it was the middle of a very hot day, and we were only halfway to Wrightsville Beach. We steered through Snow's Cut and headed north in the Intracoastal Waterway (ICW). Everything seemed to be going well until we came to an abrupt stop. Our depth sounder read 34 feet so we thought we had plenty of water beneath the hull. We stopped the outboard motor, pulled it out of the water, and everything looked fine.

Dean jumped into the water to look under the boat to see if he could find the problem. We were both surprised when the water came to just above his knees. Had we known anything about the Intracoastal Waterway, we would've realized we were outside of the channel and our depth sounder wasn't working. In this part of the ICW the water depth is less than 17 feet in the deepest parts at high tide. In the Cape Fear River, where container ships come in from the ocean, the depths can reach 50 feet. We had indeed run aground. Dean was able to push the boat into deeper water, and we started paying more attention, trying to stay between the green and red channel markers. Finally, we reached our destination and turned back to Southport.

Our trip south was not without problems. As we approached Snow's Cut, the oil alarm went off, so we stopped at Joyner's Marina near the eastern entrance to Snow's Cut and asked about getting oil.

The man at the counter in the office asked us, "Two stroke or four?"

We simultaneously looked at each other saying, "What?"

"The motor. Two stroke or four?" He rolled his eyes at us, as if we had just fallen off the back of a turnip truck.

"Not sure."

Feeling stupid, we called Alan, who told us to just bring the boat back; the engine would probably be okay.

Amazingly and despite ourselves, we made it back to Southport in one piece, and we both wanted to do more boating.

4

Our First Boat

My son explained that if we were to get a boat, we'd need a handheld VHF radio. Most boaters generally have these radios not only to call each other, but also marinas, bridges, and if absolutely necessary, the Coast Guard. They are an essential part of boating and safety. Even if we bought a boat that already had a VHF radio, it was always good to have a portable radio as back up. If the battery died on a boat, the built-in radio might not work.

In our little town we have a couple places to buy marine equipment. Dean had given me clear instructions on what I should buy. I went to Blackbarry Marine where a salesman asked, "What can I do for you, Sweetheart?"

"I need a VHF radio."

"And what are you planning to do with it, Sweetheart?"

"I'm buying a boat, and my son says we need one."

"Honey, are you going to be heading offshore or just boating around here?"

"Around here, I guess."

"Sweetheart, you don't need a VHF radio. Just use your cell phone." As he walked back toward his co-workers, I felt like they were laughing at me.

I returned home empty-handed. Dean was angry, not at me, but at the salesman. We drove to West Marine, a chain marine store, 45 minutes away. The salespeople were knowledgeable and friendly. Over the next few years, we'd only ask for Jim, the salesman who first helped us out.

I paid $1,000 for my first boat. She was an old junker, a waterskiing boat with an inboard/outboard motor—a gas hog. Unfortunately, like a junk car, she wasn't reliable. I didn't have a trailer, so we paid rent for a slip. Mostly, Dean and I would cruise the waterways together. Dean was more daring and sometimes would go out fishing alone. A couple times I took her out without Dean, but never unaccompanied. Eventually, when our junk boat died, we found someone to tow us into Deep Point Marina next to my neighborhood.

A guy in town, whom we fondly named "Yankee Bob," was great with outboard motors. Since we didn't know much, we thought he could tell us if the inboard/outboard motor was worth fixing.

I arrived at Bob's shop and explained the situation to him. "So, you don't have a way to get it to the ramp? And no trailer either?"

I replied, "No."

Bob shook his head in disbelief.

When another gentleman in the shop overheard our conversation, he spoke up, "I can use my boat to tow her over to the ramp."

Bob added, "We can use my trailer." It was settled, we had a plan.

I was grateful for the kindness of these men, whom I had never met before. "How long will it take to get my boat to the shop?"

"A couple hours."

"Oh. Well, I have to go to work, so I don't have a couple hours today."

Bob asked, "What about tomorrow morning? How early do you get up?"

I told them I could be up anytime. At the crack of dawn, the following morning, I met Bob and Dan at the marina. At the boat ramp, we pulled it out of the water and took her over to Bob's shop. Bob took one look at the motor and told me it wasn't worth salvaging. I had a worthless boat! I'd have to move it off Bob's trailer. One of Dean's friends offered to store the boat at his house until we could scrap it or sell it.

Within a month, I bought my second boat, an older 17-foot Bayliner Trophy, a fishing boat with an outboard motor. She had a small cabin with a V-berth for sleeping and room for a portable toilet. I thought Yankee Bob would be impressed with the outboard, but he wasn't. He told me I should have asked him before buying a boat with an outboard motor, as there are good outboards and bad ones.

One way or another, I had another boat in the water. Dean and I took it up to Wrightsville, up to Wilmington, and around Oak Island. My fuel costs were half the cost of what I paid with the first boat. Dean went fishing whenever he could, but I still lacked confidence in going out alone. While I was working, Dean had plenty of time to practice his boating skills, but as much as he tried to teach me, it came across wrong and I would get frustrated. One of Dean's friends went out with me to give me advice and teach me a little about boating. His friend taught me how to handle the wakes of other boats and rules of the waterway. I was learning more about current and wind.

Within a few months we had problems with the outboard. The motor wouldn't turn, so our dockmaster, Jesse, took me to

Wilmington to look for used motors. A gentleman approached us and asked what the problem was. Jesse explained the issue, and we also mentioned my junker boat, which was sitting in my friend's yard taking up space. The guy offered to take the ski boat in exchange for fixing the outboard motor on the Bayliner.

Going fast in a fishing boat wasn't my idea of a great time on the water. Nor was I a fisherman. The Bayliner handled well at higher speeds, but she wasn't a boat for moseying around to see the sights. Fishing boats are designed to get you where you want to fish and then get you home just as fast as you got to your favorite fishing hole.

After a year in Southport, during my Christmas vacation, Dean and I decided to take a road trip south to Key West in my red Volkswagen Eos convertible. On the way we stopped in small towns along the coast, following the Intracoastal Waterway. The ICW is like a freeway for boats along the East Coast. It is more protected than the ocean, meandering down rivers and manmade canals like Snow's Cut. Sometimes, the ICW crosses bays and inlets. Technically, the northern end of the Atlantic ICW is in Norfolk, Virginia, and the southern end is in Miami, Florida. We met many people who had traveled the ICW south along the Atlantic coast in their boats during the fall and traveled north during the spring. One of our dock neighbors, Mark, cruised his sailboat to Marathon in the Florida Keys.

After Dean and I left Key West, we stayed with Mark on his sailboat in Marathon for a few days. He was at the city mooring field with two hundred other boats on mooring balls. Many were waiting for a good crossing to the Bahamas. Some boats were enjoying the warm Florida winter, including Mark, who'd be returning to Southport in the springtime.

While staying with Mark, Dean fell in love with the idea of living on a sailboat. On the ride back to Southport, he looked up sailboats on his smart phone. We bought a small sailboat, a 28-foot custom cutter with a Honda 8 hp outboard motor with service records. Theoretically, she was a boat we could live on for six months. What caught my eye was the beautiful handcrafted interior. I paid less than $10,000 for *Carolina Girl*, and then I arranged sailing lessons. Had we only taken the sailing lessons first, I would've bought a very different sailboat. Buying a boat because of prettiness wasn't practical.

My boats were getting more expensive, but in reality, these boats were teaching me and Dean lessons that we'd be hard pressed to learn in a college classroom. Dean wasn't exactly college material and had dropped out of high school, so I justified the expense with giving him skills he might use to earn a living. Eventually I'd have to stop supporting him.

Dean took to sailing like a fish takes to water. When we first moved to Southport, he commented about sailors being less than manly. His attitude and appreciation for the art of sailing changed quickly; realizing it takes more of a man to sail than to run a motorboat. After a month or two, Dean moved onto the sailboat and became the live-aboard skipper of my third boat, sporadically letting me take the helm. I was funding his boating education, but not my own. My comfort level on boats was not improving as quickly as I wanted.

5

The Great Loop

For me, the only benefit of Dean living at the marina was that he met interesting people. One day, he talked to a couple doing "The Great Loop." Knowing my dreams of going sailing for six months, he told me, "Mom, I found the perfect trip for you. It's called the Great Loop. You leave from anywhere on the Loop, and your destination is where you started. For the most part you're near land."

"Okay. Start from the beginning. What's the Great Loop?"

"From Southport, it's a route that goes up the Atlantic coast, through the Great Lakes, down rivers, around Florida, then back up the Atlantic coast, ending in Southport. Waterways are connected the entire way. You'd see the eastern half of the United States from the water." He was very excited, and it was hard to get him to slow down. "When you finish the loop it's called 'crossing your wake' because you cross through the same waters which you left behind in your wake when you started the trip."

Trying to visualize a picture of the United States in my head, I asked, "How do you get from the Atlantic Ocean to the Great Lakes?"

"The Erie Canal. Look it up online where you can see a map."

As Dean learned more about sailing and went on his own adventures, I read about the Great Loop.

It was clear that the concept of "sailing off into the sunset," my original idea, was not very safe. I wasn't going to be comfortable by myself sailing through the night, into the ocean and away from anything familiar, like land. I like being around people. Sailing into the sunset was a romantic notion, but not practical. The Great Loop seemed more reasonable. I'd still see plenty of sunsets. At night I'd dock or anchor under the stars in a small cove. I could take my time and visit towns with character like Southport along the waterways. From everything I read, it looked like "Looper" boats traveled on a buddy system, two or three boats together. Most boats were 35 to 45 feet long, comfortable for couples. Single for over twenty years, traveling with somebody was not part of my plan. I wasn't going to spend my life waiting for that special person. What if I never met him? I'd die regretting all the things I didn't do. I needed to live my life now. I could buy a small power boat that I could handle alone. I entertained the idea of having Dean join me for the first month of the Loop, until I became comfortable. But could I ever get comfortable on my own if Dean were with me?

6

Ranger Tugs

One evening after work, I walked into the kitchen and found a Ranger Tug as the screen saver on my laptop computer. It was a small trailerable trawler with everything I wanted in a power boat. In the fall of 2012, there were two used 25-foot Ranger Tugs for sale near Charleston, South Carolina. One was a 2009 model, the other a 2008. The 2009 boat was out of my price range, but it was pretty and I liked the color. We decided to drive to Charleston to get onboard and see both boats.

The 2009 Ranger Tug was beautiful. The owners had invested a lot into preparing her for weekends in Charleston, like a condo on the water with brass insignias and custom monogramed towels next to the sink. However, the boat didn't look like they ever took her anywhere. A forest of growth was trailing off the bottom of her hull. We wondered when the hull was last cleaned. Were the owners more interested in the decor than in her running condition? For the Great Loop, that was over 5,000 miles, I needed a boat that ran well, not one that looked pretty at a dock.

The 2008 boat, *Pea Pod* was in better running shape, although not as pretty. Both boats had less than 100 engine hours, showing that neither had been used much. *Pea Pod* was a guy's boat, nothing fancy, just the basics. If anyone had slept on her, it was probably in a sleeping bag. The first boat had custom sheets and linens, with a soft, inviting V-berth, while *Pea Pod* had the standard, uncomfortable four-inch cushions. Outdoor speakers were mounted to the cabin frame, and the fish locker had a small attached table for gutting fish. ICK. We took *Pea Pod* for a trial run on a cold, windy, rainy day. This little boat definitely gave me something to consider. Could I live on this small of a boat for a year on the Great Loop? Dean thought she'd be an easy boat for me to handle by myself.

In December, I made an offer on *Pea Pod*. We scheduled the closing between Christmas and New Year's Day, to give me time to bring her up from Folly Beach to Southport. The boat trip would take four days during the cold, winter weather, as long as I could avoid storms. I built in extra days, just in case. The broker offered to deliver her to Southport for me, but I declined. I also refused Dean's offer to come with me. As long as I planned to spend a year on this boat by myself, I had to start by handling four days on my own.

Before arriving in Folly Beach to pick up *Pea Pod*, I installed the Automatic Identification System (AIS) to show nearby boats that transmit the AIS signal. My son and I had a close call with a container ship when we brought *Carolina Girl* from New Bern to Southport. We had left Wrightsville Beach in the evening, and as we motor-sailed south on the Cape Fear River approaching Southport in the middle of the night, we saw bright white lights. We thought they were range markers and lined up in the centerline of them. Dean called the Pilot Station to determine if there were any large ships around and found out there was indeed a large container ship at our exact location. We barely managed to get out of the way before we heard the five bone-chilling blasts warning us to get out of the way. We could feel the air shift, as the freighter moved by, barely missing us. They used their spotlights to find us after we passed. Of course, that close call was before we took any lessons, when we were still new to boating. In that moment, as we recovered from the thought of being hit by a container ship and dying in the Cape Fear River, we vowed always to have AIS on any boat we owned, no matter how big or small.

At the closing, the boat broker gave me the keys to *Pea Pod* and offered a second time to come with me to North Carolina. Maybe he sensed my anxiety. I agreed for him to crew for the first day, which would take me across Charleston Harbor and to Isle of Palms. That evening, after we signed the paperwork, we went to West Marine to buy a new radio for *Pea Pod* with an iPod port. Since I was going to spend four days on the boat, I wanted some music.

Standing in the West Marine store looking for the right radio, I answered a call from one of my friends from work. "What's up?" I usually don't hear from co-workers while on Christmas vacation.

"Did you hear about Mike?" He was one of my patients whom I'd known for many years and one of the most tormented people I'd ever met. Despite working from North Carolina through telemedicine, I still felt very connected to my patients in Arizona.

"What happened?"

"I don't know the details, but he killed himself. I guess his dad found him."

"How is his dad doing?"

"He's having a tough time. He wasn't at all like Mike had described him."

"And his daughter?" Mike's biggest fear was having his daughter find him. Over the years, we had talked a lot about her. She lived with her mom, had been a straight-A student, graduating with honors. She was his pride and joy. His eyes always lit up when he talked about her. As much as he loved her, he also felt like he was a disappointment to her and wished he were a better father. Sometimes he thought she'd be better off without him.

"I don't know."

It was bound to happen sometime, with Mike's history of suicide attempts, usually under the influence of vodka. I often wondered if he had schizophrenia, and not just severe depression; he was adamant and fearful about what kinds of medications he would or wouldn't take, not wanting to feel like a walking zombie.

My friend continued, "I hope I haven't interrupted anything."

"I'm picking up my boat in Charleston."

"Oh, I should let you go then."

"Thanks for letting me know about Mike. Give my condolences to his family. I'll call you in a couple days."

I needed a few moments to think, to get my thoughts sorted and keep myself together. I sat down on a nearby chair. Tears welled up in my eyes, and I told myself that I could cry later on the boat.

The broker asked, "Is everything all right?"

"No. One of my patients died. I knew him for many years. He was a good guy."

I stood up and we took the radio to the checkout counter. The broker took me out for a quick dinner before returning to *Pea Pod*, but my mind was elsewhere. He dropped me off at the boat and said he'd call in the morning. Major storms were coming through that night, and we weren't sure we'd be able to leave the following day.

My first night on *Pea Pod* was in Folly Beach, getting ready to move her north toward home. It was a very stormy, cold night. Between the lightning and thunder, the winds, and sleeping on the four-inch cushions that felt more like wood, I hardly slept. Of course, I also lay there thinking about Mike. I was still struggling from Vonnie's death the month before. Mike reminded me of Vonnie's second husband; both were tortured souls. Sid was a Vietnam Vet, which I believed had contributed to his suicide. I had no idea what sparked the darkness in Mike. I had never met anyone so hell-bent on killing himself, yet through his tormented darkness, I saw his kind heart.

Mike and I didn't have the easiest start of a therapeutic relationship. When I first met him, he was on court-ordered treatment. I was sent to the residential facility to verify he was taking his medicines and give him refills. As he saw me approaching, he said, "I don't want to see you, and I don't want your fucking meds."

"I don't blame you. These meds can suck."

"You should just leave."

"Mike, you're on court order to take these meds, and I'm ordered to make sure you take them. When you get off the court order, maybe we can work to reduce them or find different medications that don't give you side effects."

Month after month, Mike tolerated my visits until his court order expired, then he moved to a different city, where another psychiatric provider saw him. A few years went by, then I saw Mike again when I started working in Bisbee, after the company changeover. When I read his name on my schedule, I wondered if he still saw me as the enemy. I wondered how he'd been during those few years.

Mike still struggled, "Tanya, I knew you always cared, so I was glad to see that you were working here." He wasn't on antipsychotics anymore and refused to consider them, even though I thought it might be the one thing that could've helped him. He didn't qualify for any services except for medication management. I wanted him to have additional supports, like therapy, but there wasn't any funding in our public system for him—only medications and case management. The idea of seeing him every three months was bullshit. I met with him every week or two when he wasn't doing well. The last time I saw Mike I was a flat picture with a voice from the computer monitor. As he was walking out the door, I called out, "Mike!"

He looked back at me. "Yeah, Tanya."

"You know I love you."

"I know. Thank you." Then, he turned and walked out of the clinic's telemedicine office for the last time.

I couldn't have had that conversation with him if I were there in person—not with a guy anyway. But with videoconferencing I could get away with it. I don't know how many of my patients ever hear those words—that they are loved. I wanted them to know they always had a place in my heart.

There was a time when I didn't tell my patients things like that, a time when I tried to have better boundaries. One afternoon, as I watched a patient get a candy bar out of the candy machine, I felt like the window of heaven had just opened and I was sitting at the edge of it. I felt an incredible amount of love and wanted more than anything to tell my patient I loved her. But the rational part of my brain stopped me when I imagined the trouble I'd get into. It was bad enough that I hugged my patients. At that moment when I walked by her, I looked into her eyes, smiled, then went into my office, closed the door behind me, and cried. I had no idea where the overwhelming feeling came from. Later that day, my patient choked on a hot dog at a barbecue and died. I thought later that perhaps the window of heaven had really opened and I didn't recognize it. That day I decided I wouldn't let another moment like that slip by again.

Through the first troubled night on my boat, dreaming of friends and patients who had passed on, the morning crept up on me. The weather conditions had not improved overnight. I drank my coffee, had breakfast, and waited patiently for the storm to subside. I talked to the broker, and we decided to reevaluate the weather at 9 a.m. By then, the weather had cleared, the sun came out, the winds subsided, and we were able to leave the dock within the hour.

I asked the broker to let me do all the driving and docking, but to give me verbal directions and advice. While I was at the helm, he installed the replacement radio for me, so I could connect my iPod. We stopped three times that day, the first for fuel, the second for lunch, and the third at Isle of Palms Marina. All three docking experiences went well.

Docking always makes me nervous because there are so many things I can't control. A word of advice goes something like this, "Don't dock faster than you want to hit something." Docking is a controlled crash. Meanwhile, it is important to use enough power to overcome current and wind. I don't know that any two docking experiences are ever the same.

The broker's wife picked him up at the Isle of Palms Marina that afternoon. I left alone early the following morning with a long way to go. I'd been to Georgetown numerous times, so I decided to take my boat further north to Wacca Wache Marina, where I'd heard about a good restaurant. I arrived just before sunset. Docking alone didn't go as smoothly as it had with the broker onboard. The dockhands first wanted me in one slip, but then changed their mind when they realized which side of the boat my power was on. With the cold temperatures, the water would be turned off at the docks for the night to keep the pipes from freezing. The restaurant was more limited in menu choices than during peak season. The first three things I tried to order they didn't have. I finally settled on stuffed Portobello mushrooms with a glass of red wine. In the middle of the winter, darkness comes early, by 6 p.m. It wasn't much later than that, when I went back to my boat to study my charts for the next day on the ICW. I was neurotic about writing down each and every marker I'd be seeing, as well as any possible problems. If I read about a channel where the current was strong, I wrote it out in my notebook. Mile by mile, channel marker by channel marker, I planned out each day.

As predicted, the night was brutally cold. Fortunately, my cabin had two forms of heat. I could turn on the heat pump or portable electric heater. When the boat was moving, a small fan circulated the heat from the engine through the cabin. In the morning, ice on the wood docks made them slick. My next stop would be Myrtle Beach Yacht Club. It was New Year's Eve, and a great way to end one year and begin the next.

Approaching the yacht club filled with expensive yachts was intimidating. I hung my fenders out to protect my hull.

Fenders are inflated rubber balls or cylinders that protect the sides of boats against piers, pilings or other boats. The dockmaster gave me directions to a slip close to the clubhouse. I requested assistance as I was by myself. The slips were tight, my heart was racing and, thankfully, I pulled the bow of my boat into the slip without hitting anything. Once I was tied into the slip and had turned off my engine, I sat for a couple minutes in my captain's seat, just breathing, proud that I had docked without any boat damage. Then, it dawned on me that I had completely forgotten about my bow and stern thrusters which could have really helped.

I walked up to the office where another boater was signing in. He and his wife had docked their boat directly across from me at the same time as I had pulled into the marina. The older gentleman knew me and was apparently one of my boat neighbors from Southport. "Aren't you Dean's mom?" He startled me, as I wouldn't have expected to run into anyone I knew, or who knew of me, through my son.

He and his wife had an annual tradition of coming to the Myrtle Beach Yacht Club on New Year's Eve and they invited me to join in their celebration. I declined their generous offer, deciding to plan out my fourth and last day, when I'd arrive home in Southport. The three Southport boats were much larger than *Pea Pod*, making her look more like a Volkswagen Bug next to an RV.

I left the Yacht Club before anyone else was up. I gently floated out of my slip, quietly idled forward, out of the marina and into the Intracoastal Waterway. Early in the afternoon, I arrived at Indigo Plantation Marina in Southport, pulling into my slip as gently and as quietly as I had left Myrtle Beach that morning. I was home. I was safe. I had navigated successfully from Folly Beach. Although it was still chilly outside, the sun was shining down on me and my boat.

7

The Plan

From the time I bought my boat, I had planned one year and three months to get ready to embark on the Great Loop. Each year there are two rendezvous for Loopers—one in May in Norfolk, Virginia, and the other in October in Rogersville, Alabama. To prepare for my trip, I'd attend the October Rendezvous, then the one in Norfolk when I started on the Loop.

My three-year contract for telemedicine in Arizona transitioned to a monthly contract in November 2013, allowing me to continue working until April, when I would embark on my adventure. I researched ways to work part-time while I was on my trip because I hated the idea of leaving my patients, especially in Nogales, where I had worked for so many years. I had shared my plans with my patients and our staff, taking a "sabbatical" and calling it my "midlife plan." I couldn't count the conversations I had with my patients about achieving our dreams, planning to make them happen.

Working full-time as a nurse practitioner, my income was more than sufficient. I was able to save enough money and plan this trip, so it wouldn't affect my lifestyle. With a home equity line of credit, I knew that I could financially handle any emergencies. My daughter, Shayla, insisted that I come up with a budget. However, I knew that if there was something that I wanted to do, like go to a fancy restaurant or take an expensive side trip, nothing would stop me. I couldn't plan for the unexpected.

The Countdown List:

April 2013: Give one-year notice to work. Start preparing patients for the changes.

Prepare boat. What will I need? What do I need to change? What works for me? What doesn't?

Start anchoring out, practice docking. Weekend trips.

October 2013 — Great Loop Rendezvous at Joe Wheeler State Park in Alabama. Meet other Loopers — (Who are these people? What are they like?)

January through March 2014 —Closure with my patients for my trip; figure out how to take care of my house and my dog.

The chatter in my head went like this:

"Can I really do this?"

"Of course, you made it through the teenage years with your kids, right?"

"This is different."

"Is it? Just a different set of challenges. Probably easier."

"I can do this!"

"Breathe, just breathe. You can do it."

The reality of the situation was that I was still formulating a vision of my plan. Living in Arizona, it was difficult to envision any kind of boat trip. I knew a boating adventure was out there, but couldn't see what it looked like. My voyage was a hazy shadow of something in the mist. In moving to Southport, I was able to start sketching what a trip would look like. If I were an artist, I would have started drawing out my trip in pencil, starting with the sailboat, then using my eraser, as I recognized that sailing wasn't going to work for me. Eventually, I would paint a clear/tangible vision with acrylic paints or watercolors. My vision was becoming clearer and more tangible.

My friends and acquaintances all knew about how I planned to go on the Great Loop. I was meeting other boaters. Many people asked me about the wisdom of going by myself; mostly out of concern for my safety.

During the spring of 2013, I started going out on my boat more frequently, trying to get more comfortable. I was wary about going out if the winds were over 10 mph. Most of my trips were up and down the Intracoastal Waterway on beautiful, calm days. I paid more attention to the tides. My plans were smoothly coming together. I had moved my boat to Southport Marina where it was easier to get in and out of my slip, as well as being less expensive.

I changed the name of my Ranger Tug from *Pea Pod* to *Annabelle*, after my eight-year old granddaughter. I added feminine touches like scrolls on the side, to make her prettier. Dean helped get her ready.

One evening, I got a call from the local police. I was watching TV in my pajamas, before going to bed. Dean had taken *Annabelle* out and gotten into an accident. I threw on some clothes and drove down to the marina. Dean was not injured, but there was significant damage to *Annabelle*. He had taken *Annabelle* to Bald Head Island and hit the steel pilings outside of the entryway. Fortunately, he was able to motor back to Southport Marina. I was devastated and angry. I had left Dean with the keys so he could work on *Annabelle*, not so he could take her out on a joy ride. No matter how strong the currents or the reasons for the accident, he crossed a line by taking my boat. Dean's risky behavior and cockiness had reared its ugly head and I'd be paying the price.

Dean was preparing to leave the following week for several months as a first mate on a 67-foot trawler. Meanwhile, *Annabelle* would need to be repaired. There had to be consequences for Dean, so I decided to sell *Carolina Girl*.

Repairs would take over three months and I wanted to get everything done that I could. During the process, she'd have a new paint job, get stronger, bigger cleats on the side decks, and they'd put Weaver davits on the swim platform for my dinghy. When she was finished, *Annabelle* would be a stronger, sturdier boat. Some changes I made I'd never use, like adding cable connections to watch TV while at the dock.

I wrote a limerick as I struggled with my emotions related to the accident, dedicated to Dean:

Words of advice for your travels.
Navigate well through the channels.
The ATON you hit,
may force me to split
with cash, as my savings unravels.

Within a week of the accident, I boarded the ferry for the Bald Head Island Marina, across from Southport, to meet other Loopers, Kat and Kermit, from Ohio, aboard *Good Karma*. Kat, about my age, continued to work while on the Loop as a consultant and writer. She is considered young in the world of Loopers where most of the boaters are retired. Their boat had a comfortable salon that accommodated eight of us. Compared to *Annabelle*, their boat felt like a mansion to me.

On *Good Karma* we had a great dinner with Kat's sister, who had been aboard with them for a vacation, and two other Looper couples. Everyone contributed to the meal, from appetizers to dessert. For me, the best part of dinner was dessert, a pecan pie with chocolate chips. The three Looper boats had been traveling together for several months. This was my first glance of the Looper lifestyle. During their stay at Bald Head Island, they would ride bikes, spend time at the beach, and share meals. They planned their next stops, sharing ideas of what they wanted to do or where they wanted to go. Sometimes the women went shopping while the men watched football. They had become good friends while on their journey of a lifetime. I hoped that I could form similar friendships when I did the Loop.

April was a big month for me. It started with giving one-year notice to leave work. Dean had the accident in *Annabelle*. Last, but not least, I met people doing the Loop. A year can seem like a long time, but often flies by quicker than we expect.

By the time I got my boat back into her home waters in Southport, I'd only have a few months to practice my skills before the weather started getting cold and wintery. My trip was getting closer and closer. My list of things to do was getting more and more specific. As I crossed off each item, it felt like I added two more. Would the list ever end? Surely it would, come April 2014.

8

Great Loop Rendezvous, October 2013, Alabama

October was proving to be a busy month. I was scheduled to go to the Great Loop Rendezvous in Alabama, and the following week one of my friends was getting married in Hawaii. I'd leave a day early from the rendezvous to catch my flight to Hawaii. All the travel was overwhelming; I felt like I was running a marathon.

I arrived in Nashville, Tennessee, where I rented a car to drive down to Joe Wheeler State Park near Rogersville, Alabama. The park had a lodge, golf course, and marina; the setting was spectacular. The temperatures were cool, in the 60s. Meeting new people always makes me a little nervous. There were a couple hundred people and 30 or 40 boats. One couple had a Ranger Tug like mine, but most people had larger boats. Although a lot of people knew each other, there were also new people like me, who didn't know anyone else. Part of the Rendezvous included meals where we'd sit at large round tables sharing plans and stories.

A couple at my table, Barb and Ross, were still looking for a boat to do the Loop. After the Rendezvous, they'd buy their Loop boat, *Attitude Changer*. Another couple, married less than a year, was in the process of building a solar-powered trimaran for the trip. Although the wife had never been around boats, she nervously supported her new husband. I sought out people single-handing the Loop thinking we'd have a different set of challenges.

Each night a different group of Loopers would introduce themselves—color coded name badges distinguished where people were in the Loop process: people wanting to do the Loop, people doing the Loop, and people who had completed the Loop. Everyone was told to line up on each side of the speaker podium. People shared who they were, who would travel with them, their boat name and make, and either a fear they had or something unexpected they experienced. Some Loopers were matter-of-fact and others told a quick story. The gender roles were well-defined, with the occasional outlier. In general, the men were the "captains" of their boats, and the women were the "admirals."

I spoke toward the end of my line, hesitant to stand in front of the crowd. When I approached the microphone, I quickly said my name, my boat was a 25-foot Ranger Tug, and I'd be starting the Loop in April, from my home port of Southport. As I started to step away from the podium and hand back the microphone, the moderator stopped me and added that I was brave by doing this trip by myself. I just wanted to get back to my chair at the side of the room, near the exit. Many people in the audience stood up and clapped. Weaving through the tables, on my way back to my seat, different women stood up and hugged me. It was humbling. After dinner several men approached me, telling me how proud they were that I'd be doing this trip on my own. During the week, one gentleman suggested several times that I consider going with someone. He told me that there were moments I'd want to enjoy with someone special in my life, even as he had enjoyed the companionship of his wife on his trip. If he had a list of preparations for me to make, it would've included Match.com or eHarmony. I could tell he meant this with all sincerity, which was different than some people I had met in my town, who felt that I couldn't do this alone because I was a woman, or that boating is a man's thing to do.

During the week at the Rendezvous I did not encounter any male chauvinism; I only encountered genuinely caring people who were impressed with my desire to do the Loop.

One afternoon as I was going from one seminar to another, a woman approached me. Debi said she had a book for me about women boaters. As we were both going to different seminars, she invited me to stop by their boat for a drink. Debi was the captain of *Sea Fever*, boating was her passion, not her husband's. They had been doing the Loop for 13 years, slowly but surely, while running several businesses.

I met Jim, a Canadian, doing the Loop on his own. His wife, Wendy was working and he had recently retired. Throughout the trip, numerous people crewed aboard his boat; he rarely traveled alone. Initially, I met him at the docks as he was saying goodbye to friends who had spent the last two weeks with him. His boat was smaller than many other Loop boats, bigger than mine, but not spacious like Kat and Kermit's boat. His boat was practical with a V-berth below with room for two people to sleep. He had a bench in the main cabin, where a third person could sleep. His boat was not as well-equipped as mine, but it had been a police patrol boat that he had modified for his needs. Jim's boat's name was *Bluenoser*, and thereafter I thought of him as *Bluenoser* Jim. He'd prove to be a great friend as I did the Loop. Jim was laidback and easygoing. We agreed to keep in touch and exchanged boat cards, which are similar to business cards, except they usually have a picture of the boat and personal contact information.

One evening as I was returning to my room, I met Malcolm, almost ten years older than me, handsome and fit, who was also single-handing. He was doing the Loop very differently than I was. He had a speed boat with a small cabin and was thinking about buying a larger boat. With a few years left before he could retire, he was moving his boat along the journey short distances when he had time. Being a corporate pilot, he couldn't take a year off or even a few months. We didn't have much time to talk; he was leaving the Rendezvous the next morning. I gave him my boat card, and he said he'd get in touch with me, as he'd love to have someone to go boating with, and he thought we appeared to be the only two single people in the entire Rendezvous. I'd later tell him we weren't, and his comeback was, "The only single people under the age of sixty."

Over the next few weeks, Malcolm emailed me, and we made plans for him to come to Southport for a long weekend. He had Marriot Rewards points and could stay in a local hotel. He showed up on Friday evening with dinner from a local Italian restaurant which we enjoyed on *Annabelle*, docked next to the boat ramp. Although it was private and quiet, it still felt very public and safe.

For the next couple of days, we took *Annabelle* out. Malcolm questioned if I had tried this or that. One of his questions was if I had showered on her. The bathroom, also known as a head, had about four square feet of standing room, about half the size of my shower at home, maybe a quarter size of a guest powder room or half bath. I thought it should be called a dime bath. I had anchored out overnight, but had never showered on my boat. As we cruised down the Intracoastal Waterway, he turned on the water for the handheld shower nozzle. An incredible stench of algae had grown in the water lines, due to lack of use. The water lines looked like they had a bad sinus infection with green, smelly, snot coming out. I thought I would vomit as I reached my head out the window at the side of the helm. I could only imagine how Malcolm must be feeling inside the bathroom.

Being a gentleman, Malcolm called forward and said, "Tanya, we have to clean these lines out when we get back to the marina."

I was shocked and surprised. He didn't mind helping me with cleaning the lines. For the next fifteen minutes or so, he ran water through the plumbing, trying to flush out most of the slimy green algae. After returning to the marina, we drove to Wilmington to buy cleaner for the water lines and flushed them some more. I learned a valuable lesson about boats; it is important to take care of all the systems, including the plumbing.

Over the next few months as I prepared for the Loop, Malcolm became a close friend whom I could bounce ideas off. We became romantically involved, but knew that commitment was not on the table, at least not until after I finished the Loop. We read the same boating books and magazines, and had similar dreams for the future. Even Dean, who was usually protective of me, thought Malcolm was perfect for me.

The holidays came and went in a blur. I spent a few days at a psychopharmacology conference hanging out with two friends from Tucson, and shared my ambitions. The reality of my upcoming adventure was hitting me. For years we came to this conference together, and the next year I wouldn't be joining them; I'd be on the water.

Lucy

9

Mi Casa es Su Casa (My House is Your House)

One of the bigger decisions a person needs to make about going on an extended trip is what to do with your house and your animals.

Some Loopers return home every couple weeks or months and check on their mail and their homes, say hello to their families and friends, and then resume on their journey. For these people, they have to figure out transportation from varying spots along the way, often from remote, rural towns. A few Loopers sell their homes, buy a boat, then sell the boat when they are finished and buy a new home. Other Loopers have family members live in their home while they are gone. I knew I had to do the Loop in one long piece; there would be no breaks between. Unlike most Loopers, I had to return to work when I finished, and not working would cost me significantly more than the cost of doing the Loop. I was not comfortable leaving my house vacant for up to a year. I love my house, my neighborhood, and my community—I wanted somewhere to come home to.

My border collie, Lucy, hates water, and was too large for my little boat. It was not fair to her to take her on my trip in such a confined space. I also didn't want to be responsible for getting her to shore a couple times per day. There were times on my trip I wouldn't know where to land with her. My friends didn't want to take care of Lucy for a year, and asking for that type of favor seemed a bit much. Boarding her at a kennel would be unfair to her and costly. I asked around Southport to find a foster, but couldn't find any. Most people suggested I take Lucy with me.

What I needed for my trip was someone to watch my house and my dog.

One morning, one of my neighbors was walking by my house with her two small dogs. We talked for a few minutes, and she asked what the plan was for my house when I went on my trip. I said I didn't know, and short of finding someone to stay in my house, I'd leave it vacant. She suggested I contact the people who owned the vacant lot next to my house, as they were planning to build their home during the time I'd be on the trip. I asked her to give them my number, and I imagined that this could work out for all of us.

A couple weeks went by, and I got a phone call from Glen, my future neighbor, who was retiring from the police force in Virginia. He and his wife would be moving to Southport in April and hoped to start the building of their home, next to mine. A few weeks later, he came down to meet me and take a look at my home. We discussed the terms of them living in my house which were simple; they would take care of my home and my dog as if they were theirs. They'd cover utilities and other costs of living in my house. For instance, if there were something small that needed fixing, like a faucet, they'd fix it. If it were a major repair, like a furnace, I'd cover the cost. My furniture and belongings would stay in the house, and most of their belongings would be in storage, except for their bedroom furniture. They'd handle my mail and let me know when a bill was due. There are some bills, like property taxes, which I paid in advance, and most of my other bills were on auto pay through my bank.

Three boats were leaving from Southport for the Loop in 2014. Each of us chose different options how to handle our homes. Mark and Jane sold their home in Ohio, came to Southport and bought a lot in my neighborhood, where they planned to build a home when they finished. Tom came home to Southport periodically throughout the Loop. While on the Loop, I met people who had left their home vacant. This worked for some and not as well for others. One couple told me about going home to find their countryside home infested with mice.

As for Lucy, the plan was great for her. She felt as if she got to keep her home and get an upgrade on her owner. Glen and Beth have a little dog, Coco, which they spoil. One day while having lunch with them on a restaurant patio, Coco was sitting on Beth's lap eating French fries off her plate. Perplexed, I said, "You encourage your dog to eat off the table?" I wondered what I'd be coming home to with Lucy, who'd never eaten from the table and was told to leave the premises if she was caught begging. Lucy would be well-cared for and very spoiled when I returned.

As I was preparing for my trip, my friend Richard, who does maintenance at the marina next to my neighborhood, invited me to a sale at the marina where boaters could sell or trade possessions they didn't need anymore. He mentioned Jane and Mark on a boat called *Average Looper*, whom I might want to meet and gave me their boat card with a picture of their boat and contact information. Unfortunately, I'd be out of town during the sale. I emailed Jane and invited them to a house concert that I was having that weekend. Though my house was within walking distance of the marina, I offered to pick them up.

Average Looper was a 48-foot cabin cruiser with three sleeping areas and two bathrooms. It had enough cabinets to store food for an entire winter. The three of us were about the same age, but they had recently retired. Mark had been a fire chief, and Jane had worked in the public schools. Their children were grown and they had young grandchildren. They had sold their home in Ohio and were considering moving to Southport when they finished the Loop. Mark and Jane stayed in Southport longer than they had planned. There was no reason to cruise further south when they planned to go north for the Loop. They liked Southport and bought a lot in my neighborhood, where they decided to build their new home when they finished the Loop.

They bought *Average Looper* in Maryland and brought her down to North Carolina. They had never owned a large boat before, and most of their boating experience was waterskiing on a lake. Jane had ideas about what she wanted in a boat that she would be living on for a year. Her boat had amenities I could only dream about: a bathtub, a washer, a dryer. Mark had hoped for a slightly smaller boat, but to keep Jane happy, they bought the larger one.

We got along well and agreed to start the Loop together. I joked that I might be stalking them, following behind them throughout the journey. They laughed, knowing that Loopers will travel together when it makes sense. My boat was much smaller than theirs, couldn't go as fast or handle the seas like theirs could, but these were minor glitches. I was nervous about the Loop and thought that having a buddy boat would make the trip easier and safer. I'd feel more comfortable as I gained skills and confidence.

The winter seemed interminably long. Beth and Glen moved into my house at the end of March while I went to Arizona to finish work and say goodbye to my friends and family, who I wouldn't see for up to a year. After returning home, I stayed in the guest bedroom to finish my preparations. On April 10th, I moved onto my little *Annabelle*. I could still come and go from my house, do laundry, and run errands with my truck. The weather was cold, rainy, and windy. It was hard transitioning from my warm, spacious home into the small cabin, the size of my bathroom. Since *Annabelle* was only 25 feet long, and eight and a half feet wide, including the back, front, and side decks, I was in tight quarters.

I arranged my clothes in baskets in the front portion of the V-berth near the bow of the boat and used the three feet closer to the main cabin as my bed. Being shorter than the average ten year old, just under five feet, I slept across the three by six foot area with my head on the port (left) side and my feet to starboard (right). There wasn't any extra room to spread out, and I had to watch my head on the back corners of the dashboard. I cut a four-inch memory foam pad to fit my sleeping space, so I'd be more comfortable. Gear which I thought was indispensable filled every nook and cranny. If it weren't for the open layout, I would have felt claustrophobic. When Malcolm and I had spent time on *Annabelle*, she wasn't filled to the brim with gear.

The heat system on *Annabelle* was nothing compared to the central heating in my home. Her thin fiberglass walls lacked insulation. With windows all around the cabin, and six ceiling hatches, *Annabelle* felt like a fishbowl. The summer sun could heat it quickly, but in the winter all the warm air escaped. My boat heater worked overtime keeping the small space toasty.

My Looper friends and I planned to start our journey on April 15, Tax Day, but the torrential rains didn't stop, so we held out for better weather. During our days of waiting, my Canadian friend *Bluenoser* Jim arrived in Southport. He had completed three quarters of the Loop, and wasn't as wary of weather as Mark, Jane, and I. Throughout the Loop, Jim had different friends and family aboard and rarely traveled alone. We kept in contact through email, and he was one of my biggest supporters, encouraging me and providing sound advice. He arrived in Southport with his wife, Wendy. I was excited for him to leave Southport with us, before dropping his wife off in Wrightsville Beach, where she could fly out of Wilmington to go home.

Dean decided to come with me as far as Wrightsville Beach, where Glen would pick him up. He wanted to start the Loop with me on my boat, even if it wasn't for the first month, like we had originally thought about.

After weeks of torrential rain, we had our first clear day, April 21st. We prepared to leave Southport Marina at 9:30 a.m. With Dean at the helm and the engine powered up, I released the last point of attachment, and pulled the teal line into the cockpit. After years of preparation, the finger pier looked barren. The memories of my docking blunders fluttered in my mind, like hummingbirds around a feeder. My mind wandered ahead of me, thinking about the Cape Fear River which lay beyond the marina's entrance, and the rising tide which would boost *Annabelle's* speed. I glanced into the cabin at Dean. He was wearing a pirate-themed shirt. I wished he could come with me for the first month of this trip, but knew it was for the best to be on my own. Pushing him out of the nest wasn't easy. I had to cut the cord. I was too comfortable giving him control. The minute he started telling me what to do or how to do it, I'd get frustrated and hand him the helm, to avoid arguing. Soon, the spray from the river would be hitting *Annabelle's* blue hull and the smell of brine would be filling my lungs. With a twinkle in my eye, I inhaled the fresh air like an old man inhales a cigar.

Suddenly I heard an explosion. We weren't ten feet from the dock when Dean yelled, "Mom, get the fire extinguisher!"

I grabbed the red canister from above the sink, perplexed as to what had caused the loud noise, and ran back out the door into the cockpit. Scanning *Annabelle's* perimeter, I saw a fire coming from the outboard motor of a fishing boat at the ramp beside my slip. Dean pulled the throttle back into neutral, then into reverse, to get me closer to the fire. The top of the fishing boat's outboard motor housing had blown off.

I yelled over at the couple whose grandchildren were with them, "Are you okay?" The fire was already out. The fuel must have burned quickly; they didn't need any help. Dean pulled *Annabelle* forward and we took her to the fuel dock to top off with diesel for the trip. Frazzled and shaking, I hoped this wasn't a bad omen.

Bluenoser waited for us in the river, then we radioed *Average Looper* waiting for us outside their marina. Once past Deep Point Marina, *Annabelle* led the way up the river. Beth and Glen stood on our neighborhood pier taking pictures as we passed. As we motored north on the river, we passed the Southport/Fort Fisher Ferry Boat heading south. The ferry's captain hailed me on the VHF radio to wish me well on my journey. It was one of those moments when you just know you've taken a huge first step after years of preparation: from first making the decision to go sailing or boating for six months, to telling people about it, to moving from Arizona to North Carolina, to learning about boats, to quitting my job, to finding Beth and Glen to live in my house and watch my dog while I was away, to finally leaving on the Great Loop adventure.

I looked over at Dean, and he looked back at me. With tears in his eyes, he said, "You going to be okay, Mom?"

"I'll be fine." On the outside, I was trying to portray a calm demeanor, but my heart was racing, and my palms were sweaty as I left my home waters behind.

"I'm glad Mark and Jane are traveling with you. Stay with them. They'll watch out for you."

Before I left, Dean made sure I had things on my boat that other people might not ever think of including: folding mast steps so I could reach the ceiling hatches, and cam cleats to keep my lines pulled back to the cockpit, where I could easily access them. He had sailed through the Caribbean Islands, gone through the Panama Canal, and was first mate on a 67-foot trawler that he navigated up the East Coast. Dean learned some of his boating skills from the best of Southport, like our TowBoat U.S. Captain Jon. We had taken sailing classes together on *II Dolphins*, with Captain Ed. Although Dean was never good in school, when we competitively took the ASA Sailing tests, his 99 percent scores surpassed my own. It wouldn't have been so bad except that I was the one who had to do all the studying. For him, even the physical aspects of sailing and boating came easy. As much as we bickered when we boated together, I'd really miss him.

As we approached Wrightsville Beach, twenty-five miles north of Southport, I pulled up beside *Bluenoser*, so Dean could catch a ride to shore. Jim planned to stay at Wrightsville Beach overnight to take Wendy to the airport. After a couple days, Jim planned to catch up with our boats. Jim was antsy to get home and attend his niece's June wedding. He wouldn't be sightseeing or going to the Rendezvous in Norfolk. Having wintered in the Bahamas, his mission was to get home to Penetanguishine, Ontario, Canada.

With *Bluenoser* safely docked, *Annabelle* and *Average Looper* cruised north and went under our first bridges together with Jane obsessively recalculating how fast we should go to make each bridge opening. Many bridges only open at certain times, like on the half hour or hour. If we missed the bridge by a couple minutes we'd have to wait for the next opening, while trying to keep our boats still in the current, like treading water. The bridges weren't much of an issue for *Annabelle*, which was about half as high, half as wide, and half as long as *Average Looper*. She could easily get under most bridges.

Our first night we stayed at Harbour Village Marina in Hampstead. As I lay down in my V-berth that night, snuggled under my blankets, I looked up at the night sky. The window hatch above me perfectly framed the Big Dipper. I fell asleep looking up at the stars. *If this was what the Loop was all about, it was going to be a great year!*

The following day, we motored to Spooners Creek, just south of Beaufort, North Carolina. *Average Looper* was moving slower than usual on my behalf; Mark and Jane told me their fuel consumption would be better for the slow pace. An easy day for them was a more difficult one for me. Alone, I had to be at the helm for the duration while Mark and Jane could take turns at the helm. Fifty miles was my limit, and seven knots was my ideal speed. Fortunately, we weren't in a hurry. Our initial plan was to anchor in Spooners Creek, but when we arrived, the anchorage was already filled to capacity with sailboats. We ended up at the marina and chalked up another great day on the Loop.

From Spooners Creek, we ventured to Oriental, a great little boating town. We stayed at Harbor Village Marina, which was north of town and had great amenities. They had a loaner vehicle, swimming pool, Jacuzzi, sauna showers, and an extraordinary clubhouse. I'd never been in such a beautiful marina. To celebrate Mark's birthday, we planned to spend two nights here. Jane and I went into Oriental for coffee and shopping. On the chilly morning, we took our coffees and pastries to a park overlooking the water and sat on Adirondack chairs. So relaxing.

The marina had paddleboards available that we could use. Having never been on one before and feeling playful, I tempted Mark and Jane with a bet. Whoever could stay on the board the longest doing the yoga tree pose would win dinner at a restaurant we wanted to go to in Belhaven, a couple of days away by boat. Jane was not interested in the bet. Initially, Mark wasn't either; however, after a couple of beers while reading in the sun, Mark changed his mind. The bet was on, and Jane would be the judge.

Mark and I dragged paddleboards to the water and put on our life jackets. I was overly confident or stupid, sure that I wouldn't fall in the water. I didn't even bother changing out of my blue jeans. Mark was already in his swim trunks since he had been sunning by the pool.

We carefully got onto our paddleboards and pushed away from the dock. Holding my paddle above my head, I executed my best tree pose, with my right foot resting on the inside of my left knee. I didn't have the best form, but it would suffice. It's one thing to try this on solid land, but on water it's extremely difficult. Every ripple in the water affects your balance. I didn't fall in, although I came really close. Mark laid his paddle across his board and executed a perfect pose with his foot resting on his inner thigh. Mark regularly practices yoga to help overcome vertigo. I counted a long list of reasons I lost my yoga bet to Mark that day.

The sun was shining, and we were having a lot of fun. Jane took videos to post on Facebook. As Mark and I approached a boat on one dock, I suggested that we race back to the dock where Jane was waiting for us. I had a 20-foot head start and paddled as hard as I could, but Mark still beat me. I couldn't compete with this not-so-average Looper.

That evening, Jim caught up with us in time to visit friends of Mark and Jane who lived in the posh marina neighborhood. We spent the evening having drinks and appetizers. I learned a lot about these new friends of mine, especially Jim. When he was a young man, he started a career as a bush pilot, flying up into Alaska on floatplanes. He had also flown in South America through the Andes Mountains of Peru.

Early the next morning, our three boats left Oriental together. Jim planned to spend two more days traveling with us before leaving us behind. That evening we found an anchorage in Jordon Creek across from River Rat Yacht Club. I was able to anchor further up the creek than either *Bluenoser* or *Average Looper* since my small boat could find refuge in more protected waters than the others due to the shallower draft on my boat. Each of their boats had three and a half feet below the water line, while I only had two and a half feet of draft. A sailboat moored lazily near the yacht club, a peaceful sight.

Initially, we thought we'd enjoy dinner together. We each had dinghies, so we could easily travel between our boats. However, the winds picked up and storms were on their way. We'd each be on our own for the evening.

My iPad application, Active Captain, shows anchorages and marinas, giving descriptions and reviews. Active Captain also overlays a chart plotter application which makes it easy to find places to spend the night. A boat can't anchor in the channel unless in an emergency situation. At night, anchor lights are mandatory to keep people from running into each other. As currents and winds change, boats will rotate around the anchor point. Thus, it's important that everyone is anchored in a similar manner, so they swing the same direction and don't hit each other. In addition, there are general guidelines for how long a person's anchor line should be, compared to the depth of the water to keep their anchor from dragging and their boat from drifting downstream or into other boats. Longer anchor lines equate to larger swings on the hook. If a person expects rougher weather or sea conditions, more anchor line is deployed. I had fortified *Annabelle's* anchor in preparation for the Loop by using an anchor rated for a larger boat, with sixty feet of chain and a hundred feet of rode, or line. The anchor line barely fit into the chain locker at the bow of the boat. I had practiced anchoring a few miles from my home on quiet weekend nights in still, protected waters. Tonight, I'd see if my practicing had helped. Jim had spent the winter anchoring in the Bahamas and didn't seem the least bit worried; he preferred anchoring to staying in marinas.

By the time the sun set, the rain had started. I settled in and started reading. Within an hour, my cell phone was beeping with tornado and hail warnings. By 9:00 that night, we were in the midst of a major storm, with rain blowing sideways. In a split second, our boats were ferociously whipped around 180 degrees. The only time I could see anything outside was when lightning flashed and lit up the creek. Sitting at my table, with my book in hand, I periodically looked toward shore, to make sure I was still in line with lights from the back porch of a nearby house. After the first tornado warning Jim called to make sure I was okay. Mark and Jane didn't have cell phone reception, so the only way to communicate with them was on the VHF radio, not that we could've heard anything over the torrential downpour. The sounds of the storm came through the thin fiberglass ceilings as loud as a tin roof. By 10:00, I was sound asleep in my berth, oblivious to my surroundings.

I woke to clear skies and brewed a cup of coffee. I noticed that *Bluenoser* wasn't where she had been the night before; I was grateful *Annabelle's* anchor held, upstream of *Bluenoser* and

Average Looper. These were not ideal conditions, but the night proved that I could anchor through a storm. It was only 11 miles to Belhaven where we could walk around town during the day and have a fancy dinner at Spoon River Restaurant that night, the one I owed Mark for winning the yoga-paddleboard bet.

As I pulled *Annabelle* into the town docks in Belhaven, her anchor randomly started deploying. Before I left Southport, Dean tied paracord around the base of the anchor, with a loop to the bow cleat to prevent the anchor from going overboard accidentally. Dean's rationale was based on this exact scenario. So each time I anchored, I had to go to the bow and unloop the paracord. Many boaters told me to always have the anchor ready to deploy from the helm, in case of an emergency. Despite their admonitions, I trusted Dean and appreciated his foresight. My anchor seemed to have a mind of its own. Jim looked at the anchor foot switch on the bow deck and determined it was corroded. He sprayed lubricant/anti-rust solution into the switch. It didn't help, so I had to cut the wire. Until it was replaced, I'd need to drop my anchor manually; a minor problem I could fix in Norfolk, Virginia, at the Looper Rendezvous.

Around 5:30, we walked the two blocks to the restaurant, which had white, blousy decorations, a bistro menu with an accompanying wine store. Over dinner, the four of us reminisced about anchoring and the nearby tornadoes. Mark commented, "Wow, that storm hit hard."

Jim said, "I thought I was going to run into you."

"Was that you? I was in the pilot house, trying to keep track of the sailboat, when, suddenly, I saw a phantom ship appear outside the window. I yelled to Jane, 'Holy shit! You gotta see this.' By the time she made it up to the pilothouse, the boat started to move away."

Jim, in his relaxed, soft-spoken, Canadian way, with a beer in his hand said, "Yup. That was pretty exciting. I came within ten feet of *Average Looper* before I got full control of *Bluenoser*. It's the first time my anchor slipped this whole trip." At this point, Jim had traveled about 4,000 miles, anchoring out more than staying at marinas. "When I realized *Bluenoser* was drifting, I started the engine, and ran to the bow to remove the snubber from the anchor. Once back at the helm, I pulled the anchor up, and put her in reverse. I was worried about slipping and falling, with all the wind."

Knowing that he wore braces on his feet, I asked, "What about your shoes?" Jim had a progressive illness, Charcot-Marie-Tooth disease which affected his ambulation.

Jim said, "I had my braces and shoes on the floor beside me."

I looked over at Jane, "How'd you do?"

She shook her head from side to side, "It was our first time anchoring. I was so scared; I sat on the floor in the salon saying the rosary."

Mark looked over at Jim and added, "I thought it was another boat that had come in from the storm. I wondered how the captain navigated into the shallow creek without running aground. It reminded me of the ghost pirate ship in *Pirates of the Caribbean*."

Perhaps I had been too lackadaisical about the storm, falling asleep and trusting my anchor. I did have a stronger anchor than *Annabelle* was rated for, with extra chain. But would I have noticed if her anchor had slipped? After fourteen years of living with monsoons in Tucson, Arizona, I was used to falling asleep to lightning and thunder. Somewhere between my indifference and Jane's anxiety, was an ideal response to the events of the previous night. A tornado had touched down within five miles of our anchorage.

The following morning, Jim left us behind while we continued our leisurely pace north to Norfolk, with a few days to spare before the Rendezvous. Mark, Jane and I planned to anchor in the Little Alligator River, 56 miles away. Jim rushed to Elizabeth City, 90 miles away, and invited us to visit him when we arrived at Georgian Bay.

10

Albemarle Sound

The night before *Annabelle* and *Average Looper* headed into the Albemarle Sound, we anchored at Little Alligator River. Jane on *Average Looper* had checked the weather forecast; we'd have light winds and one foot wave heights. But for the next few days, NOAA also predicted storms with a lot of rain. If we didn't leave our anchorage that morning, we could easily be stuck at anchor for the duration. We woke up early with the idea of crossing Albemarle Sound before the winds picked up in the afternoon. At 6:30 a.m., we pulled up our anchors to cross the 17 miles. The prediction of the waves and weather were wrong.

As I put my boat into gear, a screeching sound came from the engine compartment. I thought my alternator belt could be slipping. *Annabelle* seemed to be running fine, but if my alternator belt broke or failed, I didn't want to be sitting in the middle of Albemarle Sound trying to fix it. I hailed *Average Looper* and pulled up beside her, with the waves bouncing both of our boats around. We put fenders between our boats, tying them together long enough for Mark to step off his boat and onto *Annabelle.* Jane tended the helm on *Average Looper.* Mark listened to the sound, took a look at the alternator belt, and thought my boat would be okay crossing the Sound. When we arrived later that day at a marina near Elizabeth City, we could take a better look. I pulled up beside *Average Looper* again, so Mark could jump on his own boat and then we all headed toward Albemarle Sound.

The waves were much higher than predicted, at least three to four feet. Mark and Jane called to let me know they were speeding up. Since the waves were hitting our boats broadside, on the beam, we tacked back and forth across the Albemarle, so our boats would rock forward and back, which is more comfortable than rocking from side to side. I couldn't afford to get seasick.

Multi-colored crab traps were scattered on both sides of the narrow channel. My partially bent knees felt like springs, absorbing the energy and helping with my balance. As I looked across the horizon, *Average Looper* was coming in and out of focus, like bad television reception. Sometimes I could see them, as *Annabelle* came up over a wave, at other times, they disappeared behind the water pouring across the windshield, or just looked grainy through the salty residue. I turned on my radar. I usually just wore socks but today, they'd be too slippery, so I wore my boat shoes for extra traction. I wished the water were calm. While trying to avoid crab traps, with both hands on the wheel, my cellphone rang—it was Dean. I'd rather talk to him with a steaming hot cup of coffee, but reflexively, I reached over and hit the green circle on my iPhone. "I can't talk right now; I'm being tossed around like a rag doll."

"Really, Mom? It can't be that bad. Take a video with your phone and send it to me."

"I am not taking a fucking video. I'll call you later." Irritated, I hung up. I didn't have time to debate the concept of wave heights, or how they were splashing up to the blue eyebrow trim above the windows.

As I approached Elizabeth City, on the northern side of the Albemarle Sound, I saw other Looper boats that had spent the night before at a small marina near where *Average Looper* and I had anchored.

I had scoped out Elizabeth City with my grandkids the previous summer. With swift currents and fixed pilings, I wouldn't be comfortable staying at the free downtown docks. I'd have to back into the space, with the stern of my boat, a skill I had not yet mastered. I suggested to Mark and Jane that we go further up the river to Lamb's Marina and they agreed. Soon, the other Looper boats followed, having also decided not to stay at the free docks. Altogether, seven Loopers stayed at the small marina. With changing weather, we needed safe dockage for a few days.

As soon as I docked and turned off my engine, I could hear the bilge pump running and see water pouring out of the bilge drain from my engine compartment into the creek. I dreaded what I would find and didn't want to open my engine hatch until I had someone standing by my side. I walked down the pier and asked Mark if he would look at my engine compartment with me. At first, he told me that he'd come over as soon as he got his boat situated. After I explained how much water was pouring out of my boat, he agreed to come right away. When we opened the engine hatch, we saw water pouring in around my stuffing box, a tubular structure that wraps around the propeller shaft, keeping it lubricated with seawater. A friend's boat almost sank when his stuffing box became loose. He was smart enough to run his sailboat aground and radio for help before he could sink.

Mark tightened the hose clamp where the stuffing box connects to the fiberglass housing for the prop, enough to reduce the water to a fast drip. *Annabelle* was still taking on water, but not at the sinking rate. I needed to figure out the extent of the problems in my engine compartment. I hadn't even been on the water two weeks.

My first thought was that a crab pot on the Albemarle hit my prop, which could have jarred loose the stuffing box. I was pulling at straws. God knows, I did my best to avoid those damn crab pots! However, since I could hardly see out my windows, it was a possibility, not a total shot in the dark.

Don and Ross, fellow Loopers, asked if I had been feeling any new vibrations when I crossed the Albemarle. Perplexed, I responded, "My whole boat was being tossed around. How was I supposed to feel a vibration? I could barely hold on!"

The marina sat off the side of a rural road next to a trailer park. It didn't have any mechanical services, just a gas station and a small grocery store. The marina owners were in the midst of building a restaurant. All the staff was friendly and willing to help in any way they could, but what I needed was a good boat mechanic.

Later that evening, Jane told me that Dean had called her while we were crossing the Albemarle. "Dean was really worried about you. He called to ask if I was keeping an eye on you. I told him we were, but it was hard because of the waves. I told him we had to hold onto things to keep our balance. He didn't seem to believe me and asked if I'd take a video. So, I scooched down the stairs on my butt, then crawled on my hands and knees over to the side windows to take the video."

"Really? You sent him a video? I told him there was no way I was sending a video!"

On her iPhone, the waves didn't look so bad, but she had taken the video on the calm tack, going with the waves versus going against them. When zigzagging across open water to avoid beam seas, the zig can be a night and day difference from the zag. It was the only time she could stand and actually take the video, even if it made us look wimpy.

Jane had bumped her head and fallen a couple times crossing the Albemarle. She said they'd been really worried about me. Short of calling for help, there wasn't anything they could do if I ran into trouble. Ultimately, we can only take care of ourselves.

Over the next few days, different boaters looked into *Annabelle's* engine compartment to help me troubleshoot. Larry and Jan, Loopers on *Panacea,* had hit a log coming down the Alligator River when giving room to a barge, and *Panacea* needed a new propeller. Larry called a marine service yard in Portsmouth, Virginia, to take care of his prop and gave me the phone number so I could have my boat evaluated when I got to Norfolk across the water from Portsmouth.

At Lamb's Marina, Mike, a diver, told me the propeller had a couple dings. He removed the cotter pin and prop nut, but didn't have the leverage or strength or equipment to pull off the propeller. He found a local business to haul *Annabelle* out of the water with a trailer, and borrowed the right tool for the job. I agreed to the haul out, then Mike and I took the propeller to a shop in Norfolk for repair. Additionally, I ordered a spare propeller to be delivered to the service yard in Portsmouth.

During those few days at Lamb's, busy with my boat, I hardly saw Mark and Jane except for the night when *Annabelle* was out of the water on a trailer. When in the water, *Annabelle* was next to the marina office, and I had a steady stream of people offering suggestions. I felt like the damsel in distress, bringing out the protector nature of the men at the marina, not just the Loopers.

John, a sailor about my age was preparing his O'Day sailboat to go south to Washington, North Carolina, with a friend. From Colorado, he worked as a mechanic on very fancy collectible, antique cars. He was tall, well built, with reddish blonde hair. In his spare time, he led kayak adventures and enjoyed skiing. I don't know when I noticed John, or when he noticed me, but we got along well. One afternoon, he took a look at the engine. Mark had tightened my alternator belt, and was still lying on my floor, with his head next to the engine. Mark got up and closed the inside hatch, then excused himself and went back to his boat.

John took a good look from the outside deck hatch. He informed me that I had a bigger problem than the propeller, alternator belt, or even stuffing box. One of my engine mounts was clearly broken, another had a crack in it, and a third could be broken as well; all four engine mounts would need replacing. Wow! Crossing the Albemarle, I only had one good engine mount holding my engine in place. The engine mounts must have been a bad batch, as *Annabelle* was built in 2008, not old enough to have these kinds of problems. Before I left Southport, I had worried about the mounts because they looked rusted, but the Yanmar engine mechanic told me they were fine! I wondered what else he missed.

That evening, when the Loopers were having "docktails," John came out of the marina's bathroom, freshly showered and shaved, and motioned for me to meet him outside. He gave me a big hug and wished me well. He'd be leaving in the morning. We exchanged phone numbers and agreed to keep in touch.

The night before, while my boat was out of the water on the trailer, I had spent the night on *Average Looper* with Mark and Jane. They remarked that if they didn't find me in my bed in the morning, they'd know where to find me. Apparently, my attraction to John was obvious to everyone. John never made any overtures toward me, other than just being kind and hugging me before he left. I liked him and was sad to see him go south while I was going north.

From Lamb's Marina, we motored north on the Dismal Swamp Canal. It was easy to go slow, as the entire Dismal Swamp is a "no wake zone." George Washington designed the canal which was completed in 1805 and used extensively during the Civil War. Lamb's Marina had warned us about debris from many storms in the canal. We still had a few days before the Spring Rendezvous in Norfolk, so we stayed a couple nights at the free docks in the Dismal Swamp.

Once through the Dismal Swamp, Norfolk is just around the bend. The landscape changes from peaceful nature with trees hanging over the canal to an industrial shipping channel full of military ships, barges, and tugs. *Average Looper* was ahead of me. Within a few minutes, I arrived at the Norfolk marina for the Spring Rendezvous. Despite our initial plans on buddy boating, I'd be here longer than they would in order to fix my boat.

The service manager, Ralph, showed up within an hour of my Sunday arrival at the marina. He had called daily to check on the leak from my stuffing box after I left Lamb's Marina. Tightening the hose clamps and the smooth waters had kept the dripping under control. We agreed it would be best if I took *Annabelle* over to Tidewater in Portsmouth with his mechanic onboard, for the short crossing of the Elizabeth River, so he could watch the engine and listen for any unusual sounds. Both marinas were within eyesight of each other. While my boat was out of the water at Tidewater, I could stay on my boat and take the ferry from Portsmouth to Norfolk for the Rendezvous. Once my boat was pulled out of the water, Ralph could look at the running gear, including the prop, shaft, and stuffing box. He'd already ordered new engine mounts.

When I showed Ralph my boat and a map of the Great Loop, he said to me, "This is a great boat. You could take her to the Bahamas, when you get down to Florida." Many Loopers cruise into the Bahamas in the winter.

I looked at him, and said, "I could, but I'm doing this trip by myself, so I don't think I'll be going to the Bahamas."

"Well, you should think about it. The Bahamas are beautiful."

"Ralph, I'd think about the Bahamas, if I had someone to go with, but as a single woman, by myself, I'm not going to the Bahamas."

"But you could."

"I could, but I'm not. Right now, I just want to get *Annabelle* fixed." He finally dropped it and we focused on *Annabelle*.

At the Looper Rendezvous, despite being distracted by boat repairs, I went to navigation seminars, which featured places to go during the next six months between Norfolk and Rogersville, Alabama, where the Fall Rendezvous takes place. I sat with Mark and Jane, Tom from Southport, and

Steve. Mark, Jane, and I had met Steve when he came through Southport on his boat *Atla,* a 32-foot Nordic Tug, more stout and rugged than little *Annabelle.* Like me, Steve was single-handing the Loop. Occasionally his wife or daughter would join him. With the most capable, fastest, sturdiest boat, Tom would have company for most of the Loop.

Being the only single woman doing the Loop, I met a lot of different people. I met men who were planning on single-handing, and couples who were amazed I would do such a trip on my own. From the Alabama Rendezvous, I ran into the same gentleman who felt I should have a companion aboard.

I said different things to people who made remarks like, "You're so brave to do this trip by yourself!"

My inner response was, "You're brave to do this trip with someone." Of course, my outer voice said, "It can't be any harder than raising teenagers." I tried to keep my tone light and not think too much about what their inner voices were saying. A big part of me envied the relationships these couples had. During the short time I had spent with Malcolm, I enjoyed his company, and felt like the two of us worked well together on *Annabelle.* I imagined the Loop could either make or break a marriage, and if I were ever married again, I'd want to be able to get along with my spouse in such close quarters. Most of the couples I met, who had completed the Loop, said the journey brought them closer together. Even the married men, who did the Loop alone, found new hope and appreciation in their marriages by the time they finished the Loop—perhaps it was from the long absence. Most of these men came from my parents' generation where gender roles were more defined. Steve was an exception in many ways; in his mid-fifties and retired from the military, he had spent many years away from his family.

In addition to being a single woman, I was also one of very few people who still had to return to work. Closest to my age, Mark, Jane, and Steve were retired. I couldn't afford to retire yet. Also, I missed the people I worked with and looked forward to returning when I finished the Loop. Some people told me the Loop would change my life and I would never be able to return to the same work. We'd see about that; I was determined to return to work in Nogales, and as far as I knew, they were determined to have me back.

Meanwhile, at the Tidewater Marina boatyard, I was learning more about *Annabelle*. She had more things wrong than I had originally imagined. The fiberglass tube that surrounded the shaft was smashed and broken. The stuffing box hose was oversized for the fiberglass tube, so when the clamps were tightened, the uneven pressure probably broke the fiberglass. The stuffing box hose would have been from the manufacturer. I'd need to replace the stuffing box, extend and repair the fiberglass tube, and replace the cutlass bearing, another tube-like structure that goes around the shaft. Ralph showed me the broken parts, so I could actually see the problems. The list of repairs were extensive, and mostly things that I could have addressed before I left Southport, if I'd only known.

Ralph was great. He let me assist in the repairs, handing tools to his staff, running to get parts, or simply handing them a dry rag to wipe the sweat from their brows. Each morning, I'd have coffee with him or Gaston, one of his staff, whoever arrived first. We'd discuss what needed to be done, and when I was at the marina, I'd do my best to make myself useful.

Despite the many repairs, they were finished in just over a week. I brought my boat to them on a Tuesday morning and left a week later on a Wednesday afternoon, knowing that my boat was now ready to move forward in the Loop.

The Rendezvous ended on a Friday morning. Over the weekend, I watched other Loopers leaving the marina across the water, continuing their journey northward. I wouldn't have the comfort of having someone nearby. I wouldn't have Jane to plan with obsessively. I wouldn't have Mark to look in my engine compartment if I heard strange noises. I was on my own from here on out, and I felt vulnerable and alone.

I was grateful for the physical work of putting my boat back together. Ralph, Gaston, and I worked well together and I could see the fruits of our labors. They were doing everything they could to help me get back on the Loop in a timely manner, in a boat that would be safe.

While working on *Annabelle*, another Looper boat came into Tidewater Marina with damage to their hull and swim platform from the tornadoes two weeks before. Their boat was in Elizabeth City when the tornadoes tore their swim platform off the stern when the boat hit the pier. It would take time to fix their boat and deal with insurance adjusters. They'd have to wait an additional year to complete their Loop, as they'd be stuck in the Chesapeake for the summer.

I had one shot at doing the Loop; this year was it.

Sunday morning after most of my Looper friends had left, sitting on the front of *Annabelle,* 12 feet above ground, looking out across the river at the different boats, Ralph showed up in his pick-up truck, bringing his teenage son who worked as a dockhand at the marina. I climbed down the ladder to greet him at ground level.

As he walked over to *Annabelle*, he said, "Happy Mother's Day."

"Thanks. I'll be making some phone calls."

"While my son is working, I'll take care of the fiberglass repair."

As grateful as I was that Ralph was willing to work on a weekend, I also thought he worked too hard, but I admired that he was teaching his son good work ethics.

"What can I do to help?"

"Not much. If you want to grab one of the open cans of bottom paint from the shed, you can touch up your bottom paint." He told me what kind to look for, so it would match the existing paint on *Annabelle's* hull. There were several different brands and colors.

After working on *Annabelle* all morning, Ralph offered to take me to the grocery store, which was too far to walk or ride my bike. I had been eating well with numerous restaurants within walking distance, plus I had an electrical cord running from the building to *Annabelle* to power the refrigerator.

Ralph drove me to a Harris Teeter grocery store, with deli areas, flowers, butcher shop—a place where I could find anything I wanted. I picked up a few essentials and Ralph bought a dozen roses for his mom and his wife, a Mother's Day rose for the office manager, and a rose for me to put on *Annabelle*.

I cut the stem short and placed it in a plastic bowl, half expecting it to fly across the cabin. A silk lavender plant sat on my table, but this was the first time I had a real flower, with a real scent. I liked the idea of fresh flowers and determined that when I could, I'd have them aboard. Some Loopers grew tomatoes on their boats, and although I didn't have that kind of room, I could have a couple small plants.

After returning to the marina, Ralph left, and I called Mom and, Shayla, my daughter, Shayla was worried that I was getting behind schedule. "Mom, how are you ever going to finish on time, when you're already behind everyone else? Aren't you worried? Who are you going to travel with?"

She mirrored my own concerns, ones I wouldn't dare say out loud. "I'm not that far behind. By the time the repairs are done, I'll just be a few days behind everyone else. Besides, most Loopers went to Deltaville where the marina is throwing a big party."

"I looked at a map, and you haven't really gone that far. Where are Mark and Jane?"

"They're in Deltaville. I think they'll win the dinghy race." I was trying to keep it light. I missed my *Average Looper* friends.

"I wish you had someone to travel with."

"Thanks, Sweetheart." I enjoyed buddy boating, but the reality was that most of the other Loop boats traveled faster than *Annabelle*, and problems could arise anytime for any of us. I just didn't expect it to happen this early.

After hanging up with Shayla, I called Mom, who was trying to meet me for a few days. "Where do you think you'll be on June 1st?"

"I have no idea, Mom."

"Well, do you know the general vicinity? I'd like to meet you in New York City, and go up the Hudson."

"I don't know." Ralph, Gaston and Rick were doing everything in their power to get *Annabelle* back in the water, but there were no guarantees of smooth sailing from here.

Since planning this trip, Mom wanted to spend a week with me. I was ambivalent about having Mom aboard *Annabelle*, not sure how we'd get along. When I was a kid, we used to go camping in our Volkswagen Westfalia, where my parents, my sister and I slept with our two dogs in a similar-sized area. When camping, we could wander off and hike or go fishing, so we weren't in each other's space. This would be different. On the other hand, I did look forward to having the company.

I briefly spoke with my son, who called almost daily anyway.

Finally, Malcolm called, "Hey, Sweetie, how are the boat repairs coming?"

"They're getting there. And you?"

"Busy. Flying a lot. Maybe when you get to New York, I can spend a couple days with you."

"My mom plans to spend a week with me in New York. Have you been out on your boat much?"

"Not enough. I've been too busy with work. I need to sell it and get a different boat." Malcolm had wanted a different boat since I met him at the Alabama Rendezvous. He had a fast boat, and with his limited time on the water, he'd venture out on days I would've stayed home because of weather. He had his boat in dry storage at a marina near Charleston a few hours from his home, affecting when he could use it. Even though I hadn't seen him in months, he was still easy to talk to, especially about boating. He wanted to know all the details of what was being fixed and when I expected to be back on the water.

The forecast for the next few days showed thunderstorms. As I left Tidewater Marina at 3:00 in the afternoon, I couldn't go far. I planned the short trip to Hampton, which was less than a 30-minute drive by car from Portsmouth, but two hours by water—a good distance to see how *Annabelle* ran after all the repairs. I don't know if Ralph and Gaston sensed my anxiety about entering the Chesapeake Bay for the first time without Looper boats nearby, but they offered to meet me in Hampton. Pulling *Annabelle* into the Hampton City Marina, Ralph and Gaston's timing could not have been better. They helped me with my docking, so I could have the stern toward the shore, and installed a shorter antenna on my boat, which enabled *Annabelle* to go under shorter bridges. The connection we needed had not arrived on time to change out the antenna at the service yard.

Before saying goodbye, Ralph gave me a socket driver to tighten my hose clamps and Gaston gave me a spanner wrench/deck key. Their advice was very different from the service yard in Southport, where I was told that the only tools I needed on my boat were a screwdriver and a crescent wrench. The three of us went out to dinner that evening at a local tavern, where we sat outdoors, and they gave me last minute service advice for my trip. They told me if anything happened to *Annabelle*, within a hundred miles, they'd come and take care of it. Beyond that, they were only a phone call away. It wasn't a late night, as Ralph had to get home to his family. We finished our meal quickly, and Gaston walked me back to my boat.

11

Chesapeake Bay

I stayed in Hampton a few more days due to stormy weather. At the city marina, I docked beside *Counter Offer*, another Looper boat. The owners, an older couple, mostly stayed to themselves. We both planned to leave Hampton on the same morning. We compared the charts on our iPads, sharing plans of different anchorages where we could stay on the way to Annapolis, with back-up plans should the weather or seas get too rough.

The morning went well, and I stayed close enough to *Counter Offer* to communicate through our VHF radios. During the afternoon, as the winds picked up, the seas became a little rougher. *Counter Offer* hailed, telling me that they were going to their anchorage. I responded that I wanted to forge ahead, a couple more hours. Finding a quiet inlet, Ingram Bay, I grilled dinner and relaxed for a peaceful night.

Just after 6:00 as the sun was coming up, I pulled up the anchor. The waves were choppy. The further I got out into the Chesapeake, the worse the waves. On Channel 68, I listened to boat chatter from nearby 50-foot sailboats. I watched as they tried to put up their sails, reefed their sails, and took them down. Despite their long, sleek, hull designs, none of these sailboats were riding comfortably. I listened as they considered returning to port, and it wasn't much past 7:00. Within a few minutes, I decided that I needed to find a protected anchorage.

At the next inlet, my chart plotter showed a boat poking its nose out like a turtle's head coming out of its shell, then the boat turned and went back in. I knew it was a small inlet, which looked difficult to get into, but it was better than turning around and going back to Ingram Bay.

As I got closer to the protected opening, the waves got bigger, making the Albemarle seem like child's play. Then, I saw a rogue wave coming toward me, bigger than all the others, seeming to tower above my boat, a wall of water. If I hit the wave on my beam, it could easily capsize *Annabelle*. This was not the time to be making any turns. I had to forge straight ahead into the wall. I took a mental inventory of everything I needed in case of a disaster. Life jacket on. Personal locater beacon within reach. SPOT locater device within reach. Dive knife at the helm. Windows shut. As long as *Annabelle* could get through this, I could too. White-knuckling the helm, I braced myself. I powered up the throttle to get through the wave with good steerage, wanting the momentum on my side.

In retrospect, I'm sure passing through that wave only took a few seconds, but it seemed much longer, like time was standing still. The wall of water completely engulfed my boat. After a moment of complete darkness, the light came through as the rogue wave passed over my front windshield and I could see again. *Gracias a Dios*. *Annabelle* was intact and so was I. Just a little further, a few more minutes, and I'd be in the safety of the inlet.

I pulled up beside a fellow Looper, John, on his catamaran, *Endeavor*. John, in his early seventies, was single-handing as well. He had intended on having more company, but schedules were difficult to coordinate. His wife was not fond of boating, so stayed home. Initially, I anchored near John, but after a half hour of being blown around, I moved further upstream to a small cove surrounded by trees on three sides. I'd spend the day confined to *Annabelle's* small space, despite the green hills around me. I felt trapped. I envied the other Loopers in their bigger boats during anchoring, as they had room to stretch their legs.

John told me that he tried leaving the inlet a little earlier and realized the seas were too much for his boat to handle. He was surprised to see me coming into the inlet and glad I made it safely. I was grateful I had seen him poke his bow out, so I could easily find the inlet. Having another Looper nearby made me feel more comfortable, even if we weren't traveling together. No matter where I went, I had a group of like-minded boaters nearby, each of us with our own set of challenges.

The following morning, John pulled his anchor and went out into the Chesapeake first. He radioed back to me that the waters were calm, a perfect day for boating. His goal was making it to Annapolis. My goal was stopping at Solomons Island to meet up with Looper friends, including Mark and Jane. From there, I'd go to a marina on the southern side of Annapolis, where I planned to meet another friend.

John was right about the weather and the seas. The water was smooth like glass. Just after lunch, as I was approaching Solomons Island, I overheard some Loopers hailing each other about where they were docked or anchored, with plans on gathering together for a party that afternoon. I had caught up to Mark and Jane, no longer lagging behind. Though ready to join the party, I appreciated the tranquil seas, a sharp contrast to yesterday. The Chesapeake can change from one day to the next, or even within a few hours. I felt torn between meeting up with friends or taking advantage of the calm waters. I passed Solomons reluctantly determined to do what was best for me and *Annabelle*, even if it meant bypassing a place I wanted to see and bypassing my friends. I reassured myself that I'd see them again soon.

I continued up the Chesapeake to a large marina, about 20 miles southeast of Annapolis in Tracy's Landing. The following day Jon, whom I had met at the October Rendezvous, was meeting me there. He offered to give me a portable washing machine. Originally, the idea of washing clothes on *Annabelle* sounded good, but having been on the water for a few weeks I couldn't imagine where I'd put the five-gallon sized washer. I wanted to unload possessions, not accumulate more.

Once again, I was at a marina with fixed docks. I had hoped for floating one, wanting to stay a few days. As I pulled my boat into Herrington Harbour Marina and followed the directions to my dock, I wondered if there were any floating docks in Maryland. The dockhand helped me tie up *Annabelle*. I went up to the office, where the people were very kind. They offered me a free glass with the marina's name on it, and I politely declined. I had cups; I had no space, not even for another glass. The beautiful grounds felt like a park.

While at the anchorage the day before, I had checked my alternator belt, which was loose again. I couldn't tighten it any further. I had a spare alternator belt with me, so I decided to change it. Since there was a Zimmerman Marine Repair at the marina, I called my friend Steve, from Zimmerman in Southport, for him to arrange for someone to check the belt. I wondered why it kept getting loose or stretching. Was there something wrong with the alignment that I couldn't see? In the office, I told the staff I was planning to have Zimmerman look at my boat. They explained that I needed a work order, and it would need to be scheduled a week or two away. I didn't think I needed the work order, as my friend in Southport would make the arrangements.

Steve called me back and told me that Zimmerman would be sending someone down to my boat right away. Meanwhile, my friend Jon called to tell me how to find his boat. I told him about my alternator belt and he came to wait with me on *Annabelle*.

As we visited and shared Loop stories, Jon said, "I don't know why you're waiting for Zimmerman to look at your alternator belt. It's easy to change."

"It isn't just about changing it, I'm worried the belt is out of alignment, because I continually need to tighten and adjust it."

"Get the new belt out; it will take ten minutes to change it. You'll save money by doing it yourself. He can look at the alignment afterwards."

I had already pulled out my spare belt and socket set. I pulled open the inner engine hatch, under the step leading from the cabin to the cockpit. I untightened the three bolts holding the alternator belt cover in place before taking each bolt off by hand to avoid dropping any bolts in the bilge. As I maneuvered the cover out of the way, I laid it with the inside facing upward, as the part next to the belt was covered with black dust. I rinsed it off when I was able to get up. Jon said, "Okay, now do you know which bolts you need to loosen to take the belt off?"

I pointed to the two bolts I thought should be loosened, "This one and this one?"

"Yup."

I was used to Dean getting frustrated with me and offering to do it for me. Jon wasn't going to cut me that kind of slack. He wanted to make sure I could do it on my own. The first bolt was easy. The second, I couldn't budge. I looked up at him, "I can't loosen this one."

In his wisdom, Jon said, "Use some leverage. Get the ratchet in place, then stand on it if you have to."

With the ratchet in position, I tried pushing it down with the heel of my foot. It still wouldn't budge. I tried jumping on it. No luck. Finally, with Jon stepping on the ratchet, the bolt loosened. I took off the old alternator belt and put the new one on. While tightening the new belt, Jon noticed I didn't have an extra-large screwdriver to help me with leverage. I tightened the belt as much as possible. Jon was right, replacing the belt took less than ten minutes. Just before putting on the cover, the guy from Zimmerman Marine showed up. I told him what I had done, asking if he could check if the alignment was off. He didn't see anything amiss, tightening the belt better than I was able to, with his extra-large screwdriver. He was on my boat for five minutes, and I wasn't charged anything. I just needed to check the belt regularly, learning to handle the mechanics myself.

Jon and I took his truck to a restaurant across the water from the marina for lunch. He'd drive home to Pennsylvania that afternoon. On the way back to *Annabelle*, we stopped at a hardware store, where I bought the appropriate screwdriver for tightening the belt. He also insisted I carry a small hatchet on my boat, in case I needed to cut my anchor line. It was a safety item that he thought every boater should carry. Jon told me about a time he and his brother had anchored, and when they tried to pull up their anchor the following morning, it was stuck in the branches of a large log. The only way they were able to get loose was by using their hatchet to cut through the branches. Otherwise, they would have needed to cut their anchor line, losing their anchor. A good anchor for *Annabelle* cost a few hundred dollars. For Jon's larger boat, it could cost over a thousand dollars. A small hatchet is cheap insurance.

Early that afternoon Jon dropped me off at the marina. It had been a good day. He pushed me to change the belt myself and gave me the gift of confidence. I thought about a time when my grandson was seven; the backyard was a mess from playing with his cousins. I asked him to clean up the backyard. He whined about how it wasn't fair; the mess wasn't just his. He did everything he could to get out of cleaning it. Finally, I told him that he could spend the day whining about it, or he could just get it done and over with, then enjoy the rest of the day. It was his decision either to continue being miserable, or just spend the 15 minutes cleaning up the mess. He quit whining, cleaned up the mess, and we went on with our day. I hated the idea that with mechanical issues on my boat I was acting like a seven-year-old. *Oy Vey*. Next time, I'd just have to "get 'er done."

Another time, in years past, when I worked in a psychiatric hospital, we had a physician assistant who worked with us. Before he came, I had to do all the work by myself. The administrators kept finding more for the medical staff to do, unaware of the immensity of our jobs. In the mornings, our PA and I would arrive at the hospital, review our work responsibilities and discuss our patients. He was in charge of routine histories and physicals, and medical issues. I evaluated psychiatric status and adjusted psychiatric medications. In our 16-bed hospital, we saw each patient daily, similar to any medical hospital. After our morning meeting with the nurses and social workers, we figured out what had to be done, and we'd look at each other and say, "Let's get 'er done!" We could be slammed or work could be easy. I relished the easier days, because there were some days I wouldn't get home until late at night. On Thursday nights, I was on-call and never slept well. I was in a sleep-deprived state on Fridays, looking forward to the end of the day when I could get to bed early. One way or another, the work had to be finished that day. There was never a choice of seeing a patient or not. I needed to use this same philosophy with my boat, not the philosophy of a seven-year old.

Periodically, Jon would email me regarding the progress of my trip, with pointers on where to stop. We talked about the different expectations people had in doing the Loop. I remember Jon telling me, "For some, the Loop is about going to battlefields and history museums. Your challenges will be different. For you, the mental part will be the hardest. Keep the faith." Jon was right; despite the camaraderie of Loopers I was already feeling different from them, with my own set of challenges. I appreciated his wisdom. After retiring, he'd done the Loop with his brother. The two of them knew all the places along the Loop to buy specialty beer for their mini-kegerator. On a more serious note, it was also a time for him to reflect on his marriage and how to make it work now that he was retired.

Soon Joie showed up at Herrington Harbor Marina in Tracy's Landing. The first words out of Joie's mouth were, "I love Dean. He saved my life." In her early fifties, with bleach blonde hair, she was as vivacious as Dean had described her. Joie and Dean met in Louisiana the previous year after Dean was hired to crew on her sailboat *Patience*. She inherited the 32-foot ketch rigged sailboat from her father, an avid sailor. Some of her favorite memories were sailing with her dad, but she had never set foot behind the helm or helped with any of the lines. She looked forward to learning how to sail. She hired a captain, who in turn, hired Dean to help crew *Patience* from Louisiana, across the Gulf, through the Okeechobee Waterway in Florida, and up the coast to Annapolis, Maryland, Joie's home port. Dean and the captain spent a few days preparing *Patience* for the journey prior to Joie's arrival. When they picked Joie up from the airport, she was wearing a hot pink T-shirt with the inscription, "Of course they're fake, the real ones tried to kill me." Joie planned to spend the first week of the trip aboard *Patience* then fly home to Annapolis and return to work.

The hired captain was not as experienced as Joie originally thought. Dean told me that when they lost sight of land, five hours from the dock, 12 miles from Cypremort Point, Louisiana, in open waters, the captain lost his grip on reality; he wasn't able to complete a sentence and his hands were shaky. They expected that sailing across the Gulf to Fort Myers, Florida, would take three to four days. The watch schedule was three-hour rotating shifts, in which the fuel for the small diesel needed to be filled, and *Patience* needed to stay on course. The first night they motorsailed at 5 knots, directly into the wind.

When the captain relieved Joie from the helm on the first night, he was naked, dangling his twig and berries. The nudist captain slept on a bench in the main salon, where the breeze cooled off the cabin as it blew in from the front hatch and out through the companionway—the most comfortable spot on *Patience*, and the most visible. Shouldn't there be a rule that nudists forewarn their boat companions? The cabin of *Patience* wasn't much bigger than *Annabelle's*. It was the end of August, humid with daytime temperatures in the 80s.

On the second night, the notorious captain forgot to top off the diesel at the beginning of his shift. Dean, waking to the sudden silence, stumbled up the companionway to find they were drifting without wind, sails or a motor, about a hundred miles south of Biloxi, Mississippi. At 2:00 in the morning, Dean tried to get fuel into the injector, but the stainless steel screw was stripped, making the diesel engine useless. When the winds picked up, they sailed; when the winds died down, they floated. They weren't making any progress toward Fort Myers, Florida.

Captain Dumb Ass wanted to forge ahead to Fort Myers, engineless against the wind, with battery power dwindling. With ample provisions, they still had food, but the milk was getting warmer by the day. Joie gave Dean the control of *Patience*, so they could sail north to Biloxi, Mississippi. Mutiny! Midday, the captain hit the red distress button on the VHF radio, signaling a sinking ship to the Coast Guard. Every 15 minutes, they were hailed by the Coast Guard, but couldn't respond with their weak transmitter. The built-in radio had lost power; the handheld VHF radio only carried the signal a mile or two. Late that night, with fog, poor visibility, under sail and approaching oil platforms, Dean realized the GPS didn't match the charts. Captain Dumb Ass must have changed the coordinates, so the Coast Guard was off by miles. They'd be lucky to find *Patience*.

On the fifth day, moving north at the speed of 2 knots, they heard the thrumming of an approaching 47-foot Coast Guard motor lifeboat. Joie was relieved and Captain Dumb Ass was still shaking. The large rescue boat hip towed them four miles to Sea Tow, where they were pulled the remaining fifty miles to Biloxi. Safe at harbor, Joie flew home and left Dean to prepare *Patience* for a land trip, strapped on a boat trailer.

Eight months later, Joie was still getting harassing phone calls from the captain, and the Coast Guard was investigating his credentials. While *Patience* was in a shipyard getting repairs, Joie offered up her slip to me. "You could be closer to Annapolis. I'm paying for the slip, so it shouldn't be a problem."

"You might want to call them first to check it out. Even though you pay for the slip, most marinas don't go for that kind of thing."

"It's my slip." She made a couple phone calls, and we were set. The following morning, Joie had her friend drop her off at Herrington Harbor, and she boarded *Annabelle*. I made sandwiches, while Joie took her turn at the helm. Together, we navigated to her boat slip, another fixed dock at Pier 7, on the South River. For the next three days, I got to hang out with Joie. She welcomed me with a large basket, filled with a plush, Egyptian cotton, white towel and frou-frou bath paraphernalia. She took me to her friend Wendy's house, where I was able to do my laundry, while relaxing in a luxurious hot bath, sipping red wine.

One evening, we went to Jalapenos, the same Mexican restaurant I had taken my grandchildren to the year before, while they visited me over the Fourth of July. The main difference was that Joie and I sat at the bar and met interesting people. She told me she always liked sitting at the bar. I had never even imagined sitting alone at a bar. I watched as Joie interacted easily with total strangers, and I wanted to be more outgoing like her. I enjoyed the camaraderie of another single woman. It reminded me of all the years I lived in Tucson, where most my friends were single, unlike Southport where most of my friends had been married for 30 years or more.

On Friday night, my last night in Annapolis, Joie went all out for a barbecue. Wendy picked up Mark and Jane from downtown, where *Average Looper* was in the mooring field. We had a feast of steak, lamb, salmon (caught by Wendy), green beans, corn, potatoes and fresh warm bread. It was a great start to the Memorial Day weekend.

Saturday afternoon, one month after starting the Loop, I journeyed further up the Chesapeake, anchored at Poole's Island. Sunday, I motored through the Chesapeake and Delaware Canal (C&D canal), to Delaware City, where several Loopers spent the night, including Mark and Jane. Once docked, I explored the small town with John, from *Endeavor*, and we enjoyed eating ice cream on a park bench. The following morning, I left a day ahead of the other Loopers. The weather was beautiful, a good day to travel down the Delaware Bay.

On Memorial Day, the dockmaster gave me guidance, "Stay on the other side of the bay, so you're not fighting with the incoming tide. Once you get halfway down and the tide has changed, pull away from the coast and let the current carry you the rest of the way to the Cape May inlet."

Trusting his local knowledge, I listened carefully. The Delaware Bay was not as scenic as the Chesapeake, with barren landscapes and a nuclear power plant on the northern shore. I saw a few fishing boats and cargo ships in the main channel. Southeast of the power plant, I found myself surrounded by at least fifty dolphins, more than I'd ever seen in my life. I put *Annabelle's* engine in neutral and tried taking pictures. It seemed impossible to time them. Dolphins always made me feel good. Late that afternoon, I arrived in Cape May, New Jersey, where I chose to stay at South Jersey Marina, renowned for their luxurious bathrooms.

12

Mom Visits

When I invited my 72 year-old mom to come with me for a portion of the Loop, I didn't know where I'd be. She was hoping to catch me on the Hudson River, north of New York City. She planned to fly to my sister's house in Pennsylvania, within a couple hundred miles of my intended location.

I docked in Cape May for a few days. By the time Mom met me, most of my friends had gone further north. Some had dared to take the New Jersey Intracoastal Waterway, which had not been restored to its normal depths after Hurricane Sandy in 2012. Only boats with less than a 4-foot draft could get through, and those boaters were warned against taking the chance. Most people go north from Cape May by navigating offshore into the Atlantic Ocean, up the coast, around Sandy Hook and into New York Harbor. If I'd left a day earlier with my Looper friends, I'd have to meet her in Atlantic City which she might not like as much as Cape May, as Mom disliked glitzy, gambling towns. She lives in the middle of the Arizona desert, 22 miles up a dirt road, in a small community of Quakers and ranchers. At night, she'd rather be looking up at a sky filled with stars than seeing city lights. A naturalist at heart, she volunteered as the state chair of the Sierra Club.

I was thoroughly enjoying Cape May, especially the marina's luxurious and clean bathrooms. The on-site restaurant offered great food and service. The Lobster House Restaurant next door had a deli with chowders and lobster salad. The marina staff treated me as if I were staying in a five-star resort.

They'd drive me anywhere I needed, including the local grocery store for provisions. Dockhands offered to take my garbage to the trash bins as they walked by *Annabelle*. For me, New Jersey was a garden state of bliss.

My Looper friends stayed at a less expensive marina, within walking distance, which didn't have the same amenities. Their boats were roomier with normal-sized bathrooms and showers. When they chose between public showers or staying on their boat, the choice was clear, they'd stay on their boat. My choice was simple too: I'd get off my boat to check out all of the public facilities my whole trip.

Shortly before noon, my nephew dropped off Mom. She planned to spend three nights with me, and I looked forward to having her experience anchoring out, as well as staying at marinas. We'd be leaving the following morning through the inside Intracoastal Waterway to Manasquan, a trip that would take two days. With weather and seas permitting, on the third day we'd venture out into the Atlantic Ocean, circle around Sandy Hook, and enter New York Harbor.

I quickly showed Mom around the marina, then we walked to the Lobster House for lunch on their boat-like deck bar, overlooking the water. After lunch, we dropped off some spices for the crew of *Shiver Me Timbers*, with whom I had dined the previous night. They were waiting on parts for boat repairs. I wanted Mom to meet the Looper friends I'd see along the way, so she'd feel more comfortable with me being alone on my boat.

We saw Burke and Stel, Loopers I had first met in Southport, then at the Rendezvous in Norfolk. Burke, a fit man of almost sixty, wearing a baseball cap, with sweat dripping down his forehead, was in the midst of fixing something on his boat. He explained to Mom that in boating, we all have "pride-buster moments." Mom looked at him quizzically. As we walked away, she smiled and commented that she got a kick out of Burke's humility and positive attitude. During my journey I'd experience many of my own "pride-buster moments."

In the afternoon, I called Mark and Jane, who had left the day before. They told me the New Jersey Intracoastal Waterway was narrow, winding, shallow and filled with fishermen and "no wake" zones. Their boat could have handled the Atlantic much easier than mine, due to their size, speed and power. The general consensus was to avoid the Waterway if possible, especially on weekends when everyone who owns a boat is out fishing. Larger boats may opt for the Intracoastal Waterway when the Atlantic waters are too rough, but there isn't a choice for a person with a smaller boat like mine.

The first night with Mom aboard, we had to put the table down and set up her bed, which took up most of the room in my small cabin. After moving all the gear I had stored under my table, I climbed under the tabletop to push it up and off its base, the only way I had enough strength to do so, but I soon realized I would have to make these adjustments twice a day. We would manage without the table and have less space than I was accustomed to on my own. Together, we placed the table top between the bench seats. With the table down, and the cushions in place, I inflated a Coleman air mattress, so Mom would be comfortable. The air mattress would be deflated during the day, so the front bench seat could face forward while we were underway. It was an ordeal to move the table down and rearrange my storage.

My bathroom was smaller than the average bathroom on an airplane. When we anchored, we'd have to shower in the miniscule space. The toilet could easily get clogged, so I had instructions for Mom. I pointed to the plastic bag hanging on a hook, I said, "Mom, you can't put anything down the toilet that doesn't come out of your body. Toilet paper has to go here."

"No problem, it will be like staying in a Third World country. I can do that."

"If you forget, I've placed gloves here," pointing out a pair of latex-free medical gloves hanging halfway out of the small cabinet under the corner sink. "If anything goes into this toilet that shouldn't, you'll have to remove it."

"Yes, ma'am."

I felt like the toilet Nazi, but this strict rule was the same one I always followed myself. I'd heard too many stories about clogged toilets. It was much easier to take all precautions and not allow my toilet to get clogged.

I showed Mom the pump on the side of the toilet. I explained that once she had done her business, she needed to flush the toilet by pumping the handle. She would use fresh water to pump through any waste. Salt water makes the bathroom smell like sulfur, so I regularly filled a gallon jug of fresh water on the sink. The alternative was to use the shower water, but the shower nozzle would drip for a few minutes afterwards.

In my limited space, I insisted that we both take showers daily. As Mom had gotten older, her preference was to take showers every other day. I could understand if someone was camping, which Mom did regularly, but this was NOT camping. In our cramped accommodations, I wanted to limit body odor, mine included. I told my very modest mother that it was possible we might see each other naked. I've never seen her naked, and there were only two times in which Mom had seen me naked as an adult.

Once, she was helping me paint my granddaughter's room, and when I forgot momentarily about a gallon container of periwinkle paint sitting precariously on the top of a ladder. The minute I moved the ladder, the paint can grazed the back of my head on its way to the carpet. Covered in periwinkle, I quickly stripped down and dashed to the shower, leaving Mom with the puddle of paint. She probably didn't even notice my pile of clothes on the floor, as she said, "How are we going to clean this carpet?"

Running to the shower, I said, "Don't worry about the carpet; it needed replacing anyway."

The second time my mom saw me naked, we were sharing a hotel room. She came out of the bathroom while I was changing. She yelled out, as if she had seen a ghost, or something horrible. I looked at her, "Really? That bad?" She tried to recover by saying, "No. Honey, I was just startled."

Being a nurse, I'm less modest than my mother. It isn't as if we don't all have the same body parts. Because I'm her daughter, I imagine I'm still more modest than most people. In any event, there wasn't room for modesty on *Annabelle*, but Mom was very good at changing her clothes in the tiny bathroom!

On Sunday, June 1, at 6:45 we left Cape May, heading north on the NJICW. At times, the channel markers were difficult to find. Mom helped me locate the numbered markers when they were difficult for me to see. I showed her how to use the Garmin chart plotter on the iPad, while I used the Raymarine chart plotter at my helm. Periodically, while staring at the iPad, she'd say things like, "Tanya, according to this, we're crossing over land."

I'd look at her incredulously, not knowing if she was serious, "Mom, look out the window, we're not on land. We're between the red and green channel markers."

Our chart plotters did not correspond to the actual locations of the channel markers, or to each other, since they had been updated at different times. The NJICW had not been surveyed since Hurricane Sandy, so neither chart plotter was reliable.

"Mom, do you see the next channel marker?"

"Yes," she responded, still staring at the iPad.

"Mom, I need you to look out the window and help me find the red buoy number 314. If we get out of the channel, we could run aground." I slowed down and kept one eye on my depth finder. When we located the channel marker, we'd resume heading in the right direction, then looked for the green buoy 315. Hour after hour, we meticulously followed the narrow, winding channel. My neck hurt with aching muscles from the tension.

Before Mom came aboard, I could use autopilot in straight stretches of water, while running quickly to the toilet. With her aboard, I felt like I should have the luxury of going to the bathroom without rushing, giving Mom control over the helm. One time, as I came out of my bathroom, I noticed we were heading straight toward a fishing boat and I had to sprint to the helm, a measly ten feet away. Panicked, I yelled, "Shit! Mom, do you see the fishing boat?"

"Of course I see it."

Was she steering from the chart plotter instead of looking out the window? I grabbed the helm and scooted onto the seat replacing her. "Is there a reason we are headed straight toward him? Are we trying to kill him?" There was no time to relax, not even in the bathroom.

The first day on the ICW was long and tiring. Just before sunset, we found an anchorage north of Atlantic City. I liked small coves surrounded by trees, but this anchorage had grasses growing along the edges with no trees in sight. I felt completely exposed, like a sitting duck, easily seen for miles.

I took the first shower, and even though it was only 8:00 p.m., I was exhausted and ready for bed. I explained to Mom how the hot water would be the temperature of the engine, much hotter than the water she was used to at home. I didn't want her to accidentally scald herself.

She had gone the entire day without going to the bathroom. I must have scared her with my admonitions. As I crawled under my blankets, I noticed Mom taking a very long time in the bathroom. I heard her trying to pump the toilet. Was I sensing her frustration, or my own? I knew she was trying not to bother me. If I were her, I wouldn't want to bother me. I can be bitchy after such a long day in such a cramped space. The waterway had indeed been tedious, as Mark and Jane had told me it would be.

"Mom, is everything okay in there?"

"Everything is fine! I'm just having problems with the toilet."

"Mom, have you put water down the toilet?"

"I'm trying to conserve water. I know it doesn't hold much and the holding tank is small."

"Mom, use as much water as you need. We'll be at a marina tomorrow and I can fill the water tank and empty the holding tank. Use more water."

Fortunately, it worked. *Oy Vey!*

After her shower, not accustomed to my early bedtime routine, Mom asked, "Do you want to play cards? It's still early."

"No. I just want to get some sleep. We'll be leaving early in the morning."

As usual, I woke before the sun came up, around 4:30 a.m. While waiting for the sunrise, I had enough time for coffee and a biscotti. It was my favorite time of day. Once the sun came up enough to see better, I'd pull the anchor and we'd continue our journey.

The second day was similar to the first with Mom. She continued to have difficulty looking out the windows instead of down at the iPad. As much as Mom may claim to hate technology, she really was a geek. I remember when WordStar, one of the first word processors came out, Mom said, "I don't know why anyone would want that program, when you can just write your own." She was ahead of her time as a woman with a PhD in electrical engineering and computer science. The iPad and chart plotter applications were more interesting to her than the scenery. At one point, I threatened to take the iPad away from her and turn off all the electronics, to force her to look out the window, but she agreed to look at the water while at the helm.

As we were in the middle of Barnegat Bay, I heard Mom telling her boyfriend on her cell phone, "We've just passed Barnegat Bay!"

I looked at Mom and shook my head. Would she ever get it?

"Mom, look out the window. Tell him we're IN Barnegat Bay. We haven't passed it."

Later that day, the captain of a fast, oceangoing, sportsfisher boat in front of us called on the VHF radio, "Hailing the small blue tug following the sportsfisher."

This sportsfisher was strangely out of place in the NJICW. His thoughtfulness was not a trait I normally ascribed to captains of sportsfisher boats. Most of my experience with these types of boats was trying to keep *Annabelle* upright as I dealt with their large wakes, as they flew past me, or slowing down to be kind, then plowing past me leaving an even larger wake.

"This is *Annabelle*, the Ranger Tug."

"Can we switch to Channel 68?"

"*Annabelle*, switching to 68."

"*Annabelle*, are you familiar with these waters?"

"No, I'm not."

"They get really shallow. Where are you going?"

"I am going to Manasquan."

"What brings you up here?"

"I'm doing the Great Loop."

"Cool! I've been hired to deliver this boat. If you were going to be hanging out around here, I'd give you my number. I'm going to Sandy Hook. The waters get really shallow around here. It's hard to get through them without running aground, even if you know them. I'll slow down so you can follow me."

"Awesome. Thank you."

For the next couple hours, we followed behind the sportsfisher boat and safely navigated through the shallow waters to Manasquan. I wondered if any of my friends would believe me when I told them the story about this very thoughtful sportfisher captain.

We arrived at the marina early in the afternoon when the tide was high and the current was strong. The dock was fixed, so *Annabelle* would rise and fall with the tide. I had to tie *Annabelle* to the pilings at each corner to keep her from banging. Maneuvering in the large slip was difficult, so a dockhand boarded to help. However, the way he was tying my lines to the pilings, I wouldn't be able to loosen them in the morning, and I couldn't afford to lose my lines.

Finally, I got on the bow of my boat and using my remote thruster control while reaching into the window to control the throttle, I was able to maneuver around the slip enough to tie up. Now the concern was how we would get on and off the boat. I tied an extra line around the finger pier to pull the boat closer when we wanted to get off, but it wouldn't reduce the ever-changing height from the boat to the pier.

The tidal range was about 6 feet, so the lines needed to be slack to allow for the boat dropping six feet below the level of the dock. As the tide came up later in the night, the lines would be so slack that the boat could bounce around the slip and bang into the finger pier. It would be a long night of checking the lines every couple of hours.

Anticipating difficulty getting off *Annabelle* when the tide dropped, I worried about Mom. I asked the dockmaster if he had any suggestions. His only suggestion was to get Mom off the boat, get her fed, and back to the boat before the tide fell. He made it sound like she was a pet, needing a quick walk, before heading back to the kennel.

I was so offended. Did he really say that? "Excuse me?"

More loudly, he repeated, "Get her off, get her fed, and get her back on the boat!"

Irritated with the dockmaster, I tried a different approach, "Do you have a ladder or something, for when the tide drops?"

"No, we don't have extra ladders, and you couldn't put one on that dock anyway. The restaurant is open, and you're running out of time, soon neither of you will be able to get on or off your boat."

Of all the marinas I went to, this was by far the worst. It didn't matter how clean the bathrooms were, since we'd be stuck on the boat once the tide dropped. I helped Mom off the boat. We met other Loopers who came in just after we did. They were just as frustrated with the marina as we were. While keeping track of the falling tide and our prospective abilities to return to our boats, we drank a quick glass of wine. Richard and Diane from *Halcyon* said they'd be leaving in the morning as the weather looked good for going offshore. Richard advised me on a tool so I could tie my lines at fixed docks as a single-hander; he had single-handed a sailboat to and from Australia. I'd order the tool as soon as possible.

I was worried about getting stuck in Manasquan for a few days, waiting for the seas to become calm. My plan was to leave in the morning with *Halcyon* and if the sea conditions got bad in the Atlantic, I could always come back.

Mom and I returned to my boat. By necessity, all night we'd be limited to our cramped space on *Annabelle*. The marina was next to a bridge, which blared out a loud, obnoxious horn every thirty minutes when the bridge opened. The bridge seemed to open and close into the wee hours of the morning, like a built-in alarm.

In my dazed grogginess, in the middle of the night, I heard a banging coming from the side of the boat. At high tide, *Annabelle* was hitting the finger pier. I had to tighten some lines and loosen others. A couple of hours later, I checked the lines again. Finally, at 4 a.m., I got up and stayed up. Getting a good night's sleep at this marina was delusional. I would have been better off at an anchorage. I just wanted to leave Manasquan. I wasn't waiting for slack tide, I only needed a glimmer of visibility to drop my lines to leave this damn marina behind.

As I waited for the sun to rise, I made coffee. Mom couldn't sleep while I was getting the boat ready to leave. I explained what a huge day this was for me. I was fearful about taking my little *Annabelle* offshore as I considered her an inshore boat. I explained how inlets can be very rough. It would be rougher because I was impatient and not willing to wait for slack low tide. Besides, I was irritated that I was at a marina where I couldn't sleep or get off my boat to use the restroom.

As we went into the protected break walls of the inlet, Mom decided it was a perfect time to go onto the back deck of *Annabelle* to take pictures. It was calm this minute, but soon we'd be rocking and rolling until we passed the breakwaters. As Mom shut the door behind her, I put the throttle into idle and ran after her to get her back inside. Since boats don't ever just stop, the boat was still drifting with whatever current and momentum carried it, so when I stepped away from the helm, I stepped away from having any control. Sleep deprived and cranky, I didn't want to chastise Mom, but her lack of common boat sense was grating on my nerves.

"Mom, this isn't the time to be outside. We're entering into really choppy water. Second, you aren't wearing a life jacket! Finally, you can't go outside and shut the door! How am I supposed to communicate with you if you shut the door?"

I was fuming, mostly due to factors beyond Mom's control. I just wanted to make sure we got into and out of the Atlantic Ocean safely. I had gone through inlets before on my other boats and in my sailing classes. I knew how rough they could be, especially if the wind was pushing against the current. At least the tide was going out, so we had the current with us. Mom had no way of knowing about the possible dangers, having none of the boating education or experience I had accumulated.

"Tanya, It's a perfect time to take pictures and enjoy the wildlife. Why don't you just let me be responsible for myself? I can take care of myself!"

"You may be able to take care of yourself in the desert, but as long as you are on MY boat, I'm responsible for you and your safety. So, get in here, and sit down. I will tell you when you can go out!"

We both returned to our seats, I put the throttle into forward, and we jostled our way through the breakwaters into the Atlantic. The waters were a little choppy, because the winds were blowing from the east. Waiting another hour for slack tide could have made a big difference. After ten minutes of being tossed around, *Annabelle* leveled out. Three miles offshore, I turned north and we rode the 3-foot swells up to the Hudson Bay. My auto pilot steered *Annabelle*, so I relaxed for the first time since leaving Cape May. I thought about the inscribed saying on my keepsake box: "We can never cross the ocean until we have the courage to lose sight of the shore." I stayed within three miles of shore, not exactly courageous, but I was in the ocean and breathing easily.

Mom and I talked about ancestors on her side of the family and their boats. She shared what it was like for her to grow up in Brooklyn; I never knew that she was born on Staten Island. New York City had changed since she was a little girl, when Staten Island was considered rural.

Our destination was Liberty Landing Marina in Jersey City across from Manhattan. Soon we'd pass Staten Island, Coney Island, Brooklyn, and Ellis Island, where my grandfather landed when he emigrated from Germany.

When *Annabelle* rounded Sandy Hook toward New York Harbor, a 70-foot sailing vessel, *Qingdao*, was heading in the same direction, decorated with dragons. Pointing towards the fancy sailboat, I told Mom, "Check out that sailboat. There has to be a story behind it."

She asked, "Do you think they're doing the Loop too?"

"No, it looks like a race boat. They've been crossing oceans. We'll figure it out when we get to the marina."

Within a few minutes, we were approaching the Statue of Liberty. I was excited to be seeing the landmark from my own boat. "Mom, go to the back deck and take pictures."

I slowed *Annabelle* down and tried my best to stay in one place while she took the photos. Keeping track of the marine traffic in the New York Harbor was a full-time job. The wakes from the commercial traffic made us to feel like we were in a washing machine. Boat wakes add another dimension to current and wind conditions. As I looked back to see how Mom was doing with the pictures, I noticed the camera sitting on her lap. She wasn't taking any pictures at all. We couldn't just sit in front of the Statue of Liberty forever! Once again, I lost my patience and my temper. Looking back at her from the helm, with *Annabelle* in neutral, being tossed about, I shouted, "Mom, take the pictures."

She yelled back at me, "Honey, I'm just waiting for it to be calm. We're moving too much."

"It's never going to get calm. It's a digital camera. You can take hundreds. Just take the pictures."

"I want one with you standing in front of the Statue of Liberty."

Anxiously, I left the helm and stood on the back deck across from Mom, so she could take the shot. Since *Annabelle* is only 8 feet 6 inches wide, I couldn't stand any further away from her. Feeling frustrated, I said, "Mom, quick, take the picture, I have to get back to the helm."

"Honey, you're too close. Can you move back?"

Now, I was so frustrated, "No. I can't. Forget the picture. I need to drive the boat. We can't just sit here." I was imagining the Coast Guard hailing us to figure out why we appeared to be aimlessly drifting in front of the Statue of Liberty. Inside the cabin, and back at the helm, I snapped pictures of Lady Liberty with my iPhone.

Outside the entrance to Liberty Landing Marina, we saw the crew of *Qingdao* preparing to enter the same marina. The Clipper Round the World Race was in their seventh leg of their 40,000 mile race at Liberty Landing. *Qingdao* was the last of the 12 Clipper sailboats to finish. In the annual race, crews are from all walks of life—teachers, accountants, lawyers and anyone who thirsts for adventure. People can join for all or some of the legs of the race. The only paid crew is the skipper for each boat. To keep things fair, each boat is outfitted identically and each boat has sponsors.

As we arrived, I recognized two other boats: *Halcyon* with Richard and Diane from Manasquan, and John and Joan from the sailboat *Destiny*. I had met John and Joan at the marina in Cape May.

Mom helped me clean *Annabelle* and put the table back up. Once we had taken care of the boat, we visited with Richard, Diane and their friends. I was extremely thankful to be off *Annabelle* and walking around. For three days, I had felt cramped. The only time I was able to get off my boat was briefly in Manasquan before the tide changed.

My sister and nephews came to pick up Mom and to join us for dinner, so grateful that Mom was able to experience this part of the trip with me. I was excited to take her into the same waters she saw routinely while growing up. Many things had changed during her lifetime.

As I parted with her, Mom said to me, "This was fun. Can we do it again, later in your trip?"

"No." I answered, "I think *Annabelle* is a boat meant for one person, but I'm glad you enjoyed yourself." Guiltily, I added, "I'm sorry I yelled so much." To lighten *Annabelle's* load, I sent extra bedding and other nonessential things home with my sister.

13

New York

The next stretch on the Loop would be from the Hudson River to Waterford, New York, where the Erie Canal starts. The scenery changed as I motored under the George Washington Bridge. Green vegetation gradually replaced the Manhattan skyline. By the time I passed the Tappen Zee Bridge, towering cliffs shaded the river.

My first stop was Half Moon Bay Marina near Harmon, where I docked with Looper friends. Mark and Jane invited me to go for a bike ride, but I was hesitant with all the hills. Then Don and Anita, in their early seventies, invited me to go with them. I thought to myself, surely if they can ride their bikes up and down these hills, I can ride mine. When I pulled my bike off the back of *Annabelle*, my chain had rusted solid. At different marinas, I had seen Mark diligently cleaning his bike. I was much less careful and had only rinsed my bike off a few times. Until I fixed my bike and got a new chain, I wouldn't be able to ride anywhere. Instead of going with my friends, I walked to town and stocked up on groceries.

After a couple nights at Half Moon Bay Marina, I continued my journey north. West Point looked like a magnificent old fort, with castle-like structures. As I rounded the corner, I saw huge white lettering on the top of a building, perhaps their gym, saying "Beat Air Force." Not a sports fan, I didn't know the Army and Air Force were rivals.

Beyond West Point, there are ruins of castles protruding from the steep hillsides. Occasionally, I passed small towns and marinas. My next stop was Norrie State Park. Again, on the Hudson, I was surrounded by Looper boats, and felt comfortable knowing that at the end of the day, I'd be seeing my friends. Across the river from the State Park Marina was another castle-like structure. I was tempted to take my dinghy across the river, climb up the hill, and investigate. I asked the dockmaster what he knew about the beautiful building, and he pointed to an information binder. There were rumors that it was a monastery, but it turned out to be a boarding school for the Bruderhof, which is a religion with Anabaptist origins. Per the dockmaster, they don't allow anyone near the castle, which is very secure. I stayed at the park, hiking the trails instead.

One of my biggest fears and challenges was ahead of me— going through the locks. Although I'd navigated through two locks on the Dismal Canal, I was facing 23 locks on the Erie Canal and seven in the Oswego Canal, before crossing Lake Ontario. The locks are designed to raise or lower a boat, and are usually accompanied by a waterfall because of the change of elevation. There is more than one way to get up or down a hill. Channel markers help boaters navigate into the lock and stay away from the waterfalls. The water is usually turbulent at the bottom of the lock, and there is a balance between powering through the turbulence while preparing to come to a stop next to the lock wall. The lock masters want the boats to enter the lock slowly and gently because boat wakes can reverberate between the walls, sloshing and rocking the contained boats. There is such a thing as lock etiquette.

The Dismal Swamp locks did not go well. When I entered the first one, which was designed to lift the boats eight feet, the lock master asked for a bowline and a stern line. I should have just grabbed the midship line for him, but following directions, I halfway climbed out the small window above my throttle controls to reach the bowline. Struggling to get the line up to the lock master, my knee hit the throttle, pushing it into reverse. Mark and Jane yelled at me, "You're going backwards!" The lock master dropped the bowline in the water, and I had to regain control and try again. I was grateful that only Mark and Jane saw my pathetic locking attempt. At the second lock, descending eight feet and starting at the top of the concrete walls, I easily handed the lock master my two lines. I stood on the back deck with a line in each hand as *Annabelle* was gently lowered. However, I had to drop a line or fall in because my lines were too short. By the time most of the water had drained out of the lock, I was standing on the edge of *Annabelle's* side deck, on my tiptoes with my hands spread out above my head. Mark and Jane called out, "Good job, *Annabelle*." I made a mental note to order longer lines, even though I wouldn't need them in any other locks.

In preparation for the Erie Canal, I stayed a few days at Shady Harbor Marina in New Delaware, New York. A local boater gave me advice on the best way to protect my hull with strategic fender placement that would remain in this position until I arrived in Oswego, New York. I put ten semi-permanent fenders around her, five on each side; ball fenders near the bow and stern, with three regular fenders placed sideways along the hull.

While in Norfolk, I had bought a spare propeller. The Norfolk prop shop recommended a different pitch than the boat manufacturer. With my new pitched propeller, I felt aeration under my hull because there was a new sound, like water flowing, while I was underway. That doesn't make much sense, but even the little changes become noticeable when living on a boat. I sent my spare to a prop shop so I could replace the new prop on my boat with the spare and reduce the aeration.

The prop shop could pick up my propeller on Wednesday from the marina, and I'd need to pick it up on Thursday afternoon from the prop shop, 90 miles south. Some marinas, knowing the needs of transient boaters, provide loaner cars to run errands, like going to the grocery store. The idea of going south on the New York Expressway was daunting, but the prop shop parts delivery only came by once a week. I didn't want to wait that long and chance getting behind all the other Loopers again.

Rain poured down as I left the marina before lunchtime in the white, muddy economy-sized loaner car. My hair was soaked, just from walking the short distance from *Annabelle* to the parking lot. Pulling onto the New York Expressway, I felt like a little old lady, with my hands in the nine and three position, and my neck scrunched up as I leaned forward into the dash, peering through the windshield wipers. The speed of the traffic in the pouring rain was daunting, especially since I hadn't gone this fast in a vehicle since I left Southport. I pulled off the freeway in Newburgh. During the hour and a half drive, my hair had finally dried out, and the clouds were starting to clear. I wished the shop could have brought the prop back to the marina. I navigated down the streets, like a rat through a maze, going around construction barriers. The paper with the Google map, placed beside me on the passenger seat, wasn't very helpful. At each intersection, with my nerves frayed, I struggled to find the street names. The smell of broken concrete hovered along the streets, by the orange and gray barricades. Within half a mile of the prop shop, as I entered an intersection, out of the corner of my eye I saw a black car coming from my right side and time stood still. *Shit*. My car skidded while I turned the steering wheel to a hard left and I felt the crunch of our fenders colliding, a T-bone barely avoided. We came to a stop in the middle of the intersection, with my passenger side front fender against his driver's side front fender.

Shaking and trembling, I thought he ran the red light. He pulled his vehicle out of the intersection to the curb, not leaving enough room for me to pull up behind him. The back half of my loaner car stuck out into intersection. I turned on my hazard signals, hoping nobody would run into me. The only thing worse than wrecking my own car, was wrecking someone else's. I got out and met the other driver on the sidewalk. He yelled, "What were you thinking? You ran a red light!"

"What? I ran the red light?"

"Yes. You ran the red light!" He seemed pretty certain that I was in the wrong. He was a confident thirty-something professional, dressed in designer blue jeans, a button up shirt, and a skinny tie, which matched his slender build. His dark brown hair was shoulder length, and pulled back into a ponytail. He looked like he was in a hurry and I had just ruined his day.

Holding back my tears, I looked up at him towering over me and said, "I don't go around running red lights." But, could it be? I was unfamiliar with the roads and busy looking at the street signs.

"I'm calling the police." Then he demanded, "Get your insurance information."

Regaining some composure, I said, "Sure. But, this isn't my car. Can you move yours up, so mine isn't sticking out into the intersection?"

He returned to his car and moved it up a few feet, not quite enough to keep mine out of the intersection, but better. I kept my hazard lights on.

While waiting for the police, I called the marina to let them know where I was and what had happened. The dockmaster seemed genuinely concerned, but immediately asked about my insurance. I reminded him of the photocopy of my auto insurance policy, which I gave them when I signed for the car.

When the police officer appeared, the other driver quickly walked over to him with his license and information. He told the officer he had a meeting to attend and needed to leave quickly. Then I heard him add, "She ran the red light and hit me."

I approached the officer and said, "Look, I don't run red lights!" The officer pointed to my vehicle and told me to wait in my car for him, so he could get the statement from the other guy. Obediently, I returned to the loaner car.

When the officer appeared at my window to talk to me, I explained to him that I didn't know which of us ran the red light. I also explained that under the circumstances, I thought we both did everything we could to avoid the collision. He checked my driving record, and issued me an accident form, and said it was a "no fault" accident. Neither of us would be cited.

My hazard lights had been on for about 45 minutes. The car wouldn't start, so I asked the officer if he had jumper cables.

"Ma'am, we can't jumpstart cars. I can call a tow truck for you."

I accepted his offer, and he called a towing company.

When the tow truck arrived, the driver was moving so fast, and started to get it ready for towing. Feeling completely rushed, I said, "Wait, I might not need a tow. Maybe I just need a jumpstart."

"Ma'am, I don't have cables in my truck. I also don't have a lot of time. You want your car towed or not?"

"You don't have jumper cables?" He had an AAA tow truck. How could he NOT have cables?

"It's $150 to tow the car to our shop. We'll give you an estimate for repairs when we get there."

I had no choice at that point. The car wouldn't start and I wasn't sure it was drivable. I agreed to have him tow my car and climbed into the cab of his truck. I called the marina to give them an update and ask about the propeller. The prop shop was willing to bring the propeller to the auto mechanic. I told the dockmaster that I'd call him from the auto shop to give him an update, and we'd figure out how I was supposed to get back to the marina.

Not only was I shaken up from the accident, I was shaky from being hungry. I hadn't eaten lunch and it was now midafternoon, without any prospect of lunch in sight. I asked the tow truck driver if he could stop at a gas station, so I could buy a candy bar. He agreed to stop, as long as I was quick. I wondered if he was finally having a moment of compassion. I still found it hard to believe he didn't have jumper cables. If only I could've casually looked over the back of the seat, to see if there were any lying on the floor of the cab.

Once we pulled into the auto shop, he dropped the car off in the parking lot, and told me to wait inside. A minute after arriving, the prop shop guy showed up so I wrote him a check and thanked him for bringing the propeller to me.

The auto shop mechanic said it would be a day before they could figure out the damages on the car and give me an estimate for repairs. Meanwhile, I read a text from the marina, "We want the car fixed at the auto shop next to our offices in Schenectady. Have it towed there." Seriously? They wanted the car towed 45 minutes further north than the marina? A hundred and fifty miles away?

I asked the tow truck driver about towing the car to Schenectady. He explained it was two and a half hours each direction, not even considering traffic, and would cost almost as much as the repair. He wouldn't have anyone to tow it until the next day. I had already spent $150 on towing.

I called the marina and asked for the dockmaster. I was told that he was busy, on another line, he'd call me later.

Frustrated, I texted him, "Why can't I have it fixed here and save the money for the tow?"

"You can have it fixed there, if you can bring the car back to us when the repair is done. Otherwise, it needs to be done up here."

I thought about how it would work to have the repairs done at this shop, who claimed they didn't carry jumper cables in their trucks. I thought about the cost of staying in a hotel while the repairs were done, or even taking a taxi back to the marina. "Do you have any suggestions for a towing company who could tow it that far?"

He texted me the number of a towing company from Schenectady, who gave me an estimate of $900.

My next text from the dockmaster said, "Have the tow truck driver drop you off on the side of the road at the New Baltimore exit. We'll pick you up there."

My head was spinning. I couldn't believe he wanted me to be dropped off on the side of the expressway! I was still shaking from the accident, and everything seemed to be happening way too fast for me to think about what I needed to do. I had been in reaction mode all afternoon, like a leaf being blown every which way in a tornado. I needed to stop and think.

I asked the auto mechanic if he'd help me jumpstart the car. I might have difficulty turning the car in tight spaces, but if I could drive it back, I'd save $900. We walked out to the car and pulled the front fender away from the tire. With the cables, the car started right up. The wheels turned enough to get me back "home" if I was careful. I didn't even bother responding to the dockmaster's last text, I was too pissed off.

In the drenching rain, I arrived safely at the marina. As I walked in the door, the marina staff told me they assumed the car had been totaled, but they were glad I was back; other people needed to use the car that evening. A young man introduced himself as Tim. He needed to pick up his grandfather, Tom, from the airport. Tim had been making repairs on their boat, *If*, while his grandfather had gone to a wedding.

The next day, the dockmaster and I drove up to Schenectady for an estimate on the repair. They told us it would be about $2,100. While waiting, I noticed a bike shop across the road and asked about buying a new chain for my bike. For less than $20, I had a new chain.

We stopped at the marina's corporate offices, and while the dockmaster was in a meeting, I ate pasta with a glass of merlot. I looked forward to having the car accident behind me and moving forward. At the attached Italian bakery, I bought enough cannoli to share with other Loopers at the marina. If the rain stopped, I could leave the following day to Waterford, about 25 miles north.

When I left the marina, my thoughts were more about leaving the car accident behind me, than what might lie in front of me. Ahead was the Federal Lock in Troy, the gateway to either the Erie Canal or Lake Champlain. I expected to arrive in Waterford by lunchtime. Heading north on the Hudson before the lock passage, I realized how literal was the old saying, "When it rains it floods." With the current pushing against me, stronger than I had encountered, *Annabelle* struggled to make headway. In the early morning, her speed was 3 or 4 knots, less than 5 mph. Later, the speed was only 2 knots. This 25-mile stretch could take me all day. It didn't matter though, I was not turning back. I was moving forward. As I approached Albany, about halfway to Waterford, I saw a couple of my Looper friends. They hailed me and asked me to stop and join them for a cup of coffee. I figured I might as well, since I wasn't going very fast anyway. Would half an hour make a difference? I pulled over and tied up to their boat and enjoyed a relaxing cup of coffee with Barb, Ross, Larry and Jan. They told me which Loopers were up at Waterford and explained that, because of the flooding, the lock at Waterford was closed. They planned to stay in Albany until the flooding subsided.

After coffee, I finally reached Troy and the Federal Lock. Approaching the lock, I saw another Ranger Tug, like my boat, docked at the Troy Free dock. I was tempted to go there and tie up with the other boat, just to say hello to another person who has a Ranger Tug, but decided against it. It was a long day, going so slowly. I was within a couple miles of my destination. I hailed the lock master and requested permission to lock through.

Federal Lock in Troy, New York

The Federal Lock in Troy is considered Lock 1 of the easterly-heading Erie Canal, even though it is on the Hudson River, and also the entrance point to the Champlain Locks, which are further north. It is built like all the locks on the Erie Canal and operates in the same way. They are designed to bring boaters up or down waterways where there is a change in elevation. The change in elevation can be a few feet or 50 feet. The Troy Lock raised my boat 14 feet. As much as the locks assist boaters, they also serve to regulate flood waters and produce energy, much like the Hoover Dam in Nevada. Each lock on the Erie Canal has a small dam beside it, which can be adjusted to determine how much water is allowed through the dam. Nearby, there is a power generating station.

At Shady Harbor, I had put ten fenders on my boat, five on each side to protect my boat hull from hitting the sides of the concrete locks, which can be covered with sharp barnacles and algae. Compared to other Loopers, I was over-prepared, but I didn't have the luxury of a partner to put out my fenders at each lock, or to prepare one side versus the other. Both sides of my boat had to be prepared for anything, at all times.

Several feet of logs floated in front of the heavy metal gates to the Federal Lock. The lock master suggested I push through the logs gently. If they stayed on the surface, they wouldn't get into my propeller. If I rushed through them too quickly, I could inadvertently push the debris under my boat. Meanwhile, a very strong current came off the waterfalls beside the lock. I had to approach the gates quickly to avoid the turbulence of the falls, which could throw my boat into the rocks or walls at the side of the entrance. It would take impeccable timing.

As I entered the lock, I saw pipes on the sides of the locks. I pulled to the side of the lock, where I could reach out my helm window and put a line around it. It went smoothly. With just the one access point of holding my boat, I still had to use my thrusters to keep my boat against the side of the lock, but I managed. As the water level rose to the level upstream, I felt good. This lock wasn't so bad. It went better than the two locks in the Dismal Swamp. When the gates opened to let me through, the lock master hailed my boat and wished me a safe journey.

Once through the lock, Mark and Jane hailed me. Larry and Jan called them to let them know I was on my way and then they had listened on the VHF radio to know when I was at the lock. They told me the docks were full, but there was a small spot in front of the dock office, which my boat could barely fit. Boats had moved one way or another to make room for my *Annabelle*. They told me that the spot was in front of a large green boat. With the strong current, moving slower than most people can walk, I motored the last two miles to Waterford. I docked *Annabelle* in the swift currents and Mark helped with my lines.

I realized how high the flood waters were after I docked; some of the channel markers were almost covered in water. I found the last spot on the free wall at Waterford next to the dock house.

14

The Erie Canal

The day the Erie Canal opened after the flooding, many of us said goodbye to our friends. Mark and Jane would be heading north through Lake Champlain, the same way I had originally planned because I heard it was more beautiful than the Erie Canal route. When I called the Canadian Locks in Quebec, they told me I needed a second person on my boat if I wanted to go through ANY of the locks in their province. My friends offered to have me tie up to their boats as they went through, but that wouldn't suffice for the Quebec authorities. The man on the phone suggested I could still navigate through the Quebec Locks and find random people to go through them with me. I wasn't going to take that kind of chance. Half the Loopers would head north; the rest of us would head east through the Erie Canal.

Waterford Lock, Erie Canal Lock 2

The first group of seven boats entered Lock 2 at Waterford. Many of us went up to the bridge overlooking the lock to watch. I decided to leave later in the morning. I was in no hurry; I'd feel more comfortable taking it slow. My friend, Jim, the harbor host of Waterford, stood beside me to watch the boats. *If* was the last boat to enter the Lock, struggling to find room on the starboard wall behind a grimy sailboat. As Tom, a fit man of 79, reached out with his boat hook to grab the line on the lock wall, he fell off his boat into the water. People watching yelled, "Man overboard!" My heart stopped for a moment. I felt completely helpless. Tom's grandson, Tim, sprinted from the helm to the swim platform, leaving the boat floating freely. The crew on the sailboat in front of *If* hollered in panic, "Your boat is going to hit ours!"

Geez. Didn't they notice that Tom had fallen in? Luckily, Tom swam to the back of his boat and pulled himself onto *If's* swim platform. Tim ran back to the helm. Breathing a sigh of relief, I saw Tom standing safely on the side of his boat, dripping wet. He remarked that since this lock had been problematic, perhaps the rest would go smoother. We all had fears about the locks. I had heard stories about boats getting blown about by the current or wind.

Once all the boats were safely tied up, the back gates closed, the lock started filling with water at 1200 cubic feet per second. In locks 2 through 6, the water level would rise by 34 feet each. In the Erie Canal our boats would slowly climb in altitude a total of 420 feet to their highest level, then be lowered down until we arrived at Lake Ontario in Oswego.

The locks can feel like large Jacuzzi bathtubs filling with water, with jets of water pouring in on both sides of the lock.

Each of these jets causes turbulence, mostly when the water is being raised. When the water is lowered, the turbulence is gentler.

Ideally, a boater can grab two securing lines in a lock to hold a boat steady, but the lines in the Erie Canal were spaced too far apart for me to hold two lines by myself. There are three types of securing lines: poles, cables, and free hanging ropes. The poles and cables run from the top of the lock to the bottom, secured on both ends. The free hanging ropes are only secured at the top of the lock, swinging freely down to the lowest water level. I could put my line around the pole and cable and be left with one pivot point, hoping to overcome any other turbulence with my bow and stern thruster. With a second line, one can hold close to the wall at two points, which is much more secure.

Jim offered to come with me for Locks 2 through 6. These locks are all close together, within a couple miles of downtown Waterford, a short walk from where Jim lived. The remaining 17 locks were spread out across 152 miles to Brewerton. I agreed to have him come aboard and accompany me through a few locks. I felt excited; this marked my passage into new waters, and I'd have a friend aboard. However, since I would encounter over a hundred locks on the Great Loop, I needed to get through most of them by myself. I didn't want direct help, only words of encouragement or suggestions on how I might be able to do something differently or better. I only wanted words, nothing more.

As *Annabelle* motored into Lock 2, I made it clear to Jim that I wanted him to be there with me, but not DO anything for me, unless absolutely necessary for my safety, *Annabelle's* safety, or the safety of other boats in the locks. I was nervous. Jim had gone through these locks hundreds of times and was calm as an oak tree on a still night.

In the first lock, I eased my boat to the starboard side, lining my window up with the cable. Halfway leaning out my small window, I reached out and wrapped my line around the cable. So far, everything was going well, just like it had in the Federal Lock. Jim went to the back of the boat and grabbed a hanging line with the boat hook. Although he was only holding the line, I told him to let it go. He said, "I'm not exerting any strength or anything, I'm just holding it."

"I won't have you when I get past these next few locks, when I have to do everything myself. If you really aren't doing anything, let go of the line. Please, come back in here and sit down. I don't want you holding any lines."

I was very uncomfortable and becoming bitchy. I was afraid if I didn't do this by myself now, I'd be in trouble down the waterway. I needed confidence in my own abilities. Jim didn't think he was "helping" me when he grabbed the line, but I felt like he was. If I needed help, I'd ask for it. Locking was not my strength. He sat facing forward, looking through the windshield like a reprimanded child, clearly annoyed with me.

As we negotiated the next four locks, Jim and I talked about the differences in our boats, the different tools we each had, and how we'd each have different strategies in tying up to the lock. We talked about the differences with having crew aboard and how much easier it is to lock through with two people. Smaller boats are thrown around more in the locks, but wind might affect larger boats more as they approach the upper height of a lock. Our conclusion was that every boat is different and how each of us approaches the locks depends on many factors.

We passed through the next four locks quickly. Jim dutifully stayed in the cabin the whole time. I assumed he was avoiding my wrath and hoped he'd forgiven me. At the top of Lock 6, I dropped him off and thanked him for his company. As much as I felt guilty for being so forceful with him, I was grateful he was with me. If I could have figured out a way to have someone with me for all the locks, it would be much easier. Unfortunately, I knew that wasn't going to happen. After dropping off Jim, I went eleven miles and through Lock 7 before tying up for the night. So far, I'd done well.

On the second day of locking through the Erie Canal, Lock 8 went well, but Lock 9 did not. I was confronted with hanging ropes. Gus and Row, on *Summerland*, were beside me on the portside wall of the 40-foot wide chamber. *Annabelle* was on the starboard wall. There was a boat in front of me and another behind me. As long as our boats stayed in position, we'd be fine with several feet between us. I needed to keep the 20-foot dangling lock rope taut, to minimize the distance I could move away from the wall. With only vertical leverage from the lock rope, I relied on my thrusters to push *Annabelle* horizontally against the wall.

The steely, gray gates closed behind us. Using my right hand to hold the rope in place with a half loop around the midship cleat, I used my left hand to control the bow and stern thrusters. I knew the Jacuzzi-like water would come in through the sides of this lock. Suddenly, the water started spewing into the lock against *Annabelle*'s stern; she was thrown sideways and my right arm seared in pain, like it was being ripped from its socket. I released the line and grabbed the throttle. My shirt was drenched in sweat. I wished I were in the lock alone as I tried to avoid colliding with *Summerland*, two feet off my stern. Now the boat which had started in front of me was dangerously close to my port side. My heart raced like a greyhound. I thrusted the throttle forward, thinking I could grind the bow into the scummy, barnacle-infested lock wall. The smell of burning diesel wafted around my little blue boat. *Annabelle* was like a small child in grown-up waters. I wanted to scream. *Annabelle's* thrusters were no match for the turbulence created by the 1200 cubic feet of murky water pouring in each second and I was terrified, operating in damage-control mode.

As the lock finished filling with the murky, brown water and calm was restored, I maneuvered *Annabelle* back against the lock wall, fearing what lay ahead. Thrown sideways, a larger boat would have hit *Summerland*. I had gotten my ass kicked, but there was no boat damage, just some serious arm bruising. What the hell was I going to do the next time I came to a lock with ropes?

The lock master came over and asked if I was okay. I was badly shaken and my right arm was swelling purple and red from my shoulder down to my elbow. The water level only went up 15 feet. I'd go through similar-sized locks that would raise me much higher.

I had one more lock to go through before stopping for the night at Riverlink Park, which had a good restaurant. At dinner I talked to Gus and Row who told me they had considered the possibility of *Annabelle* slamming into them and had chosen to focus on their lines versus trying to defend themselves against my boat. There was nothing they could've done. Their job was keeping their boat safe on their wall.

Another couple, who had joined us for dinner, had also lost control of their boat in Lock 9. Alone in the lock, they didn't sustain any damage or worry about other boats.

Before I went to bed that night, I studied the remaining locks for the Erie. So far, just the one lock had caused me problems—one out of ten. I had managed two locks with just ropes without problems, but I didn't have a different strategy for getting through the locks. I thought about what was working. I had to focus on something positive so I wouldn't feel too overwhelmed with self-doubt. I thought about the 12 upcoming locks and obsessively took notes on how many more had ropes. Six locks would be challenging: Locks 11, 15, 16, 17, 18 and 20. Of these, Lock 17 might be the hardest with a 40-foot lift, nicknamed the "Guillotine Lock" because of the way the gate comes down from overhead instead of closing from the sides like a normal gate. The other lifts ranged from 8 feet to 21 feet. I was not looking forward to any of them. Could I do it? I had my doubts.

On Thursday morning, I eased into Lock 11 with three other boats. SHIT! It happened again. My boat was thrown around like a rag doll. My arm got even more bruised and battered. I couldn't do this. For the 12-foot lift, sideways and throttling forward into the lock wall, I was doing everything in my power to avoid hitting the boats around me. Once the water settled and I maneuvered *Annabelle* against the wall, the lock master came up to me and asked if I was okay. I shrugged it off, "Just a few bruises." I didn't confess feeling traumatized, helpless and discouraged. *Annabelle* was managing better than I was. Losing control in one lock was an understandable mishap, but losing control in two was a disaster.

Manned by Barb and Ross, *Attitude Changer* went through the lock with me. Exiting the lock, I hailed them and explained that I needed to take a break. I'd anchor off to the side of the canal to regroup and catch up with them later. I couldn't hold back my tears, pretending to be brave any longer. I knew the next couple locks would have cables and I'd be okay. Still, I needed time to pull myself together.

I maneuvered *Annabelle* between two islands, dropped anchor, and lay down on my bed and cried. Should I turn around and go back? Nobody would blame me. Maybe I shouldn't be doing this Loop. If I went back, I'd have to go through Locks 9 and 11 all over again, this time down instead of up. Shit! I never wanted to see those locks again. How long could I just sit here peacefully at anchor? What if I didn't do anything?

My mind went into fantasy mode. Maybe, *Annabelle* and I could get airlifted out of here? I wouldn't even have to start the engine. I could imagine a big rescue helicopter, sending lines down to attach to my boat, lifting us out of the water and safely back to land.

At which point, my phone rang. It was Malcolm. Damn him. I swore he had a way of knowing when things were happening. I didn't answer the phone. I didn't want to talk to him. I'd call him later, maybe tomorrow. As much as Malcolm was supportive of my doing the Loop, I still harbored resentment toward him. In his last email, he mentioned his new girlfriend, and how they were pretty serious. Paragraphs about boating surrounded that sentence which screamed at me like it was in a bold 48-inch font.

Back to reality. I had to decide one way or another. Would I go forward or turn back? There wasn't much of a choice. I'd have to move forward. Still, I had nearly a hundred locks to go in the Loop, including the next eighteen in the Erie and Oswego canals before crossing Lake Ontario. How would I manage them? Worst case scenario, I could ask Dean to come up and help me. Meanwhile, I'd check all the other locks, from the Oswego Canal, through the Trent-Severn Canal in Canada, and down the Illinois, Mississippi, Tennessee and Tombigbee Rivers to see how they were set up. Thirteen locks down and 99 to go. I tried not to feel overwhelmed.

Anchored by Lock 11, I could put off any decisions to bail for now. On the front deck, I relaxed for a few minutes and took some deep breaths before pulling up the anchor. I mixed up one of my favorite Starbucks lime refresher drinks. I could put off my decision to bail for now. Somehow, I would get through this. Just then, I heard my VHF radio. "*Annabelle, Annabelle*, this is Lock 12."

I responded, "Lock 12, this is *Annabelle*."

"You can come up to lock 12. You'll be okay, we have pipes. We'll be gentle. Are you okay?"

"I'm okay. I was just pulling my anchor to come up there. I wanted to wait until I could lock through by myself. I'm on my way."

"We'll be ready for you. You'll be fine."

The lock master at Lock 12 was about as compassionate as anyone could be. Once I got tied to the pipe, he came by to make sure I was set. He filled the chamber gradually with water, so I didn't feel the current in the lock. As I reached the top of the lock, he came by again. We talked a little about the upcoming locks, and he said he'd radio ahead to ask them to be gentle with me and let them know I was on my way. He wished me luck in my journey. There were only two more locks to go through today, before I stopped in Canajoharie, and they'd have pipes.

At the following lock, divers were doing repairs. The lock master asked if I minded waiting half an hour while the scuba diver finished. I told him it was no problem for me to wait and asked if he could talk to me at the wall before the lock. At the entrance to the lock, there was a rock wall with cleats on the port side and the current from the waterfalls was on the starboard side. I was able to maneuver my boat into a position to have the port side of my boat against the wall, which I held in place with my left arm hanging out the portside window. The lock master lay down on his stomach on the top of the wall, so he could be closer to eye level with me. I asked him about the locking with the ropes. While explaining to him what happened in Locks 9 and 11, the current from the river whipped my boat around, just as it had been done in Lock 11, but reverse. This time my left arm took the brunt of the force. Unlike the previous situations, I was able to let *Annabelle* float safely away from the wall and then downstream. Now, I had matching bruises. Although it wasn't intentional, I couldn't have explained the situation better to the lock master. He saw what could happen when the current was stronger than I could manage.

From downstream, I called the lock master on the radio and told him I'd await his call to enter the lock. Within a few minutes, he called and opened the lock doors. Once I had gone up the lock and was waiting for the steel doors to open on the other side, he came to my boat to talk to me once more. As much as he may have felt badly for me and my bruised arms, he didn't have much advice.

In Canajoharie, I tied my boat to the free town wall. I saw my friends Row and Gus (*Summerland*), and Barb and Ross (*Attitude Changer*). We'd share dinner that evening. I brought my favorite peach cobbler, made with Cherith Valley brandied peaches. As we prepared for dinner, *Shiver Me Timbers* approached, with Andy and two crewmembers: Karen and Mike. There wasn't room on the wall, so they tied up to *Summerland*. I had seen *Shiver Me Timbers* in Norfolk and Cape May with different crew aboard. Andy was taking his boat through the Erie, then up the St. Lawrence Seaway, then back down the Atlantic Coast to return to Florida.

While we were eating, I brought up my struggles with the locks. Sometimes, people are so nice that they offer things that they don't expect to follow through with, but I still had five more rope locks before getting to the summit, including the "Guillotine Lock." Andy offered to let his friend, Mike, crew with me for the next three days to help me get through the rest of the rope locks. Politeness seemed to rule the day, and Mike didn't have much of a chance to back out before I quickly jumped at the offer. I could use all the help I could get even if this wasn't what Mike had signed up for with Andy and Karen. *Shiver Me Timbers* would set the pace, and I would follow along. I'd be their shadow, stopping wherever they wanted. At night, Mike would stay on the sailboat; during the day he'd be with me on *Annabelle*.

The crew of *Shiver Me Timbers* planned to get breakfast, go to the local museum, and leave after lunch. This plan worked for me since I wanted to walk to Lock 14 and talk to the lock master. Barb and Ross would leave in the morning, ahead of us. Row and Gus planned on staying a couple days to do some minor repairs on *Summerland*.

As I approached Lock 14 from land, I saw numerous "NO TRESPASSING" signs. I thought to myself, Really? What was the worst thing that could happen if I trespassed over there? They'd call the police and I'd be asked to leave the property. I could live with it. So, I trespassed.

I approached one of the men working at the lock. He pointed to the person in charge, and I walked over to the lock house. I apologized for trespassing, but showed the guy my painful, deep purple bruises, which covered the backs of both of my arms. I explained how my boat had been tossed around in Locks 9 and 11. Although Lock 14 had pipes, did he have any suggestions for me on how to get through the rest of the rope locks? At first, he didn't think there was anything more I could do. He said, "The lock master at each lock makes the decisions about their lock."

I responded, "I've heard that you've got some control over how fast the water fills."

"That's true. In general, there are expectations of how fast it should be filled, and it's important to keep the traffic moving through the locks."

"Can't the locks be filled slower to keep the boats safe?"

After a short pause, he said, "When you approach a lock, ask for an 'easy lift.' I'll radio ahead to the locks in my section, and we'll do everything we can to get you through safely."

I thanked him for his help and started back toward *Annabelle*. I could do this. I had Mike and I had the magic words.

Walking back to the dock, I passed a beautiful stone house that I first noticed on the way to the lock. An older man was working in the yard. I stopped to tell him how much I admired his house. He asked where I was from. I told him about my boat, *Annabelle*, and said that I was sailing the Great Loop. He said he enjoyed going down to the water to see the boats as they went through the Erie Canal. I let him return to his work, and I walked back to the dock. I needed to make my lunch and get ready to leave. I was feeling much more optimistic!

Shortly after I arrived on my boat, a tall man, about my age, approached. He liked my boat and mentioned that when he was young he'd been in the Coast Guard. He introduced himself as Michael. I invited him onto *Annabelle* to take the ten-second tour of my living quarters. He thanked me for letting him aboard and strode up the hill to the parking lot. Five minutes later, he started back down the hill with the older man from the stone house. Watching them come down the hill, I could imagine each of them a good forty years younger with the older man dragging a young boy down to the water. Only, here they were two adult men. Clearly, the older man was not happy about Michael returning so quickly to the car. Shaking my head, I wondered what would be next. I was amused to watch them approach *Annabelle*. The younger man was practically being forced down the hill.

I smiled and said hello to both of them. The older gentleman said to me out of frustration, "This is the deal. Michael has never been through any of the locks. I thought it would be nice if you could take him with you through a lock. He was supposed to ask you himself!"

Practically laughing, I said, "Okay."

Michael, looking down and blushing like a ten-year-old in trouble, said it was true; he'd been on many ships, out at sea, but never in the Erie Canal and never through a lock.

Looking him in the eye, I said, "Michael, I would love to take you through the next couple locks. I can drop you off at St. Johnsville."

As the older man hiked up the hill he looked back, smiling, "I'll see you in St. Johnsville." His mission seemed to be accomplished. I offered Michael a sandwich. I called Row and Gus to tell them I had Michael aboard and what the plan was. I had a stranger aboard. Sweet Michael!

As we finished our lunch, Andy, Karen, and Mike came down the hill toward their boat. I dropped my lines and told them to meet me in St. Johnsville. They pulled off the dock a couple minutes after I did. Michael would be hanging out with me through a couple locks, which would take two hours, at the most. Then I'd have Mike aboard. A part of me felt like God must have heard my prayers, or at least felt my pain, as he sent two good men to help me.

I explained to Michael I'd need for him to grab a line as we approached the wall, the exact thing I admonished Jim for in Lock 2. The lines would be too far apart for us to grab them both while the boat was stopped. He'd have to grab his line first, giving it slack, so I could get to my line. Reaching out my window only gave me 10 inches to work with. He agreed to my plan. As we approached the locks, we asked for an "easy lift." It worked. I felt exhilarated. In St. Johnsville, I maneuvered *Annabelle* alongside the dock, and Michael stepped off. Smooth. Back in the waterway, I pulled alongside *Shiver Me Timbers*. While heading up the canal, side by side,

Mike came aboard, stepping over his railing and down onto my boat. Smooth AGAIN!

The locking from that point on became much easier. Having a second person aboard and asking for the "easy lift" made all the difference. Even the "Guillotine Lock" went well. Mike complained that the lifts seemed much slower than they had been. They were and I was grateful. These locks could go as slow as molasses in January, and I'd be thrilled. Mike didn't understand how brutal Locks 9 and 11 had been for me. He wasn't dealing with painful, swollen, bruised arms. It would take a month for my arms to heal, while I looked like the poster girl on domestic violence billboards. "If your arms look like these, call 911."

For the next couple nights, while having dinner with the crew on *Shiver Me Timbers*, we'd make plans for the following day. Ideally, Mike would get onto my boat in the morning before we left. Somehow, I felt like they kept trying to sneak out ahead of me. In the morning, I'd walk over to the sailboat and ask about Mike. I'd be told that he'd be right over. A few minutes later, I'd watch *Shiver Me Timbers* pull off the dock with Mike aboard. I'd radio over and ask about Mike and be told they had forgotten. Seriously? Forgotten? Did they think I was that gullible? I'd pull up beside them, and Mike would come aboard, like the first time, side by side, heading upstream.

I felt like an annoying little sister, whom *Shiver Me Timbers* couldn't shake. I just had to get through these lift locks. Mike may not have liked me, and I wasn't always thrilled to have him aboard either, but damn it, I needed him! The only time I was frustrated with him was when he made comments about how simple these locks were, and he didn't see how ANYONE could have problems in them. Even with his comments, I was on my best behavior. When he said things like, "Tanya, when you lose control of your boat, just let go of the helm, and let your boat take care of you." I showed restraint and sucked it up. I wanted to rip his head off for saying such stupid things. It was okay, though; he would leave, and I'd never see him again. I hated the idea of desperately needing someone who didn't even want to be with me.

On our final day together, Saturday, June 21, we approached Sylvan Beach, on the eastern shore of Oneida Lake. It was late in the afternoon. I needed fuel at the marina, and *Shiver Me Timbers* would go a little further to the free docks. At the marina, I asked if they had any slips available. In addition to fuel, I needed to do laundry. The dockmaster told me they had just rented their last slip. Disappointed, I'd motor to the free docks.

Then, a couple of guys said, "Wait. Are you on your own? Is this your boat?"

Was it that obvious that Mike really wasn't "with" me?

The guys said, "We have a spot next to our boats. Our boat neighbor has anchored out for the night, so his slip is open. You can stay there."

"Thank you. Is it a far walk to the free dock?"

"No, about five minutes."

Mike said, "I want you to drop me off on *Shiver Me Timbers*. I don't want to walk."

Incredulously, I looked over at Mike, "No problem. I'll drop you off." I took Mike across the water, pulling aside the sailboat, and let Mike climb aboard. I waved goodbye to Andy and Karen, thanking them for loaning me Mike, then thanked Mike for coming with me.

When I docked *Annabelle* at the marina, the guys were waiting with their wives, and welcomed me to their summer playground. "Sorry we were a little pushy, insisting you stay here with us. We didn't think it was a good idea for you to stay at the free dock. It's Saturday night and you would've been stuck in front of all the bars. You wouldn't have gotten any sleep. We felt you'd be safer here."

"I appreciate it. Thank you so much!" I meant it with all my heart. I was incredibly grateful. A peaceful, quiet night, and a place to do my laundry, was everything I needed. I wouldn't even need to worry about other boats in the morning. I could wake up and leave when I wanted to. Literally, it was downhill from here to Lake Ontario.

As the sun was rising the following morning, I left the marina and was so grateful to have *Annabelle* back to myself. The locks from here to Lake Ontario would be descending and much easier. I crossed Lake Oneida, passing *Shiver Me Timbers*, and went into Brewerton. In the last of the Erie Canal Locks, I'd be dropping down 7 feet. Many of my Looper friends had been docked in Brewerton. Lock 23 was filled with five Looper boats, including *Attitude Changer* and *Estrellita*. We were ready to head north through the Oswego Canal, with seven locks to bring us down to the level of Lake Ontario in Oswego, New York. The challenges of the Erie Canal were behind us.

On the way to Oswego, I noticed a town called Phoenix, which had a free town dock. This town was different than the Phoenix I knew; small enough to ride a bicycle around. I pulled my boat over to the docks, tied *Annabelle* up, and walked around. According to the Active Captain app, a group of young people, the "Bridge House Brats," worked to make sure the boaters were very comfortable, including bringing breakfast to the boats from local restaurants. I imagine I would have actually seen these people if I had docked on Friday or Saturday night, but it was Sunday, and nobody was in sight. Up the road, I found a local bar/restaurant and ordered a cheeseburger. I asked the bartender if there were any grocery stores nearby, within biking distance. She explained the only place around was the food mart at the gas station. She gave me directions, and after lunch, I rode my bike there. If running low on supplies, these food marts would at least replenish my supply of peanut butter. If I were lucky, they might have decent bread. Usually, they had the Wonder Bread of my youth, which could compete with Twinkies for shelf life and cardboard for taste. The only item I was ever really worried about was half-and-half for my morning coffee. One way or another, I could always pick up a Hershey Bar with almonds. With a basket full of bacon, eggs and bread, on my way back to *Annabelle* I passed a roadside vegetable stand where I bought fresh strawberries, lettuce, cucumber and tomatoes. My grocery excursion was a success.

The afternoon sun beat down on *Annabelle*; it was hot and she felt like a dry sauna. I closed all the shades, covered all the hatches, turned on the air conditioner, and washed her down. Inside, she felt like a cave. It was a relaxing afternoon in Phoenix. I took pictures of the sign, sending it via text to my friend Susan, whom I visit every time I fly into Phoenix, Arizona. On this day, the only thing this sleepy little town had in common with the one in Arizona was the heat.

The morning came quickly and I had just a few more locks to go through before Oswego. They were all easy. I would lay over in Oswego for a few days while waiting for storms to pass through before crossing Lake Ontario. The Oswego City Marina was within walking distance of the downtown area and I met up with Barb and Ross there. The staff there was very helpful and arranged a haircut appointment for Barb.

The hair salon was a full service salon. I decided to walk up the road and find out what their specials were. I wanted much more than a haircut. My body needed some tender loving care. The salon was beautifully appointed with roses outside the front doors. The young woman greeting guests listed the different services they offered. I wanted them all: the haircut, facial, manicure, pedicure and a massage too. The whole package was less than $300. I arranged to come by the next day after an early lunch. I felt lucky they could fit me in.

Back at the marina, I noticed a large sportsfisher, *Knight Life*, with a gold burgee of the Loop, signifying they had completed the Loop. I was interested in meeting these "Gold Loopers." I approached their boat, knocked on their hull, and when they came out, I introduced myself. This couple had done the Loop a year or two earlier and were going up the Trent Severn waterway, then planned to return to New Jersey, where they lived. Pat and Dick, a couple about the age of my parents, were waiting in Oswego for better weather, as I was.

After a relaxing "spa day," I saw Sylvi and Michael had arrived on their sailboat and were docked beside me. That night, I went over to their boat for a glass of wine, cheese and crackers, while we watched a magnificent lightning storm. Along the Erie Canal, they had engine problems that turned out were fairly easy to fix. Something had clogged their water intake for the engine, causing it to overheat. Once they removed the foreign object, their boat ran well. This was the second time I saw them since meeting them in Waterford. They were almost done with their journey. They'd make one last run to a town called Sackett's Harbor, just up the St. Lawrence River from Lake Ontario. They boasted about this charming town, where they kept their boat. I decided to make their town my next stop as well. While sitting on their sailboat, protected from the pounding rain, we talked about what kinds of trips we would like to do next.

Sylvi said, "We plan to sell our sailboat and buy a canal boat in Europe."

From there, she told me about the canals and the narrow, long shapes of the boats. Their next adventure was waiting for them. I had learned something new. I hadn't even thought about what to do after the Loop.

15

Lake Ontario and Into Canada

I was lazy on the morning I crossed Lake Ontario. Usually, *Annabelle* was one of the first boats off the docks, leaving just after the fishermen, but I left after Sylvi and Michael. They were in a hurry to get to Sackett's Harbor, New York, where they had friends meeting them. It was the last day of their trip. I'd meet up with them later, barely being awake enough to help with their lines. Well, they were in as much of a hurry as anyone can be with a sailboat. They'd motor across the lake, as their mast had been dropped to their deck prior to going through the Erie Canal because sailboat masts are too tall to go under most bridges, which are only 20 feet off the water. They'd raise their mast when they got home. Once the mast is taken down, the pole-like structure can either be shipped to a destination, or laid lengthwise along the sailboat, cradled by wood supports like on Sylvi and Michael's sailboat. The masts take up a lot of room on the sailboat and usually hang over the ends.

Within an hour or two, I released my own lines and headed out into the Great Lake. It seemed more ominous than it really was. Technically, I was just cutting the corner of the lake, and I'd never be more than three or four miles from shore. Barb and Ross would follow behind me. On this windless day, the lake was smooth and glassy. The fog rolled in quickly, within a mile of passing through the Oswego Inlet. The fog was so thick that it looked the same all the way around the boat. It was difficult to tell where the water stopped and the air began;

the transition from water to air was blurred in the whiteness. Visually, there were no clues of any movement except for the chart plotter, which showed *Annabelle's* location. I could hear the chugalugging of the diesel engine, but nothing else.

I turned on the navigation lights and wondered how long the fog would last. *Annabelle's* radar was not working; it had been sketchy the whole time, like it had a mind of its own. In addition to the radar not working, I noticed the autopilot had also quit working. Radar was meant for days like today, when I couldn't actually see. Autopilot was something I needed every day. Without autopilot, I couldn't just leave the helm and go to the bathroom or make a sandwich. *Annabelle* could get turned around if I wasn't at the helm. Some systems on *Annabelle* seemed to work very randomly, especially the electronics. The wiring behind my helm station, which I could access only through the V-berth, looked like a rat's nest. I'd have to look for loose wires when I got into port. I was steering like my Mom had in New Jersey, looking down at the chart plotter instead of looking out the window. I couldn't see where I was going, but I knew my direction, forward toward the Thousand Islands in the St. Lawrence River.

The heavy fog lasted an hour then gradually started to clear. I was able to see a little way into the distance. I didn't see Barb and Ross until we had both cleared the fog, and they were about a mile or two behind me. It was a short day; I'd only log four and a half hours on the engine, getting into Sackett's Harbor around lunchtime.

Sylvi and Michael helped me tie my lines when I pulled into my slip at Navy Point Marina in Sackett's Harbor. The neighboring boats were helpful as well. I was in a covered slip with other smaller boats around me. At the T dock, at the end of our slips, was a massive 60-foot yacht that I had seen a couple times coming up the Erie. Within a few minutes, Barb and Ross came in. Their initial slip was covered, but their boat was too tall and they were moved a few docks over to an uncovered slip. Sylvi and I went over to help them tie up.

I returned to my boat, made a sandwich, and noticed a faint humming sound. In Waterford, I had replaced the switch to my bilge pump, and the noise I heard now was similar to that noise, but it wasn't coming from the engine compartment. It was louder in my small bathroom. The only motor in the bathroom was for the shower sump pump, which is housed in a clear container under the sink, through an 8-inch round access panel. After opening the small cabinet, I emptied the cabinet, opened the access hatch, and the sound got louder.

The clear box holding the pump, where the water drains from the bathroom, is larger than the access area. Tubes and wires ran above, around, and into the box. One tube ran from the drain into the box and another tube ran from the box to a drainage hole in the hull above the water line. Wires are attached to the small motor for the pump. *Annabelle* was so small, though, it was difficult to access these connections. Lying on the floor awkwardly, it was difficult to get my hands into the small area to get the lid off. Being larger than the access hole, the lid had to be maneuvered to the side. First though, there were four screws that had to come off, two of which were not visible. I had a thumb screwdriver, which is about an inch long, which I could turn between my thumb and index finger to loosen the screws. I contorted my body into position to loosen the top, with my torso on the bathroom floor, and my legs in the narrow companionway. Getting the screws out was the easy part; maneuvering the lid was more difficult. As I was lying on my floor, wrestling with the lid, Ross and Barb knocked on my window.

In a loud voice, Ross said, "Tanya. You in there?"

I scrambled to my feet and opened the door to my cabin. "My shower sump is broken; I was trying to get it out."

Barb chimed in, "Have Ross look at it; he's good at that kind of thing."

"I don't know; it isn't exactly easy to get to."

Ross countered with, "Well, let me have a look." He poked his head around the corner into the bathroom, seeing the cabinet door open with all the cleaning supplies lined up around the edges of the bathroom and the small access hole inside the cabinet. He could hear the motor running, but there wasn't anything to pump out. "You need another pump. You're right; it isn't easy to get to."

Earlier, Barb, Ross and I had made plans to walk around town, so I asked them to give me time to get the information I needed for the pump. I took my iPhone, positioned it above the box and took a couple pictures. This gave me the information I would need for a replacement. The motor was still running, but it wouldn't hurt anything. I closed up *Annabelle* so the three of us could walk into town.

As we were walking down the dock, the boater from the boat diagonally behind me asked, "I overheard you talking; is there anything I can help you with? I have my car here."

"Is there a West Marine store around here?"

"Yeah, it's about fifteen minutes away."

"My shower sump is broken, I need to replace it." He must have sensed how torn I was feeling, between wanting to go with my friends and wanting to get *Annabelle* fixed.

"I've got to get my boat cleaned up, but I'll be around all afternoon. When you get back, I'll take you over there."

"I appreciate it. My name is Tanya."

He nodded and held his hand out to shake mine, "Tom."

A quick handshake, "Thanks, Tom, I'll be back soon."

Barb, Ross, and I walked around the small town, which reminded me a lot of Southport. Pan Galley was reported to be one of the best restaurants in town, with a one man band, the owner, who entertained the guests at night. We hoped to make reservations for dinner that night. The only reservation available was at 5:00, just after they opened before the music started. Because of their reputation for great food, we took it. When we got back to the marina, my kind neighbor had finished washing his boat and was ready to take me to West Marine.

Nothing was more important than my shower sump pump. Without it working, I couldn't shower on my boat. "I'm ready to go. Thanks for taking me."

"No problem. I know what it's like to be on a boat without a vehicle. It happens to all of us one time or another. Where are you going?"

"I am doing the Great Loop."

He quizzically looked at me with his eyebrows furrowed, "By yourself?"

"Yup."

"I don't mean any disrespect or anything, but I don't like boating by myself, and can't imagine doing what you're doing by myself. Why didn't you go with someone?"

"I've been single a long time, and I figured if I had to wait around for someone to go with, I'd never go. I thought about having my son come with me, but he needs to move on with his life and not be hanging out with his mom."

"I can't believe he let you go by yourself. I guess you've been boating most your life."

"No, just three years, I had to learn about boating to do this trip."

"You didn't grow up on the water?"

"I grew up in the desert. Just over three years ago, I had an opportunity to live wherever I wanted, so I chose to live near the water so I could learn about boating."

At West Marine I found my parts quickly, and we went back to the marina. He offered to stop by the grocery store for me on the way back, but I had plenty of groceries from Oswego. When we got back to our boats he offered to help me put in my shower sump, but I explained it was a very small space, and probably easier for me to do myself. He'd be leaving that afternoon. I thanked him for his generosity, and we parted ways. Throughout the Loop, I'd meet strangers who would go out of their way to help me in whatever way they could. I felt very fortunate.

After fixing my pump, I had a short time to get ready for dinner. Barb, Ross and I walked up the street to the Pan Galley, where we sat in a beautifully landscaped garden for a delicious dinner. I ordered lamb with asparagus; Barb and Ross ordered a salad and burger to share. I was a little surprised they were willing to go to this high-end restaurant, as they had been very clear from the first time I met them that they wanted to show that ordinary people could do the Loop on a shoestring budget. When we were together at Lamb's Marina, Barb and Ross looked for a Golden Corral, joking that they might find all the inexpensive buffets on the Loop. In Cape May, at the Lobster House restaurant Barb and Ross ordered burgers, while other Loopers ordered seafood. The three of us had a wonderful dinner at Pan Galley, even if we missed the night's entertainment.

After dinner, an older couple at the end of the dock, on a 60-footer, invited me to their yacht for docktails. *Annabelle* was damn cute and noticeable and they had seen her on the water a few times. I felt a little awkward as I didn't know this couple, who had been boating for most of their lives. Their son joined them for part of their journey. "We'd see your boat, and we were just so impressed with how you handled her. Our son was with us, and well… he is single, and we kept telling him, he needed to meet a girl like you."

"Thank you. That's very kind."

"Do you mind if we give him your information; maybe he can email you?"

I felt even more awkward. "Sure." They had my boat card, so they could give it to anyone they wanted. It also had my blog address listed on it.

As the sun set at 9:00 p.m., which was getting later and later, I got off their large yacht and walked over to where Barb and Ross were hanging out with their new friends. I wanted to find out the plan for the following day. After quick introductions, we decided to leave for a small town in the Thousand Islands, called Clayton, known for three things: River Rat Cheese, the Antique Boat Museum, and its proximity to Boldt Castle on

Heart Island. We'd stay in Clayton two nights before crossing into Canada.

We left midmorning and arrived in Clayton midafternoon. On this Saturday afternoon, the free city docks were full with small fishing boats lined up just inside the break wall, all in a narrow lane leading to the boat ramp next to the dockmaster's office. The city dockmaster told me I'd have to wait for the smaller boats to go home for the evening before I could find a free spot. On the other side of the lane of boats was a marina, which appeared to have many empty slips. Barb and Ross arrived before I did, and pointed me in the direction of the marina, to an available slip beside the public dock.

I had a choice to anchor in the choppy waters outside the marina and wait, or go to the marina next door. I pulled into the slip beside the public dock, so I could be close to my friends. I worried that I was in someone's slip, but nearby boaters assured me that nobody was renting it and nobody was available in dock office until Monday. I felt like I was parked illegally; I wouldn't park a car in someone else's driveway without permission and using someone's boat slip felt sketchy, but nobody around me seemed to care.

On the other side of the city dock, across the narrow water lane, was another Looper boat, *Midas Touch*, named after the couple's golden retriever. Clayton was a beautiful little town and everything was within walking or bicycling distance. I found a great little restaurant for breakfast; the only seating was at the bar. An older man sat next to me and the waitress knew immediately what he'd be having. She brought his coffee, asked if he was having "the usual," to which he replied a brief, "Yep." Then she brought him one egg and a piece of toast. He was a man of few words. I sat quietly having my eggs, bacon, and hash browns, quietly eavesdropping on the waitresses, as they ran from table to table making sure the tourists and regulars were all taken care of.

One afternoon in Clayton, I rode my bike to the grocery store. I could manage a full supply of groceries in my bike basket with a small, lightweight backpack, made from the same thin material of rain ponchos. The backpack could be crunched up and put into a four by six-inch pouch. Barb and Ross invited Marian, Pat, and me to dinner on *Attitude Changer*. I had seen Ross at the Antique Boat Museum earlier in the day. Barb wasn't as excited as we were looking at these older boats. At the grocery store, I bought fresh berries for dessert.

Making dessert for five people in my little boat took some doing. The dessert called for berries, whipped cream, lemon curd, and one-inch cubes of shortcake, layered. I only had small bowls, nothing large enough to whip the cream in. When I first started, the cream splattered all over the cabin. Finally, I managed to get the hang of it. My friend, Deb, who had given me the recipe, was a diehard, make-it-from-scratch baker, so she made the lemon curd herself. I was cheating by using store-bought curd from a specialty shop. The dessert was delicious and I was glad I had something to share, but I wouldn't make it again, not with the mess I had to clean up.

On our last night in Clayton, in typical Looper fashion, we discussed travel plans for the next day. We'd go up to Boldt Castle and walk around the island for a couple hours, then go to Gananoque, Canada, to check into Canadian Customs. We talked about the procedure of checking in, what we heard and what we had read.

Barb made a comment about the Canadian flag, "I don't see why we should put the Canadian flag above our United States flag. I'm an American first."

I responded, "Because it shows respect. It's tradition throughout the world to fly the host country's flag above your own."

"I don't want to put their country above mine; my loyalty is to the States."

"I guess you'll do whatever you want. I'm not sure I'll fly my yellow flag for customs." A yellow flag is used to signal that a boat has just arrived in a new country and has not been approved through customs. It stays in place, clearly visible above all other flags, until the captain of the vessel has been given approval to be in the country. I explained, "I heard it's a quick phone call; the custom's officer gives you a number, then you're done. If I only have to fly the flag for ten minutes while walking over to the videophone, then it isn't worth climbing up and down from *Annabelle's* roof. If they tell me they want to search *Annabelle*, then I'll put up the yellow flag."

"We don't have a yellow flag, but Ross has a yellow shirt we can use."

Our three boats—*Annabelle, Midas Touch,* and *Attitude Changer*—left Clayton, the birthplace of Thousand Island dressing, around 9 a.m. We navigated our way through the many islands of the St. Lawrence River, and found Heart Island, the home of Boldt Castle, which was on the United States side of a seemingly imaginary border with Canada. It's quite a tourist attraction for Americans and Canadians, with ferries ushering passengers to and from the island from Alexandria Bay and Gananoque. George Boldt started building the castle for his beautiful wife, Louise, in 1900. Four years after construction began, Louise died, and the castle died along with her. Construction stopped and what remained was left to the elements.

In 1977, the Thousand Islands Bridge Authority bought the island for a dollar for the purpose of restoration, with the provision that all money from the island revenue would be spent toward restoration. Since then, they have spent millions of dollars renovating the island. There is a small fee to tour the castle and they have a free public dock. Different buildings include a boathouse on a separate island with its own ferry. Barb and Ross, who pulled up to the dock just after me, weren't sure they could manage some of the steep stairs of the old castle and wanted to have lunch before wandering around the island. They told me to go on ahead of them; they'd catch up with me later. I was left to my own devices wandering the island. I took many pictures of the beautifully manicured gardens and buildings, but what intrigued me the most was the border patrol station.

Next to the ferry terminal, the cedar siding on the small building was inviting and warm. It exists on this island for the Canadians who need to check into the United States to visit Heart Island. The station was a one room office, with a counter and a small desk. When I looked in the window, there was a nice-looking young man sitting at the desk. If I were to walk in, it seemed like he would've offered me a cup of coffee. This was such a stark contrast to Nogales, Arizona, where the U.S. Customs and Immigration Service, part of Homeland Security, feels like a police state.

In Nogales, the border officials drive four-wheel drive vehicles, carry automatic weapons, and are everywhere. For years, while commuting between Nogales and Tucson, I'd go through the checkpoint on my way home. I was used to the lines, with canine patrols sniffing each car for drugs. With my English-German heritage, it was more of an inconvenience than anything. I was always waved through, with minimal conversation. They'd ask, "Citizenship?" A brief response, "U.S." Then, they'd motion me forward, and I'd drive home. It was simple. My car was never searched and I always felt respected.

The first day I started commuting with staff of Latin heritage, I learned that my "white experience" did not match theirs; the color of our skin and hair mattered. As we approached the checkpoint, my three companions started rummaging through their purses for their licenses and passports. Mili frantically said, "Tanya, get your ID out!"

Calmly, I replied, "I don't need to."

"Please, just get it out, so we don't get pulled over. I want to get home at a decent hour tonight. I'm tired."

"Mili, I've never had to show my ID before, why should it be any different now?" The three of them glared at me. If I caused a delay, this might be the last time I was invited to commute with them. But I was stubborn, and I thought the whole precaution was absurd. I'd been through the checkpoint a thousand times.

As we approached the patrolmen, dogs sniffed the cars as we slowly progressed forward, one car at a time. When we arrived, the border patrol agent took a quick look at their licenses, and then with his flashlight aimed in my face in the backseat asked, "Citizenship?"

I responded "U.S."

He motioned us forward. We made it through without any problems; I'd still be allowed to carpool.

Mili looked back at me from the front seat, shaking her head, "Ay, Tanya. You had me worried."

"Mili, we're all Americans, it shouldn't be that difficult."

"But it is." For Mexican Americans and Peruvian Americans, like my three companions in the car, border checkpoints can be difficult, especially in the conservative state of Arizona.

I almost felt guilty walking by the checkpoint on Heart Island without anyone asking my citizenship. I imagined I could point to the U.S. flag on top of *Annabelle*, flapping in the breeze.

After spending three hours at Boldt Castle, I returned to *Annabelle*. I had seen my Looper companions, who told me they'd be along shortly. I'd have time to make lunch before leaving. I took my Canadian flag from its storage place in my cabin, climbed to the top of my cabin and on tiptoes placed it above my American flag. I was ready for Canada. On our three boats, we dropped dock lines and convoyed to Gananoque, where there was a large marina, and more importantly, our Canadian entrance point.

Barb hailed the city marina, and made reservations for our three boats in adjacent slips. High school-age dockhands came running to help with our lines. I was proficient at docking by myself, but Barb was always looking out for me. I overheard her tell the dockhand, "You make sure to help *Annabelle*; she is single-handing." The dockhands came to my boat first. I had all my lines and fenders ready, so all I needed to do was step off my boat and tie off. In reality, these teenagers were almost more in my way, but they were trying hard to be helpful. I suggested they help the other two boats, which were bigger, and in my estimation, more difficult to dock. The dockhands showed me where to go to sign in and call customs, then ran to help *Attitude Changer* and *Midas Touch*.

I was the first into the office to sign in and pay my dockage bill. The dockmaster told me that I should be calling Customs first. Behind the building, I found the videophone on the wall with a number posted beside it. I called the number. The phone was too high for me to see it well. I felt as if I had to jump for them to see anything more than the top of my head. I had brought a piece of paper and pen to write my entrance number. The official on the other end of the line had only a few questions for me.

"Who is on your boat?"

"Just me."

"Just you?"

"Yes." I gave him my full name and date of birth.

"What is the state and registration number of your boat?"

I gave him the information.

"How long do you plan to be in Canada?"

"About a month."

"Where will you exit Canada?"

"I'm not sure; I guess Drummond Island."

"Write this number down and put it on the dockside of your boat. It needs to be visible by any Canadian official at all times while you are in Canada."

By then, Ross was standing behind me for his turn to use the phone. "Can you check in my friend, who is here on his boat as well?"

"No, ma'am. He has to call separately, there's a queue of calls, and it isn't allowed."

"Okay. Thank you." I hung up and let Ross make his call. After paying for dockage, I returned to *Annabelle* and put my numbers inside of the main cabin windows on both sides of her. I never had to put up the yellow flag; I never saw a Customs official. Barb had meticulously hung Ross's yellow shirt above their flag and was awaiting her official captain's return. Per protocol, only the captain of the vessel is allowed to leave the boat to call Customs. Once the captain has declared the crew members of the boat and it's been approved, the crew is allowed to leave the boat. I was surprised I wasn't asked anything about my passport, not even my passport number. We were told that we couldn't bring fruits, vegetables, plants, or more than a liter of alcohol across the border. However, I wasn't asked about any of that. Along the way, I'd run into other people who were asked many more questions than I was.

Canada is very strict about guns. Theoretically, a person can bring a gun into Canada for hunting and only if it is documented correctly. I'd even been told to call my flare gun a "signal launcher." A Looper friend had filled out paperwork to bring a shotgun with him. In trying to be upfront and honest about the gun, he initiated the conversation about having it aboard and told the official he had filled out the paperwork. Within minutes, Canadian Border Patrol was searching his boat and confiscating the gun. In addition, Border Patrol searched another Looper's boat which had previously been cleared.

Canada was the only place people didn't ask me if I had a gun aboard, which was probably one of the most common questions people asked me on the trip. My strategy was to stay away from places where I didn't feel comfortable. So far, I felt very comfortable and surrounded by people watching out for me.

After Ross and Pat returned to our three boats, the five of us relaxed and talked about how simple Customs was, the different questions we were each asked. Then we tended to the normal business of boating, discussing our next day's plans. Many of our friends would be staying in Kingston for the Canada Day celebrations, held July 1, the following day. With all the celebrations, it was difficult to get into a marina in Kingston, so we opted to go further to a smaller marina in a town west of Kingston. One way or another, we were starting a new chapter in this journey—Canada.

Peterborough Lift Lock

Healey Falls Flight Lock

Lindsay Lock 33, Lock Workers

16

Canada and the Trent-Severn Waterway

Arriving in Canada was a milestone and would bring new challenges. Communication, which I took for granted in the States, would be more difficult here. I called Verizon ahead of time and added the "Mexico/Canada plan" to my service, allowing for free texts and 1,000 minutes per month. The minutes would help me get in and out of marinas, making whatever arrangements that needed to be made, but nothing more. Data was simply too expensive. I couldn't use my Verizon mobile hotspot for Internet; I'd only have access to public Wi-Fi at marinas.

On July 1, Canada Day, our three boats left from Gananoque toward the Trent-Severn Waterway. We originally hoped to stay in Kingston, but the marinas were full for the Canadian celebrations, so we went further west to Collins Bay Marina. On our third day in Canada we arrived in Trenton, the gateway to the Trent-Severn Waterway, which would take us inland to the Georgian Bay, covering 240 miles. The Trent-Severn Canal system that connected Lake Ontario to Lake Huron was primarily used for recreational purposes, although it had roots in industry and logging.

Having struggled so much with the Erie Canal, I was worried about the Trent-Severn Canal with its 45 locks. Canadian lock rules were different from the rules in the Erie, and even different from one province to another; I knew there were three locks that would be very different from any I had seen. Two had large containers of water which either moved up or down with a hydraulic lift, like one sees at Jiffy Lube. However, these were massive, with large rectangular pools of water. The third unusual lock, second to the last, would be on railroad tracks, lifting the boats out of the water and over a road, then down on the other side. A couple of locks were flight locks, meaning the first lock would take the boat up one level, then the large gates would open at the top of the lock and the boat would go into a second lock to lift the boat even higher. As much as I had read up on these different locks, I was still afraid. My two-week old bruises were still green, albeit fading, covering the backs of both my arms.

The dockmaster in Trenton was very helpful. Because of weather, I'd stay there two days. The first lock was a couple miles away. I didn't feel safe taking my bike on the busy road, so I walked through a beautiful park on the side of the canal. At the lock, I bought my one-way seasonal pass that would allow me to go through all the locks heading west and allow me to tie up to lock walls overnight. Many of the locks are in small towns which makes it cheaper than paying for traditional marinas. Although I could have paid for my lock pass when I actually arrived in the lock in *Annabelle*, I needed to figure out how I'd get through. More than anything else, I wanted advice.

As I approached the lock, I noticed the sign that gave basic information: Engines must be turned off. Life jackets were mandatory. I didn't have any problem with the life jacket, but turning my engine off was a scary concept. How could I get myself out of trouble if I didn't have my engine running? I already knew the locks had cables attached at the top and bottom of the lock, so tying on shouldn't be problematic like the dangling lines of the Erie.

As I paid for my passage, I asked the lock master if there was anything else I needed to know.

"You have to tie off on two cables."

"Two? But I'm only one person. Throughout the Erie Canal, I reached out my window and just tied onto the one cable."

"We don't allow that here. It's safer with two."

"But how can I control my boat, if I'm not at the helm?"

"Your motor won't be running anyway."

I was on the verge of tears and felt panicked. "I don't understand why can't I keep my motor running?.."

"These are small locks; we don't want anyone having problems with carbon monoxide from the motor fumes."

That made sense to me. I didn't want to be getting headaches as I went through the locks. I could see his point. I think he must have seen the fear in my eyes. He tried to reassure me. Finally, he said, "Look, ma'am, I'll let you go through with just the one line through your window, if you really want. I don't think anyone else will though. We'll do our best to help get you through these locks safely."

"Can I go through them with just my boat, not with other boats?" I was pushing my luck.

"Ma'am, we're short staffed and need as many boats going through together as possible. Our staff has to go from one lock to the next. My staff here is responsible for the three locks. Once we get boats through here, we drive up to the next lock, then the one after that. After we get everyone through, we come back here and start all over. This isn't like the States, where they have staff at every lock."

I guess I'd been selfish to think I might get lucky and go through on my own. "Can you tell me if the water is filling more from the front or the back of the lock?"

I could tell he was getting frustrated with me. He probably wondered how on earth I had made it this far. "Are you coming through today?"

"No, tomorrow."

"I'll watch for you." Then, he turned his back to me and returned to his paperwork.

I thanked him for his time. He briefly glanced back up as I walked out the door. Out of the corner of my eye, I saw him shaking his head.

Returning the couple miles back to the marina, I worried how I'd make it through these locks with all the new rules. If I had a system that was working for me, why couldn't I just stick with it? Not that it worked for me all the time.

The following morning, I unhitched my boat from the dock at 8:30, giving the first boats a head start to the first lock, which opened at 8:00. I hoped to show up after everyone else had already gone through. I'd be back to traveling alone for now. If I ended up in the same marina as my Looper friends, it was good, but if I didn't, I was okay with that too.

These locks could hold four to six boats, depending on the size. The locks were smaller than the ones on the Erie. The gates had hand cranks, or body cranks, depending on how you looked at them. The lock workers would lean into the two levers, turning a large cog wheel which opened the lock gates.

I had put a lot of thought into how I was going to tie off on two cables. I decided to start the way I was used to, by reaching out my window and hooking a 6-foot long fender line around the cable. Then, I tied the line around my cleat, even though everyone says not to ever, ever, ever cleat off the line. There were stories about cleats being ripped off the side of boats, leaving gaping holes. In the Erie Canal, I would've ended up with a hole in the side of *Annabelle* had I not released the line when she was thrown about. It took all the strength I had, just to release it from being looped halfway around the cleat. I went to the back of my boat, and with another fender line, tied off the stern of *Annabelle*. I'd have to keep a close eye on both lines, running back and forth between them, checking on the tension. The cables in this lock were much closer together than in the Erie. The lines were about 15 feet apart, which worked for my 25-foot boat. After tying off, I went back into the cabin and turned off my engine. I thought to myself that it wasn't so bad. Maybe I could handle this, especially if all the locks had cables so close together. Two other boats entered the lock just after me. I was tied off before either of them. The lock gates shut behind us, and the lock started filling with water. As I approached the top of the lock, the lock master from the day before came over and asked how I was doing.

I smiled at him and said, "I like your locks. I think I'll be okay."

As I turned the key to start up the engine, he smiled back at me and told me to go up the canal slowly, as his crew would be helping me through the next couple locks. I felt happy that I could do this. These locks would be much better than the Erie. By the time I finished the seventh lock, I was relaxed. I practically felt like I was friends with the lock workers, who drove from one lock to the next. One of the workers came to my boat and asked how far I'd be going that day. I told him

I'd stop in Campbellford for the night. He told me about their farmers' market and suggested I go to a specific bakery.

Around 7 p.m. I pulled into Campbellford, with another two hours of daylight. The canal went through the center of town, with a couple bridges over the small river. On both sides of the canal, boats were docked against the walls. On the left side, I recognized *Knight Life*, the sportsfisher boat from Oswego with the Gold Loopers from New Jersey. I pulled in front of them and tied to the concrete wall. Signs directed boaters to the office to sign in if they were planning to stay the night and needed power or bathroom facilities. The free wall, which didn't have these amenities, was on the other side of the river. After registering, I asked if they had recommendations for dinner; I was hungry from my day's journey. The nice young lady pointed out a local food bistro at the corner that served organic vegetables and free range meats. I walked straight to the restaurant deciding that I could say hello to Pat and Dick on *Knight Life* afterwards. At the Bridge Eatery & Public House, I ordered buffalo meatloaf with potatoes and veggies. It doesn't sound much like a summer recipe, but this was Canada. Chilly evenings reminded me of winter in Tucson. The buffalo meatloaf was delicious and I saved some for the next day's lunch.

When I returned to my boat, a note from Pat said, "Come over for a glass of wine." I stuck my leftovers in the refrigerator and walked over to their boat. When I arrived, they asked what I had done so far in Campbellford. I explained I had just gotten here and had dinner. I told them about the bakery suggested by the lock worker. They told me to go to the Butter Tart Factory instead, with pastries so delicious they were tempted to stay another day just to buy more. They gave me a butter tart which they had saved from the morning. It was like a small pecan pie, but ten times better, and I love pecan pie. I was told to go to the Butter Tart factory as soon as they opened because when they sold out they closed for the day. I'd walk to the bakery in the morning.

From Oswego, Pat and Dick had traveled up the Trent-Severn to the Georgian Bay and were on their way back down to return to New Jersey. They were traveling much faster than I was, and it amazed me that I had run into them again.

First thing in the morning, I found the Butter Tart Factory, but they didn't open until 10:00. I had hoped it was like those bakeries that opens their doors at 5 a.m. I had time to cross over the bridge and go to the farmers' market and have a full breakfast at a family restaurant. I was at the door to the Butter Tart Factory the minute they opened, and bought a half dozen butter tarts. I'd have to make them last. I wondered if you gained more weight by eating them quickly or savoring them over a few days. I'd limit myself to one a day. Later, I'd regret not filling my freezer with them. Who cared about a few pounds when it came to something so delicious?

After the Butter Tart Factory, there was no reason to stay in Campbellford. *Knight Life* left early in the morning, and I was ready to continue my journey east. Stocked with fresh lettuce and tomatoes from the farmers' market, and leftovers from dinner, I left around noon.

The next few locks were close together. At 1:30, I arrived at the first of two flight locks at Healey Falls. Their size is intimidating, because they have two compartments for water, like two stair steps. Since I had started the Trent-Severn locks a couple hours behind everyone else, I was going through most of the locks by myself. Passing through the lower gate, *Annabelle* was lifted 24 feet. Then upon entering the second gate, she was lifted another 24 feet before the final gate opened to exit the lock. When I got to the top of the flight lock, I asked if I could leave *Annabelle* there for a few minutes so I could take pictures. The view, looking down at the green valley with the river flowing through it, was spectacular.

The lock master took pride in the garden outside his office, and planted flowers beside the doors. I asked him why his lock walls were so clean. In previous years, he power washed them in preparing for winter. With reductions in funding and help, he couldn't be as meticulous, but they were still the cleanest that I had seen.

The lock masters coordinated the timing of opening and closing the locks. They'd call each other, and by the time I went from one lock to the next, the subsequent lock would be ready and I'd be invited in. At the entrance of each lock is a wall with a blue stripe, where one can wait until the lock opens. In addition to the waiting wall is another wall where on a first-come, first-serve basis, one can tie up for a break, a picnic, or to stay for the night.

I had relaxed enough with the locks that I was sitting on the bow of my boat while locking. I'd get the stern tied up first, then go to the front and relax while holding the line. I enjoyed these moments, as it got me out of the cabin and away from the helm. They were perfect breaks.

Big Chute Railroad Lock

17

Georgian Bay

One of the highlights of approaching Georgian Bay is going through the Big Chute railway lock. This "lock" is the only one of its kind in North America. A massive, steel, open-ended railroad car, three stories high, carries boats over a road on two sets of tracks. Boats are floated into the railway car and held in place with straps and airbags. Once on the other side of the road and back in the water, the straps are released and the boats float out. When several boats are in the lift, the largest boat rests on its keel. The lift can hold a 100-foot long boat, up to 24 feet wide, or several smaller boats.

At the Big Chute Lock I docked at the free docks, a short walk from the public marina and restaurant. It was midafternoon, and I was famished. I decided to eat lunch before figuring out how this lock worked. I walked into the small diner and noticed how empty it was. This wasn't a normal hour for people to be eating; the lunch crowd was gone, and the dinner crowd hadn't arrived yet. The owner didn't seem bothered. He approached me from a table on the far side of the dining room, which had papers spread out, as if he was in the midst of monthly reports. He told me to sit wherever I like and handed me a menu. I asked if I could take a table on the patio and if they had Wi-Fi. I had brought my iPad and wanted to check my email and the weather. I quickly ordered fish and chips, and the owner went to the kitchen to fix it for me. I felt a little guilty that he was going through all this trouble. Once he delivered my meal, he returned to his table and continued his paperwork.

I had an email from *Bluenoser* Jim. He had a friend who could drop him off the next day around noon at Little Chute, the last of the Trent-Severn waterway locks at the entrance to the Georgian Bay. He hoped the timing worked for me and gave me his cellphone number. The weather report for the following day showed rain in the morning. I wouldn't be leaving under ideal circumstances, but I rationalized that the waterways were well-protected from wind. *Annabelle* could handle rain better than strong winds.

At 5:00, I walked over to the lock to watch the large railcar lift the boats over land from one side of waterway to the other. I climbed the stairs up the three story building to the observation deck and lock operators answered my questions about the locking. I imagine they sensed my discomfort and wariness. They asked about my boat, and I pointed it out on the free dock. They encouraged me to go ahead and do the Big Chute then, as it was quiet and they could put *Annabelle* "front and center" with the best views. As if I needed further convincing, they explained that the free dock on the other side of the lock was quieter and more peaceful during the night. I thought I'd have to take off all my fenders, but they said to just remove the large red ball fenders from the bow and stern; they'd work around the others. Excited, I jogged over to my boat, brought the ball fenders into the cockpit, and motored over to the loading area. A small fishing boat arrived there a few minutes before I did, and they were already waiting. Over a loudspeaker, the lock master announced that the fishing boat needed to wait and let me into the lock first. Lock operators determine where the boats will be, not the skippers.

I steered straight into the railway lift, front and center with the view I had been promised. I was surprised how quickly the lock workers strapped and secured *Annabelle*. They told me to turn off my engine. As I stopped the engine, I asked if I could leave my helm and sit on the front of my boat. I was told to sit wherever I wanted; they had no concerns about my walking along the small side deck, a few inches wide, holding onto the top railing. I grabbed my camera and threw the strap over my neck.

As I made my way to the bow of *Annabelle*, I thought back to my childhood, when my mother called me a monkey. I had lost that agility years ago, but easily managed climbing around on my small boat. Once at the front of my boat, I thoroughly enjoyed the ride. For many people, it may not seem like a big deal—to go up over a small hill and down the other side, but my boat was dangling in straps and I felt like I was about two stories above the ground. It was an adrenalin rush. The ride was over quickly, less than ten minutes from start to stop. By the time I scrambled back to my helm, my boat was floating in the pool on the lower, western side of the lock.

I tied *Annabelle* to the free dock on the lower end of the lock, which was allegedly more quiet and peaceful than the upper free dock, although it was beside the power station. There were at least a hundred stairs to climb to get to the road. The weather was changing, and it started raining. I realized it would be an early evening. As I contemplated the Big Chute Lock experience, I thought that the only thing better would be to have done this with company. All my Looper friends would be going through this lock with their spouses and friends. The sky darkened, and the rain poured down. Nights like this were perfect for bundling up in my little bed. Despite any reasonable concern about lightning, I had found it easy to fall asleep to the sound of thunder and the smell of fresh rain.

For breakfast, I hiked up the stairs and across the road to the marina restaurant. A couple of lock operators came in for coffee. They said it would be a slow day, due to the rain. It had been raining most of the night and didn't look like it was going to stop. I told them how much I had enjoyed going through the lock, and they suggested I get a day pass if I wanted to go through it again. For $40 I could go back and forth all day long, a cheap thrill.

After breakfast, I walked over to the lock. A man, close to my age, was talking with one of the lock operators about how slow it was because of the weather. I asked the man if he had ever been on the Railroad lock. He said he hadn't, but he had been watching boats lock through since he was a small child and today he had ridden his motorcycle to watch the boats go through. He was disappointed there wasn't a line of boats waiting for passage. Remembering the night before, thinking how much better the Railroad Lock would have been if I had someone to share the moment with, I asked the stranger if he'd like to go through the lock with me. He looked down at me, and said, "Really? You don't mind if I go with you?"

The man agreed to meet me at *Annabelle* fifteen minutes later, long enough for me to buy my day pass. He showed up, I gave him the ten-second tour and handed him a life jacket. The rain wasn't too bad, just slightly more than a drizzle. At the Railroad Lift, *Annabelle* was the only boat to be carried up the hill to the other side. I sat on the bow with the stranger, both of us silently taking videos with our iPhones. On the other side, I floated *Annabelle* out, turned her around, and steered back into the Railroad car, one last time. By then, it was pouring. For the return trip through the lock, my nameless companion chose to stay on the back deck, protected from the rain. I sat in a puddle on the bow to take more pictures. As we finished our thrill ride, I returned to the free dock and let the stranger off. Although we didn't say much to each other, both entranced in the moment of locking, it felt good to have someone aboard for those few moments.

Before releasing my lines, I changed out of my dripping wet clothes into clean dry ones. My laundry bag was full.

Bluenoser Jim planned to meet me at Little Chute, the last of the 45 Trent-Severn locks. From there, he'd accompany me into Georgian Bay and his hometown of Penetenguishine, which we called Penetang for short. With the rain and fog, I made my way to the final lock in Port Severn, Ontario. As I pulled into the waters above the final lock, the rain died down, but the winds gusted. Jim showed up with his bright smile, and we went to the Dam Restaurant, overlooking the waterway. After a customary lunch of fish and chips, we took *Annabelle* through the lock and into Georgian Bay.

I took advantage of having an experienced boater aboard and relaxed as Jim took the helm for the first hour. By midafternoon, we had crossed *Bluenoser's* starting place for the Loop, where Jim completed his journey and crossed his wake. In his home waters, we pulled into Bay Moorings Marina, within walking distance of Jim and Wendy's home. I looked forward to seeing their town, about which I had heard so much.

After docking and getting settled, Jim told me, "Get your stuff; you're staying at my house."

I fully intended to stay on my boat. "No, that's okay. I'll stay on *Annabelle*."

"Nonsense, is this your laundry?" He grabbed my laundry bag. "I'll carry this. Grab an overnight bag."

"Jim, I can stay here."

"You'll stay in our guest room. Wendy's going to be happy to see you."

I saw it was a losing battle. I'd have to get over my separation anxiety from *Annabelle*.

Jim and I had a lot to catch up on, and he wanted to make sure I had good pointers on where to stop while still in Canada. He had finished the Loop in time for his niece's wedding, a month before I arrived. Wendy was still working, and the two of them were still figuring out the division of labor since Jim's return. Although she had spent her vacation time with him, she had the sole responsibility of taking care of their home while he was gone.

Jim told me of his struggles since being home. "It's hard to figure out what to do. I can garden, fix this or that, but it isn't the same as having new places to go each day, like when I was doing the Loop. Wendy is very organized, and wants me to take more responsibility for things at home and do more of the planning. I want to go have adventures, and she is focused on her career. I feel like my time is limited with my health, so I want to make the most of it. It's been a struggle." Jim's neuropathy from Charcot-Marie-Tooth disease wasn't making walking any easier.

Jim was excited I was there because I understood the driving force of the Loop, how it forces a person not to take things for granted, but to be open to change and more relaxed about the little things. Perhaps I was a distraction to their problems. Jim could focus on helping me with my boat for a few days.

That night, when Wendy got home from work, Jim fixed dinner. As I shared stories from the trip, I told them about the sailboats from the Clipper Round the World Race at Liberty Landing. In one of those small world moments of six degrees of separation, the son of Wendy's best friend was the skipper of the winning boat, *Henri Lloyd*. In addition to boating skills, the young captain, Eric Holden, must've been a great team leader with crew members of varying skills for different sections of the race. I showed Jim and Wendy a YouTube video the crew of *Derry Londonderry Doire* made with Pharrell Williams's hit song "Happy."

The next morning after Wendy left for work, Jim and I checked on *Annabelle* and changed her oil. Jim ran errands and I stayed aboard to check the alternator belt. The service manager walked by the stern, and seeing me working with the engine hatch open, asked if he could help me.

"Where can I get rid of this old oil?"

"I'll take it for you." I was in luck. "Is there anything else we can do?"

I hadn't expected to get any repairs done in Canada and didn't plan to stay for more than a few days. Jim and Wendy were leaving on Friday to meet their daughter for a family vacation, and it was already Wednesday. "I have a couple problems on my boat; I'm not sure if you can fix them."

"We can try. What's the problem?"

"My autopilot isn't working."

"I'll send a mechanic over to take a look."

When Jim came back, I let him know that I was waiting for the mechanic and I'd meet him back at his house once I figured out if they could fix anything. It was a long afternoon. The mechanic wasn't exactly rushing to my boat, and my hopes were diminishing as the afternoon progressed.

Finally, around 4:00, the mechanic showed up. As he walked down the pier, I noticed he only had a simple voltage tester, but no other tools. I had already asked other service yards along the way to look at my autopilot, and each time the mechanic looked at the wiring behind the helm I was told it was a mess, which I already knew. Then, the mechanic would tell me it would take a couple days to clean it up, which they never had time for, and they'd send me on my way. However, I had also talked to Dean, and he thought it was the motor, not the electronics. The electronic displays were responsive and showed the direction, so my faith was in Dean's assessment. As the man approached *Annabelle*, I said, "Where are your tools?"

"I don't have time to fix anything right now; I have a concert to go to with my girlfriend and need to get out of here early."

Pointing to the voltage tester, I said, "I don't think it's the electronics, I think it's the motor."

He looked at me as if I were some strange creature. "Where is the control box?"

I pointed to the electrical panel. "It's behind here, but you have to get into the V-berth to get to it."

"I'd rather start here." He pointed to the electrical panel. I handed him the square headed screwdriver to pull off the electric panel then crawled into the V-berth and pulled off the fuzzy headboard panel, which sufficed for the wall between the helm and the V-berth.

It didn't take long for him to figure out I was right about getting to the control box, and he crawled into the dark V-berth to look at the black metal box between the hull and the inside wall of the cabin. He found a fuse which wasn't showing any voltage. "It must've been a loose fuse."

"Maybe, but I still think it's the motor. I guess we'll see if that fixed it." I wondered if he didn't just loosen the fuse himself to prove his point.

I took him to the stern of the boat, where I had previously uncovered the autopilot motor. As I sat at the helm, following his directions, he acknowledged the motor wasn't working. "Do you have a hammer?"

"A hammer?"

"It could be stuck."

I handed him the hammer, and he smacked the motor housing a couple times, then it started up.

I was just over a third of the way through my trip, "I've got another 3,500 miles to go. Is it going to keep working?"

"I don't know. We might have another motor in stock. Our parts guy can check on it."

It was a quiet and quick walk up to the office, as he checked and rechecked his cell phone. He clearly didn't have time to bother with me since his focus was on texting his girlfriend.

The parts manager checked his computer and found they had the exact autopilot motor in their sister marina, a half hour away, a rare coincidence. They could have it delivered the following day. "Is there anything else we can get for you?"

"I could always use a spare alternator belt. Oh, and my stern thruster isn't working."

The mechanic looked at me. "You didn't say anything about the stern thruster."

"I doubt it's something that you guys can fix anyway. I can't imagine you'd have the part, and it's almost impossible to reach."

The mechanic told the parts guy, "Look, I've gotta go. We can haul her boat on Friday. It won't take long to replace the pump."

As the mechanic walked out the door, the parts guy asked, "Do you have the manufacturer information on the stern thruster?"

"It's a Side Power. I'll grab the owner's manual. I had someone look at it. The motor runs, but the blades don't spin. I was at the Peterborough Lift lock when it stopped working. It worked fine when I tied up at the bottom of the lift, but when I got to the top, it stopped."

"You sure nothing got into the prop blades?"

"I had a diver look at it. Then I took it to a repair shop he recommended. They hauled the boat and said it was probably just a pin, but they didn't have one, and it would be a couple weeks before they could get one."

"You sure you need it fixed?"

"Obviously, I can manage without it. But, it will have to get fixed sometime. If I ever sell my boat, the buyer will expect the thrusters to be working. If you can get the part, it'll make my life easier. I have a long way to go."

Within fifteen minutes, I returned with the instruction guide for the thrusters and the part number for the alternator belt, barely making it into the office before they closed.

Thursday, Jim showed me around Penetanguishine, telling me the history of the small town. Friday morning, he and Wendy left. They offered me the use of their house while they were gone for the weekend, and Jim told me he hoped I'd still be in town when he got back. It all depended on how fast they repaired *Annabelle*.

Friday felt like a long day. Changing out the autopilot motor was easy enough for the mechanic. Then, he pulled *Annabelle* out of the water and checked the stern thruster. The problem was just a small pin, which their sister marina had in stock. *Annabelle* sat on boat stands on shore, in the shade of large trees, while the parts manager drove to fetch the minuscule part. It cost a few hundred dollars to replace the two dollar pin. Having been through a similar repair at Tidewater Marina in Virginia, I tried to give the mechanic some pointers on how to make the repair easier. He was determined to make the repair by himself, but I knew one person could hold the thruster motor in place with a rope or cable, while a second person bolted it in place. The small space to reach the thruster was at the stern, through a 12-inch cabinet door, through a hatch, and down further than most men could reach, without a shoulder dislocation. As the clock approached 5:00, the lift operators were waiting for the mechanic to finish. On Friday night, nobody wanted to get stuck at work. Finally, the mechanic let one of his co-workers help him and they put the stern thruster back together in time to launch *Annabelle* before closing time. As I took her back to her slip, I checked the auto pilot and thrusters; she was back in working order.

The boat behind *Annabelle's* slip was a party boat, or at least that was my perception. Peter, the owner, had come by *Annabelle* several times while I waited for the mechanic. He lived a mile away, enjoying his boat during the warm summer months. One evening I had seen him take off in his fast boat with a case of beer and a few young people aboard. He invited me to join them, but I declined, grateful for having Jim and Wendy's company. Despite being close to my age, Peter seemed like he was in the party mode of someone in his twenties. The young women on his boat looked like they could be his daughters.

Saturday morning, Peter drove me to the local grocery store so I could provision for my trip through Georgian Bay. Jim had given me charts with a list of beautiful, scenic anchorages. Both Jim and Peter agreed the first place to stop would be Henry's Fish House. Peter thought *Annabelle* could motor there in an hour or so, until he found out I'd only be going 7 knots. His preference was much faster. I left the dock that morning around 9:30, and Peter helped me with my lines and gave me his phone number, just in case I should ever find myself back in Penetang.

18

From Penetang to North Channel

Henry's Fish House is famous amongst boaters. There are no roads to this famous diner; one must get there by air or by boat. The docks are filled to capacity for most of the boating season and boats share the docks with the floatplanes.

As I approached this landmark, I could tell I was close, because for the first time I had to share the water with an airplane. I wondered if they had the same rules of the road as I did. There must have been a dozen docks with dockhands, each with a VHF radio in hand. I throttled down into neutral to assess the situation. Was I supposed to be calling a restaurant on the VHF radio? I didn't really know, but it was midafternoon, so I decided to tie up to a dock which didn't look busy. I checked my fenders, made sure my lines were easily accessible and free, so I could grab my bow and stern lines as I stepped off *Annabelle*. I gently motored forward like a turtle to one of the docks, which all stuck straight out from the shore, and pulled *Annabelle* gently alongside. I put the throttle into reverse for a half second then back into neutral, stopping *Annabelle's* forward movement and stepped onto the dock with her lines. The windless day was peaceful, temperatures in the mid-seventies, and the waters were still. Unlike the narrow rivers, where water is flowing downhill, or the tidal waters of the coast, there isn't much of a current amongst the many islands in the Georgian Bay.

As I stepped off *Annabelle*, a young dockhand came running. "Ma'am, do you need any help?"

"No, thank you. I have it. Am I okay here? Or do you need me to move?"

"You're fine there. You handling this boat by yourself?"

Just then an older gentleman came up behind the teenage dock hand. He was probably in his early sixties, tall, and very well fed. He had an air of authority. "Tanya! It's good to see you!" He reached out and gave me a great big bear hug.

I was surprised and confused. *Did I know this man?* As he released his hold, I said, "And who are you?"

"I'm Paul. I own this place. Some people call me Henry. I've been expecting you. I saw your friends earlier today. They're anchored on the other side of that island over there." He pointed to the one of the many forested islands nearby. "You have to go around to the backside of the island. When you get to the inlet, they'll be on the right side. It's a good anchorage."

I remembered the text conversation with Steve earlier that morning. He had asked where I was and thought the cost of dockage at the restaurant expensive, considering it didn't include electricity. Steve was traveling with his daughter Claire. She was a beautiful, smart graduate student, who had produced shows on NPR. They had stopped here in the morning and waited for the restaurant to open, so they could have an early lunch. Steve almost always anchored out. He was traveling on a tight budget, downloading movies and books whenever he found free Internet, only staying at docks if he absolutely needed to do laundry. A town library was usually his best bet for downloading. Most marina Wi-Fi connections had limited access.

After I got my bearings on how Paul knew me, I had more pressing questions. "How do I get a ride on one of those floatplanes?"

"Georgia Bay Airlines. They have an office in Parry Sound. Let me introduce you to the owner."

We walked over to a young man who might have been thirty. The young pilot told me to stop by in the morning to reserve a flight. I excused myself from these two entrepreneurs and went upstairs to the restaurant overlooking the docks and ordered their signature fish 'n' chips.

Before I left, I thanked Henry and bought a bright, lime green T-shirt. I was proud to have docked there. If I had arrived closer to either lunch or dinner, I wouldn't have found a spot.

As I powered up my engine I checked out the anchorage Paul had pointed out to me on my iPad. I pulled away from the dock and navigated the narrow channels. Echo Bay anchorage was shaped like a butterfly. No boats anchored on the left, but there were at least ten in the cove on the right. Most boats were anchored with Mediterranean moorings, meaning they had dropped an anchor off the bow of their boat and tied the stern to the shore, allowing for more boats in tighter spaces. *Atla* stood out from the rest, not just because the red Nordic Tug had a similar shape to mine, but with only the bow anchor out, *Atla* could swing freely. She was not lined up with the other boats. As I pulled alongside Steve, he told me there was a $10 fee for doing anything on land, whether tying off, going to the nearby dinghy dock, or hiking. I dropped my anchor about 40 feet away from his boat. Since we'd both be swinging the same direction and were far enough away from other boats, we wouldn't hit each other or anyone else. Despite

Steve's reassurances, I was still skeptical, as the general rule about anchoring is to anchor like the people around you, so everyone swings the same direction, or doesn't swing at all. This anchorage was mixed. My personal preference was to anchor as far away from any other boats as possible and not worry.

Steve pushed his kayak over to my boat. It was attached with a rope to *Atla* so he could pull me back. I clumsily climbed into his kayak and he tugged the line back to his boat. There is no graceful way of getting in and out of kayaks. I was lucky I didn't fall into the cold water.

At 6:30 I left Echo Bay anchorage, excited about the day ahead. I had a one track mind. Parry Sound was about 20 miles away, and I expected to arrive early. If I was lucky, I'd be on a sightseeing flight that afternoon. It was all I could think about, and I felt like I couldn't get there fast enough. I wanted to be at the floatplane office when they opened, before any tourists showed up. I looked over at Steve's boat, and saw he'd taken his kayak out for an early morning row. He'd be leaving the anchorage early, like me, while Claire slept.

Shortly after leaving the anchorage, the fog rolled in. The evergreen islands and channels became difficult to navigate, slowing me down. It was dangerous negotiating these narrow channels with poor visibility and granite rocks under the surfaces ready to take a chunk out of a boat or a propeller, but I was on a mission. I slowed down and diligently watched for the channel markers, staying safely between them. The red markers were easier to see than the green, which blended into the surrounding landscape. Canadian channel markers are very different than the ones in the States. They are red or green 4-inch posts, called spars, which stick out of the water about

4 feet. The top of the green spars are pointed, while the top of the red ones are squared off. Channel markers in the States are larger and easier to read, with 3-foot triangular signs for the red markers and 3-foot square signs for the green markers. One of my friends ran his boat aground outside of Orillia, when he accidentally navigated outside the channel on the wrong side of a marker. Rumor was it cost about $30,000 for the repairs to his hull and props. Beyond the financial strain, the repairs took a month in Southern Canada where the boating season only lasts two or three months. Running aground in Georgian Bay should be called "running-a-rock." The shallow, sandy bottoms of North Carolina waterways are much more forgiving.

Soon I received a text from Steve. He'd left the anchorage shortly after I did. He warned me about three speedboats coming my way, and I warned him about the fog. Because the channels were so narrow, speedboats would fly by *Annabelle*, sending a large wake, which could throw her out of the channel. Aware that they were behind me gave me that little bit of extra knowledge to avoid being caught off guard when they flew past.

By 8:30, the fog had lifted and I was pulling into Parry Sound. Steve was a half hour behind me. The local marina managed the city wall with dockage, clearly meant for boats larger than mine, as the wall was four feet above my railings. My goal was to stop long enough to book my flight and eat a good breakfast, then go to the marina. I pulled up to the large wall at a ladder, where I could climb out of my boat and onto the walkway. Just the top of *Annabelle* was visible. From the city wall, I could see Georgian Bay Airlines and their floatplanes in their private docks.

I made a beeline to the small floatplane building but they were closed. I looked in the darkened windows and saw a large gift shop. Two small single-engine planes were behind the building in their slips. One plane looked like a four-seater Cessna with floats for landing gear, but I wasn't familiar with the other one.

When I was young, my father had bought two planes, a Cessna and a Beechcraft Bonanza. My mother had struggled to support our family as a school teacher. After I entered high school and my sister had graduated, she got divorced and was able to return to school to further her education. While my parents were married, my father mostly went to school and frequently asked my grandma to give him money for investments that always ended badly. Once he even bought a brothel, but that's another story.

Mom had told me how she learned about the planes, which my father called a business expense. At dinner, my father's best friend asked Dad if he liked his new plane. Mom said, "What plane?" Dad responded, "Which one?" Dad was not a pilot, so he hired one and took lessons. I went flying with my father a couple times in each of his planes before they were either sold or repossessed. I enjoyed small planes and once in southern New Mexico flew in an open cockpit biplane, doing loops. A floatplane would be a whole new experience. Like my boat, these planes had dock lines.

Disappointed, I walked back to the city dock and watched Steve pull *Atla* in behind *Annabelle*. I offered to help with his lines, but he has his own system for docking. He tossed a short line with a loop over the dock cleat, then attached the bitter end to his midship cleat. From there, he could maneuver enough to attach his bow and stern lines. The Nordic Tugs have large rubber bumpers on the port and starboard sides to protect the hull. *Annabelle* would get scratched up without the fenders laid out ahead of time. Steve had a door at his helm, so he could step outside, and with one hand still on his wheel, loop the dock cleat. I had to leave my helm, go out the back door 10 feet away, and catch the dock cleat from the back of my boat. Maybe if I had practiced a few rodeo skills while in Arizona, Steve's technique would be easier from my small window. His docking strategy wouldn't work for my boat, and my strategy wouldn't work on his.

Once Steve was docked, I explained, "The city wall is ten dollars a day and you have to pay at the marina." Some city walls were free.

"I promised Claire a shower and we have to do laundry. Any facilities?"

"No bathrooms, no electricity, and no laundry at this wall. I'm going to the marina after breakfast."

"We'll join you. What do they have around here?"

"We can find a bakery or coffee shop." The three of us strolled up to the main street, lined with shops and restaurants.

After breakfast, we walked back to the city dock. Each of our windshields had a note to pay the marina for docking. Steve called the marina on his VHF radio and let them know to expect both our boats. The dockmaster asked if we needed help with our lines, and Steve told him that we would get our own lines. Listening to Steve make these arrangements for both our boats was different from when I approached docks with other couples, who'd usually tell the dock hands to help me because I was by myself. In most cases, I found it was easier to dock *Annabelle* alone than it was for them to dock their large boats, even with two people aboard. Communication sometimes contributed to the difficulty, with one spouse or the other yelling out directions. The dockmaster told us where the two slips were located, and Steve told me to enter the marina first and pick my slip, then he'd take the other one.

Once docked, I hightailed to Georgian Bay Airlines, leaving Steve and Claire to do their laundry and chores. The office was now open, but the clouds were causing delays with the small airline. I made my reservation for later that morning, but hour after hour the flights were delayed. While I waited, I walked into town and looked at the different shops; every hour, checking back with the airline. Finally, at 3:00 in the afternoon, my flight would be going out. I'd be flying over the Georgian Bay with another couple. Including the pilot, there were four of us. This was not the entrepreneurial pilot I had met the day before. This young pilot seemed bored with his job and lacked personality. He told us general safety information and how to put on our seatbelts. He was matter-of-fact and answered questions curtly. Maybe he was frustrated by the delays, or just having a bad day.

The couple flying with us were about my age, and about as opposite as two people can be. As outgoing and vivacious as the wife was, the husband was reserved and quiet. She wore stripper heals, black leather pants with a white blouse, with bold make-up and bleach blonde hair. Her husband wore khaki slacks with a black golf shirt and vest, with black and white tennis shoes. They lived in Toronto, but were originally from some Middle Eastern country. I couldn't understand or pronounce their names. After two or three attempts, I gave up trying.

The husband got in first. He had to maneuver himself into the back corner of the four seat airplane, which didn't have much more room than the backseat of a 1972 VW Bug. As the wife stepped forward onto the floating pontoon, I winced, fearing she was going to slip and sprain her ankle or land in the water. I couldn't walk ten feet in those shoes. I was fortunate to be in the front seat next to the pilot. For once, being single worked to my advantage. I had views out the front and side windows. With my iPad GPS, I tracked our flight and compared it to where I had navigated in the waterways.

After we were buckled in and the engine had started, the pilot slowly increased the speed, and we accelerated down the waterway. It was exciting to reach the magical speed of liftoff. Unlike landing gear on normal planes, the pontoons stayed down. My Canon camera had a zoom lens, and I took videos with my iPad. As we climbed a few hundred feet above the ground to our cruising altitude, I could see the large granite cliffs just under the water, which caused such grief for boaters. Up here they were clear and dangerous. My level of respect for these waters skyrocketed. Maybe I shouldn't have left in the fog this morning. It was one thing to be told about the rock ledges, hiding just below the surface of the water, but it was another thing to see them. In the Georgian Bay, the hairpin turns made more sense from the air, while the evergreen islands and crystal blue waters bestowed a false sense of tranquility. At times, the clouds cast shadows over the waterways, obscuring the dangers. With this new perspective, I had a magnified appreciation for Georgian Bay, as if I had just seen it for the first time.

The flight lasted an hour. While the jubilant wife was on cloud nine, her husband seemed preoccupied. When we got off the plane, I asked if they knew where the local Starbucks was. They offered to drive me there, as it was too far to walk. I wanted to restock *Annabelle* with my favorite lime drink and hadn't seen a Starbucks since Annapolis. On the way back to the marina, the wife asked if they could see my boat.

"Of course." My verbal filter was intact, as I didn't add, *as long as you don't fall into the water with those heels.*

I bought the last of Starbucks lime drink mix and added the strawberry-lemonade drink mix to my coffers. I spent almost $200 ensuring I'd be well-stocked for the next three months.

As we arrived at the marina, the husband told his wife to be quick, "We don't have all day. We need to get back to Toronto."

"I'll just be a minute, Sweetheart. You sure you don't want to come?"

He kept the car running. "I'll wait here."

We walked down the pier to my boat. She loved *Annabelle*. She asked if she could have her picture taken at the helm, then beside the boat, and in a dozen more different poses on top of the boat. With her phone in hand, I clicked picture after picture. It didn't really matter what anyone thought; she was smiling, happy, and hadn't sprained an ankle or broken a fingernail.

After a few minutes, we saw her husband marching down the pier. "We have to go! Enough already!"

"Okay, okay, just one more. Come here, stand beside me for a quick pose."

Sternly, he ushered her off my boat and thanked me for allowing the imposition. As they walked away, Steve poked his head out of the door to his boat. "What was that about?"

"I went on my flight with them. She wanted pictures of *Annabelle*."

"She was all over your boat!"

"Yeah, she was." I had been accustomed to people asking me to take pictures of me and *Annabelle*, but these photos had had gone to a whole new level. I was just grateful she kept her clothes on.

I smiled, went inside, and prepared dinner. That night I met Loopers from *Le Hooker*, who were also docked at the marina. I thoroughly enjoyed Parry's Sound. This one day would be one of the highlights of my trip. I couldn't imagine being here without the airplane ride. On my blog I posted a couple of pictures soaring above Georgian Bay to illustrate just how beautiful and dangerous the channels could be. Now that I'd seen the granite cliffs waiting just below the surface, I'd have to be more careful in these Canadian waters.

Before going our separate ways, Steve and I traveled one more day together. He took Claire to a nearby town, to catch a ride on a bus to the airport in Toronto since she was on her way to England for graduate school. I navigated the channels up Byng Inlet to a town called Britt, renowned for a great restaurant at Hotel Britt. I was excited about going to the fancy restaurant at Britt Inn which was highlighted in the cruising books and recommended by *Bluenoser* Jim. This wasn't exactly a culinary tour, but I did look forward to good restaurants. Peanut butter and jelly sandwiches had become my standard fare because they were the simplest lunches to make while at the helm; not exactly the spice of life.

Of two local marinas, I chose to stay at St. Amanti's Marina which was closer to the Britt Inn. In addition to their proximity to the Inn, they advertised Wi-Fi, a restaurant, and grocery store. The weather was changing, so I might be here for two nights. I filled my tank with fuel, and was told to settle my bill for the fuel and dockage in the grocery store. In the store, I was given a code for the Internet, which changed daily.

I asked the woman behind the counter, "Where is Britt Inn?"

"Down the road, but it's closed."

"What?"

"The owner died a few months ago, and it hasn't reopened yet."

The restaurant at Britt Inn was the only reason I had come up this remote narrow channel to this marina. How is it that nobody seemed to know about the guy dying? Why'd he have to die this year? How many people had told me about the restaurant? How many times had I read about it? The guides said it was place not to miss. Hell, they were just published this year.

"Are there other restaurants here?"

"The one upstairs."

"How is it?"

"It isn't the Hotel Britt, but it's okay."

I was very disappointed. I trudged back to my boat. It was still early in the day. I needed to know about the weather. I couldn't get online because the Wi-Fi wasn't strong enough. I looked out my window, seeing that a catamaran had just pulled up. *Joint Adventure* was also doing the Loop. They had come here with the same hopes of going to Hotel Britt. I asked if they had tried the Internet yet. They weren't having much luck either.

Within a few minutes, *De De* pull in. Who knew that this isolated spot would be such a hotspot for Loopers? I always enjoyed seeing Henry and Diane. They had built *De De* with their own sweat and blood. Although the same age as most other Loopers, they were the newlyweds of this Loop, having only been married a year or two. Most couples I met had been married for thirty, forty, or even fifty years. These two had a smaller boat than most, a couple feet longer than *Annabelle*, with a similar floor plan. Another difference between our boats was that *De De* had an outboard motor, while *Annabelle* had an inboard diesel motor. Their boat could go faster than *Annabelle*. They were so proud of their boat, their creation. I wondered how they managed to get along in such a small space.

I often felt that *Annabelle* was a good size for one, but I doubted how comfortable it would be for longer than a weekend with two aboard. It was hard enough for me to spend four days on my boat with Mom. The only man who'd ever been on *Annabelle* overnight was Malcolm. Although the two of us got along well on my boat, we looked at bigger boats with envy. I wondered how he was getting along with his new girlfriend, who wasn't a boater. I'd hear from him soon enough when I got back to the States, or through an email. He continued to keep up with my blog postings and would usually contact me soon after a post. Since I was in Canada, email was the best means of communication.

Boating in small quarters seemed a great way to decide if two people should be together. Mom and her significant other, Jimmy, had spent a couple weeks on his 24-foot trailerable sailboat, which had much less space than mine. Jimmy couldn't stand up straight in the boat, but had to hunch over. Mom and Jimmy slept on either side of the cabin on benches. I was surprised they didn't want to kill each other by the time they got off. Mom told me that while they sailed, she would generally get comfortable with a good book and let Jimmy do everything.

The summer I looked at buying a house in Southport, Jimmy stayed on his sailboat for two months at a marina in Washington, North Carolina. Mom enjoyed the weeks she spent with him on his boat, which was mostly moored at a dock. With a vehicle available, Mom was able to come to Southport and help me look for houses. At the end of that summer, Jimmy towed his sailboat to San Carlos, Mexico, where he cheaply kept the boat out on a trailer, in a secure yard a good day's drive from where they lived. Occasionally, he'd go down for a few days and sail her. According to Mom, it wasn't the same as being in North Carolina, and she stopped going with him. He sold the boat this year to a couple who want to sail her to Australia. I can imagine that extensive of a trip in the right-sized sailboat, with the right person; definitely not in Jimmy's tiny boat.

De De fueled up and took a spot behind *Annabelle*, closer to the river, as the piers stuck out from the shore, each holding two to three boats. I welcomed Henry and Diane. It was time to catch up and I was getting frustrated with the Internet. Henry and Diane had also heard about Hotel Britt. In lieu of being able to dine at the famous restaurant, we went to the one above the grocery store.

After ordering overpriced hamburgers, Diane asked, "Have you seen *If*?"

"Not since Waterford, when Tom fell overboard. Have you?" Visions of Tom climbing onto the swim platform while the rest of us were helpless ran through my mind. I thought Tim and Tom must be far ahead of me by now. How was it possible that we didn't run into each other and I was in front of them?

"We saw them at Parry Sound last night. They're supposed to come here tonight."

"I hope they get in early, or stay put. It looks like a storm is coming in; the wind has picked up. They might just want to find a safe anchorage."

After we caught up on travel stories, we went back to our boats. On the way, I stopped in the grocery store to take a better look around. Surprisingly, boaters were sitting in the aisles, trying to connect to the Internet. Their advertised Wi-Fi only worked in the building. *How did they expect us to get weather and be safe?*

That evening, *If* arrived safely at the docks. It was dark and the wind was howling. Henry, Diane and I walked over to welcome Tim and Tom. They invited us all onto their boat and offered dinner. We weren't hungry, but we enjoyed their company. Tom was excited to see me; he relayed how quickly news travels both on and off the Loop. "I've been keeping up with your blog since Waterford."

"Really? Why?" I hardly had time to write my own blog, much less read anyone else's.

"The day after I fell overboard, friends called to see if I was all right. Somehow, they'd seen your blog." I was surprised at how quickly word traveled. From different parts of North Carolina, Tom and I had never met before the Loop. The last thing he said to me in Waterford was not to put it on Facebook. I told him I wouldn't, but I'd put it on my blog.

"I'm sorry." I felt badly that his friends found out about one of those moments he didn't want publicized.

"Don't be sorry; it's all good. I appreciated how you wrote about it."

Then Tim, his grandson, added, "And I liked the way you portrayed me in the blog."

I was relieved when our conversation got back to the present and how they made it up the channel to this little marina with the wind gusting. Their boat handled well and was built for bigger waves than mine. It was a much faster boat, traveling three times faster than I could go. I asked if they had considering anchoring, rather than risk the bad weather. They had not anchored yet on their trip. "What about the Bustard Islands?" These islands were my next stop and had no alternatives to anchoring.

"We're going straight to Killarney." One day of travel for them was at least two for me.

Diane and Henry added that they were going to the Bustard Islands too. Once again, Tom and Tim would get ahead of me. We parted for the evening and looked forward to the next day. The wind was still blowing and the rain was pouring down. I hoped the morning would be calm and peaceful. I thought about Steve and Claire, and hoped they found a safe anchorage.

As I navigated toward Bustard Islands, *De De* got stuck behind me. The channels were very narrow, only wide enough in spots for one boat. At times, I thought I could reach out and touch the granite rocks, as they poked out of the water. Once through the channels and out into the open bay, I enjoyed using my autopilot for the first time since it was fixed in Penetanguishine. My bearings were on the small island that *Bluenoser* Jim had told me about.

Entering the cove on the north side of the Bustard Islands, I was surprised at the number of boats anchored there. *De De* was right behind me, and the deeper I went into the cove, the more boats I saw. I found a spot toward the back of the cove and dropped anchor, but *Annabelle* drifted dangerously close to the granite wall. I pulled up the anchor and went back to the entrance. Following me into the cove, *De De* anchored close to my first spot.

My new anchor spot was just inside a second entrance to the cove. The waters were shallow, and there were rock walls and boulders just under the surface. Once *Annabelle* was anchored, I walked around the stern and sides with my extendable boat hook to make sure I had enough depth, measuring the distance from the visible boulders and rocks. I'd be safe tonight, but it wasn't ideal.

The scenery was beautiful. The waters were clear. The main problem I had with anchoring was that *Annabelle* was so small that I didn't feel like there was anywhere to stretch my legs. I could handle claustrophobia for a night, but not much more. I was hesitant to take down my dinghy and explore the island. I worried that I wouldn't get back to *Annabelle*, or I'd have problems with handling the dinghy.

Planning my next day's journey wasn't taking as much time as it once had. I wanted to go to Killarney, and there were two routes. The first route was direct across open water; the second route was through narrow channels. *De De* was going through the channels because of the fjords, which are high cliff walls on either side. The route would definitely be more protected, even if it was longer. I postponed my decision until morning when I'd have a better idea about the weather. Crossing the open water and using the autopilot was definitely relaxing.

19

Mayflies

I first started seeing mayflies in Penetanguishene in mid-July where they'd congregate on the boats and docks. It seemed they were attracted to anything white, like the topsides and decks of most boats. Locals assured me that mayflies were harmless, dumb, and slow, and that they smelled when they started to rot. These insects are a shorter, stubbier version of a dragonfly, without the beautiful colors. They come from the water, where larvae have lived for almost a year before maturing into their adult bodies, when they grow wings to fly. They must come up from the water in the middle of the night, because in the mornings they'd lie patiently on the surfaces, waiting for death. Unlike most insects, that sense danger and scurry away, these insects don't budge. They are as fragile as rice paper. Spraying water at them is enough to kill them. They disintegrate into a grayish-brown muck, with their translucent wings being the only structure left to snag onto crevices and clog the drains. The mayfly season is short in Ontario, usually only lasting a couple weeks.

When I arrived in Kagawong on July 25th, it must have been the height of mayfly season. With no room at the docks in Little Current, I had forged ahead to this small town, where the marina has only a few finger piers. Prior to arrival, I called the dockmaster and he told me he didn't have room for me either. However, after finding out how small *Annabelle* is, he offered to make adjustments. He expected a sailboat later that day and figured we could share the finger pier.

As I approached Kagawong, the dockmaster helped me tie off *Annabelle*. I immediately noticed three large boats, one trawler and two cruising boats. The dockmaster said they'd been there for a couple days and were planning on leaving the following morning. As I looked closer at the boat beside me, I noticed a gold Looper burgee flying from her bow and she was named *Good Karma*. I looked forward to the day that *Annabelle* would sport the gold burgee. I wondered if it was the same couple I met in Southport who'd invited me to dinner in April 2013 while they were doing the Loop.

At the dock office I paid for the slip. The dock house was like a small warehouse, with a saggy, old couch and a wooden coffee table. A few supplies hung on a wall. An old oriental rug lay in front of the couch. In the back corner next to the cash register, was an ice cream refrigerator. Ice cream was sold everywhere in Canada.

I handed the dockmaster my credit card and said, "I hope I meet my dock neighbors. I recognize the boat name."

"I saw them walking up the hill a little while ago. I doubt they're back. The three boats are traveling together. They're leaving in the morning."

"I heard the weather's turning bad."

"Yeah. High winds and rain."

"I'm going to stay here till it gets better."

He ran my card through the machine and said, "I hear Little Current is pretty busy with the Regatta."

"A cruise ship came in too, so there wasn't any space, not even at the fuel dock. I stopped just long enough to have lunch with friends. Another Looper let me raft to their boat." It was the first time I was turned away since starting this journey three months earlier. After I was told there wasn't any space, the Loopers from the *Joint Adventure*, which I had seen in Britt, offered to let me tie up to them, so I could have lunch with Tom, from Southport, and his companion.

"Where'd you eat?"

"At the Anchor Inn. One of my friends from Southport told me they had the best fish tacos he'd ever eaten. He's gone back there a couple times."

Outside, I stood for a moment looking at the sterns of the adjacent boats, and at the contrast between little *Annabelle* and the much larger *Good Karma*. I knocked on *Good Karma's* hull and saw a familiar face, "Are you Kermit?"

"Yeah." He had a confused look on his face.

I extended my hand, "Tanya, from Southport. Remember? I had dinner with you and Kat at Bald Head Island almost a year and a half ago."

"That was a long time ago. What're you doing here?"

"The Loop," I said as I pointed to *Annabelle*.

"Wasn't she in the shop when we were in Southport? I can't believe you did it. Kat will be glad to see you. The girls have gone into town. You'll have to come by later for docktails, so we can catch up."

It was surprising and wonderful to see familiar people. I thought back to when they came through Southport the previous year, I was curious that Kat continued to work as a consultant while doing the Loop. She used Skype occasionally, but did most of her work on her computer while they were traveling, which I had researched doing. I missed my patients and was all too aware of how difficult even one day a week would have been on a trip like this.

Kat was one of the few Loopers who still worked, not because she had to, because she loved to. Kat was about my age and her retired husband seemed to be about ten years older. After spending a winter cruising the Bahamas and being from Ohio, they decided a boating life might suit them better than land life.

Good Karma had been upgraded from the boat I saw in Southport. She was the same brand of boat, but new and larger. Kermit had put her name on her stern the day before I got there. I wouldn't have recognized the new *Good Karma*, as it was her name that caught my eye.

After settling in, the dockmaster offered to drive me one mile up the large hill to a convenience store. It was a hot, sticky day. I appreciated the ride, but decided to walk back as one of the highlights of the town is their bridal veil waterfall.

The convenience store was minimally stocked. I hoped to pick up a dozen eggs, meat, or fresh vegetables, but they carried mostly chips, soda, and, of course, ice cream. Leaving empty handed, I walked down the hill, detouring through the park with the waterfalls. At the bottom of the falls, families were swimming in the freezing cold water. *That's not for me; I like my water hot.* When I lived in Tucson, I would lounge on my air mattress in my hot tub, spinning slowly, while listening to music and dreaming of being out in the ocean. I took a few quick pictures of the falls then walked down the hill to the marina.

In the marina office, the dockmaster asked if I found what I needed. I explained they didn't really have much in the way of real food, just snack food. He offered to drive me to Gore Bay, the closest larger town, a half hour away. I thanked him and told him I had enough food onboard for a few days. With meat in my freezer and a few potatoes, I could easily get back to the United States with my supplies. I was constantly over-preparing. In Waterford, New York, I had met a gentleman with a similar boat, who was also single-handing the Loop. He managed to get by with a jar of nuts, coffee, and a few protein bars, mostly eating at restaurants. He had one set of silverware, one plate, and one change of clothes. *Annabelle* looked as if she belonged to a hoarder, with extra supplies everywhere. I had more tools on my boat than most people have in their garages, rationalizing two drills with three batteries. It made sense because I only had one charger. I did send the sewing machine off with Jane, who had plenty of space on *Average Looper*.

While sitting working on my blog, Kat came by. It was time for docktails. She took the ten-second tour of *Annabelle*, and I told her I'd be there in a few minutes. Docktails were on the large trawler, which their friends had rented. With a large salon on the fly bridge, it was a time to relax and talk about the day's journey, the trials and tribulations, the beauty of the Northern Channel, and the ever-present "pride-buster" moments, which Burke had mentioned early on. My humbling experience was learning that I couldn't always rely on having a slip for *Annabelle*. Kat and Kermit were traveling the opposite direction from me. Similar to when I had seen them in Southport, they were traveling in a group of buddy boats. They were as surprised to see me as I was to see them.

Kat asked, "Is it lonesome traveling alone?"

"It seems like I run into people everywhere I go. Even when there aren't other Loopers around, the other boaters have been great."

"Have you had any company on your boat?" Kat and Kermit seemed to always have company. When I saw them in Southport, Kat's sister was with them. Now, they had a neighbor aboard.

"My mom came with me for a few days. I thought about having my son come along, but he takes too many risks. I asked my daughter about having one of my grandkids come for part of the trip, but she wasn't comfortable with them being on a boat. It was probably for the best. I would've hated going through the Erie Canal with either of them aboard."

Kat and Kermit had their routines of who did what on their boat, and the Erie wouldn't have been a problem for them. Each had duties, whether locking or docking. In general, I saw the wife, aka "admiral," getting the lines and fenders ready, while the husband steered the boat. Once docked, there were more chores, whether cleaning the boat, paying the marina, getting pumped out, or hooking up to water and power. Docking was a time to connect the boat to shore and to connect with friends. When traveling in caravans, it was also a time to plan for the next day.

Kat and Kermit planned to stop at Little Current the following day. I asked them about weather, but they weren't too concerned. I still hadn't decided if I was going down the coast of Lake Michigan on the Wisconsin or Michigan side once back in the States.

Kermit was clear on the better choice. "Definitely head down Michigan. There are safe harbors every twenty-five miles. The lake can change quickly, and you'll be glad to know you aren't any further than twelve miles from a harbor."

Kat added, "The towns in Michigan are great. We'll get you a list of the ones we really like."

"What about the prevailing winds? I heard the winds are mostly coming from the west, so the shore of Michigan is affected much more than Wisconsin." Wave heights build up as the wind crosses the large expanse of water, creating the worst waves on the Michigan shore. My preference was to be on the protected lee shore, where the land forms a barrier to the wind, and the waters are calmer. I used the same principle in determining a good anchorage.

Kermit acknowledged this, but added, "True, but on the Wisconsin side you have big cities with ship traffic, like Milwaukee. If you're a 'Packer fan,' then you might want to go that way." Then, he reiterated, "They don't have the safe harbors over there, like in Michigan."

My mind was made up. I'd go down the Michigan side and take my chances with the winds. I liked the idea of having safe places to dock or anchor my boat every 25 miles. Kat and Kermit told me to come by *Good Karma* in the morning with my iPad and they'd show me their favorite stops. I got back to *Annabelle* late that evening as the sun was setting after 9:00 p.m., then slept soundly. Once again, I was in an unfamiliar town surrounded by friends.

Awakening at 5:30, as the sun started rising, I prepared my coffee; when I looked out the window, *Good Karma* was covered in a brownish-gray blanket. I opened my back door, and my boat was also covered. I squinted and looked again. The sides of the marina building were also covered. GROSS! The mayflies were bad in Penetanguishine, but they were just a sampling of things to come. I finished my coffee, determined to walk over to the marina bathroom and shower. The bathroom was separate from the dock building, closer to the road and further from the water. Sprinklings of white showed through the brown covering on the small concrete brick bathroom facility. I grabbed my shower bag and stepped out into the cockpit, which was bug-free because of my custom top. When I looked at the finger pier, though, it was covered with mayflies, much harder to see because their color blended with the wood decking. Once dead, they'd be washed back into the water from whence they came. Squishing them in my Keen sandals would take some doing, imagining their wings getting caught in the crevices of the soles. As I stood frozen, a humorous thought came to me. *What would the Dalai Lama do?*

I was pulled out of my imagination by the sound of a young lady. "They aren't going to move."

I looked toward the sound of the young voice. She was on the dock in front of me with a large push broom, the kind used for garage floors or commercial buildings. She was sweeping the ugly bugs off the sides of the building, carefully avoiding them as they fell into piles on the dock.

"They die when you touch them. You just have to walk through them."

"Do you do this every morning?"

"For a couple weeks."

Wincing out of disgust with shivers up my spine, I took my first step onto the dock, crushing mayflies under each step. The small bathroom across the parking lot had fewer mayflies, but there were still too many for my comfort. Only the metal door knob had escaped their descent. I took my shower, and by the time I finished and was returning to my boat, I saw Kermit hosing off *Good Karma*. Her pristine whiteness returned. I'd be using the hose next. *Maybe I should've waited for my shower.*

Calling over to Kermit, I remarked, "I see you've started early with cleaning."

"We'll be leaving soon."

"The weather seems pretty good right now, but we're supposed to have storms this afternoon."

"We'll be fine. It doesn't take long to get to Little Current from here. Kat's having coffee. Get your iPad, and the two of you can figure out the best stops in Michigan."

After boarding *Good Karma,* Kermit told me about the marine stores and Kat focused on the shopping. Faithfully, I marked each quaint town on my app.

Kermit advised me on returning to the States. "The best place to go through border patrol is through Mackinac Island. They have a video phone. It's really easy."

"Don't most people go through Drummond Island?"

"But you have to wait in a line of boats and the officers come aboard. It's easier through Mackinac Island. You'll need reservations to stay there."

As if it were a foul word, I repeated, "Reservations?"

"It's a busy marina. Make them in advance, online. Trust me. It's better than Drummond." He handed me a copy of the Michigan State Park and Rec guide, which had layouts and phone numbers of all the state-run marinas. "Keep it, we have another one."

"I hate the idea of reservations."

"This is the one time you have to. There's nothing like having your boat right there at Mackinac. You can ride your bike around the island, eat fudge, and you have to see the cupola at the top of the Grand Hotel."

Kat added, "You know. Where they filmed *Somewhere in Time*, with Christopher Reeve and Jane Seymour."

I still had no idea what a cupola was, but agreed to make the reservation. A short while later they were ready to leave. I watched the three boats pull out of the small harbor, smiling to myself and thinking about our paths crossing. What a small world. Except for the few small local boats, I had the marina to myself.

The remainder of the day was quiet until the storm blew in that afternoon. Making the reservation was tedious, and I ended up calling the Michigan Parks Service. Mackinac Island didn't have a reservation available for the day I wanted to be there, which would have given me extra days to spare. Having looked at the weather, I'd be in Kagawong for a three or four more days, and it would take two long days to get to Mackinac Island if I really pushed it. Weekends were booked months in advance, I could only get a reservation for Wednesday through Friday. All my experience so far had taught me that plans have to be flexible, not set in stone, for the sake of being safe. Despite my apprehensions, I forged ahead with the reservation. Worst case scenario, I'd be out dockage fees for a couple nights.

For three days it was cold, windy, and rainy. The dockmaster introduced a friendly, older, local couple to me. They had lived on their trawler when they were in their sixties and now that the husband was in his eighties, they split their time between a home in Kagawong during the summer and one in Florida during the winter. The following day, they invited me to join them for a late breakfast in Gore Bay. While there, we also stopped at the local marina which had a marine store, and then drove to a grocery store. I was counting down my days to crossing back into the States and didn't want to have to throw away any fresh food. Although I'd be entering at an OARS (Outlying Area Reporting Station) station by video phone, there was still a chance for border patrol to inspect my boat. With my luck, even thinking about breaking the rules was enough to get caught.

At night, the winds howled. By the third night of bad storms, the dockmaster offered to let me sleep on the couch in the office. After I declined, he offered to let me stay with him and his wife at their house. Canadians are very hospitable. I declined his generous offer and explained that if the winds let up the following morning, I'd be gone by the time he got into work at 8:00. Because of the bad weather, I was cutting into my time for crossing the North Channel and getting to Mackinac Island. Before he left for the day, he asked one last time, if I had changed my mind. I thanked him again. From experience, I'd always be more comfortable on *Annabelle*, no matter what the weather was like.

The next morning, the sunrise was beautiful. The clouds had dissipated, and with them, they must have taken the last of the mayflies. *Annabelle* was clean and so was the dock. The sunlight glistened off the water and off the sides of the building, which was pristine white from all the rain. The waters weren't as flat as I would have liked, but they were calm enough. I left the dock at 6:20 a.m. I had picked out a few anchorage spots where I might spend the night on the Canadian side of the border, both in the North Channel and the northern border of Lake Huron.

As I left Mudge Bay and navigated into the larger waters of the North Channel, the seas became rougher. The only other boats I saw for the entire day were five large fast boats, each in the 50-foot range, traveling together in a pack. They all flew by me, within less than 100 feet, sending their wakes my way, as if dealing with the choppy waters wasn't enough. At times, the seas were rougher than the Albemarle. I wondered what would happen if my boat sunk. I was miles from land and didn't have cell phone reception. I wondered how anything survived the long, harsh winters here, where the waters froze solid. In case of emergency, I had my SPOT finder and a personal locater beacon. Feeling very isolated, I turned on my radio to distract myself from the "what if scenarios" of drowning alone and never being found in the ice cold waters. Thousands of times I had told patients to not play the "what if" game, and if they were going to, to think of positive "what if" stories. I needed to heed my own advice and focus on getting back to the States.

I had been in Canada a month, and the hardest part was the limited communication back to my family and friends. With limited minutes on my cellphone and rare Internet access, I missed making phone calls when I wanted, something I had taken for granted. Despite the friendliness of the Canadians, I felt isolated and lonely.

Every hour I wrote down my coordinates (46.00'.190N, 082°59'.035W), how fast I was going (7.7 nm/h), and my engine speed (2200 RPM). I charted the islands as I slowly passed them. Around 4:30 p.m., I arrived at the final anchorage on the Canadian side of the border. I entered the cove, but didn't like the protection from the winds. It was still early enough to forge ahead to the next anchorage, a good hour away, even though I was exhausted from being at the helm for ten hours. I left Wagash Bay and crossed the imaginary boundary into the United States, where I anchored in Scammon Cove behind Meade Island. This was a peaceful, protected area with large houses on the shores. I was finally in the States, but I couldn't call, text or email anyone to share my joy. I still didn't have a Verizon signal. Here, I was truly alone. I hit my SPOT, which transmitted my GPS coordinates through the satellite to my list of family and friends. At least they could see where I was anchored, and I would sleep easy, knowing they knew where I was and that I was still safe.

That night, I looked up at the full moon; it was the last day of July. I wondered if it was a blue moon, the second full moon during the month. Blue moons reminded me of Annie. Before her, "once in a blue moon" was just an expression, nothing I ever paid attention to.

Although she wasn't my patient, she lived at the residential facility where I worked daily during my first job as a psychiatric nurse practitioner. I saw her every day at the residential facility, which was in a grand old house in the older part of Tucson.

Annie was one of the most tormented people I'd ever met, with more suicide attempts in her lifetime than Catholics attending Mass, but during the few months I worked at this facility, she seemed to do well. She shared her art work with me, and we talked about normal stuff—the weather, or things she picked up at the store during an outing with the staff, and such. It seemed to me like an ordinary interaction. On occasional weekends, I brought flowers from the local nursery—petunias, daisies or whatever was in season —to plant in the backyard garden. Annie would never get her hands dirty. Once, I went overboard and brought a Palo Verde tree, so there'd be shade from the desert sun for the residents. Annie thought it was a hilarious feat as my friend and I got the large tree out of the back of his pick-up truck and dragged it to the backyard. I'm not sure which was harder, getting the tree in the backyard or digging the large hole in the caliche ground, a common problem for southern Arizona gardeners. It took a few of us to get it planted in the desert soil.

Months passed, and I was offered a new job in rural Arizona that paid much more. When Annie heard that I was leaving, she told me she didn't want me to go. "I haven't attempted suicide since you've been here. I haven't even been to the hospital."

I acknowledged how well she had been doing and encouraged her to take the credit herself. I wanted her to know her stability was because of her efforts, not mine. Now, so many years later on the anniversary, looking at the full moon, I recalled the goodbye party, the cake, and good luck wishes from the staff. Annie showed me a picture she was painting which looked like a sunset in various shades of blue.

"It's a blue moon," she said. "I'm not done, but it's for you. I'll make sure you get it."

That evening, as I drove home, I was pleased about the work I had done at the residential facility, and I was excited about starting my new job in rural Arizona. The following day, I received a phone call from a co-worker. "Did you hear about Annie?"

With a sick feeling in my gut, I asked, "What happened?"

"She stepped in front of a train yesterday, after dinner." As I sunk to the floor with tears running down my cheeks, I thought about the picture she drew for me. The sunset. The full moon. We didn't just talk about ordinary things.

How many years would I agonize over her death? More than a decade later as I looked up to the full moon, Annie's picture was etched into my memory.

After a restless night, I left at the break of dawn. I was on the north shore of Lake Huron and had only a few hours ahead of me before arriving at Mackinac Island. I was excited to get there. On Lake Huron the fog was thick and the water was smooth, which reminded me of Lake Ontario when I left Oswego. As I hadn't seen anyone out the day before except five fast boats, I didn't figure I'd see anyone today either. My radar decided to work, which was sporadic, but useful on a day like this. The fog lasted most of the morning.

Around 11:00, I decided to be more responsible, as I was getting into a more congested boating area. I couldn't remember the proper signal for fog. Was it one long and two short? One short, one long? But, I knew it was written down somewhere. I started rummaging through the pages of a navigation book and stumbled onto a section about U.S. Customs and Border Crossing. Completely distracted, I skimmed through the paragraph. One sentence caught my eye about a $5,000 fine for not checking into customs when entering U.S. waters, including anchoring. Shit! I had illegally anchored. I frantically searched for the Customs phone number. Of course, I didn't have any way to call them the night before, or even this morning. I would tell them. Surely, they'd cut me some slack. Finding the number, I called and got through to an officer. "I am calling because I've entered U.S. Waters."

"Where are you checking in, ma'am?"

"Mackinac Island."

"This is the Sault Sainte Marie Border Station. You'll have to call a different number."

"But, I thought I was supposed to call."

"Ma'am, are you in your boat?"

"Yes."

"Where are you?"

"Lake Huron. On my way to Mackinac Island." My breathing was slowing down, as he asked his methodical questions.

With a slow, calming voice, he replied, "Just check in with the phone at Mackinac. You don't need to call."

"But the book said I could be fined for not calling."

"Ma'am, you're not getting fined."

"Okay. Thank you for your help."

I hung up. I was relieved and realized I must have sounded like a frantic, ditzy blonde who shouldn't be operating a boat, or any machinery for that matter. I was surprised he didn't ask me to put my husband on the phone. As my head cleared, I looked out the window. In the midst of my self-inflicted craziness, the fog had lifted. I could see Mackinac Island in the distance.

20

Michigan

I pulled into the Mackinac City marina just after noon. When I radioed the marina, I was told it was too early to check in, but if my slip was available, they'd let me dock. Otherwise, I'd have to wait in the anchorage with the rest of the boats. I had reservations for two nights, which were difficult to get in July and August. I waited a few minutes while they checked on my slip, and fortunately, it was open—a fixed dock facing Fort Mackinac. Being with all the smaller boats, *Annabelle* was placed next to the green lawn. I was 50 feet from the main road which circled the island, where all the horse-drawn carriages waited for passengers. The smell of horse shit permeated the air, along with wafts of Mackinac's famous fudge.

As I pulled into my slip and started to tie up, I saw a familiar face. Steve, from *Atla*, was there with his wife, Wendy. I had met their daughter, Claire, but this was the first time meeting his wife. Steve helped me tie up and waited for me to check into Customs through the OARS videophone, which only took a few minutes. Once I was legal, the three of us walked down the street to an open air hotdog stand just past the main shopping district. Sitting at a picnic table, Steve and I caught up on the events of the last couple weeks since he had pushed ahead to meet Wendy. They were staying at St. Ignace and had taken the ferry over to the island for the day. Purely coincidentally, they walked by the marina at the exact time I arrived.

After lunch, I left the two of them to enjoy their time together and went back to the marina where I had seen other Looper boats, including *Estrellita*, *Serenity*, *No Compromises* (from Southport), and *Sanctuary*. I hadn't seen this many Loopers gathered in one spot since Waterford and felt grateful to be reunited with them. Tom, my Southport neighbor, and his companion invited me aboard for dinner that evening. Stel and Burke invited me to ride bikes with them around the island. Meg and Jim invited me to visit them in Harbor Springs, where they'd be crossing their wake the following day.

When I had time alone, I walked to the fudge shops and picked out boxes to send to my friends and family at home: my mom, my children and grandchildren, friends, and an extra-large box for my clinic in Nogales. I felt grateful for all the people in my life, whom I loved and cared about and who had supported me along this journey. In Canada, I bypassed many of the places that Jim had told me about because I missed being in the States, where I felt more connected.

On Friday morning, my Mackinac Island reservations expired. The fog was so thick in the morning, that I couldn't see the boats two piers away from mine. The visibility in the water couldn't have been more than 50 feet. Hour after hour, I waited for the fog to lift. I went to the dock office to see if I could stay another day; the concept of being on a schedule still made me uncomfortable. The dockmaster told me I had to be out of the marina by 1:00, whether fogged in or not. The harbor was filled with boats which were anchored and waiting for their reserved slips, even if we couldn't see them. Any argument I made about safe boating practices didn't matter. If a tornado was coming through, I'd still have to vacate my slip by 1 p.m., so I returned to my boat and waited.

I tried reading, but couldn't focus. On the VHF radio, I listened to the boat traffic in the background. With Wi-Fi working, I revised my plans for a shorter day, not sure I could make it all the way to Harbor Springs during daylight with reports of choppy seas. I'd have to stop at Mackinac City, on the north shore of Michigan, less than an hour away.

Just after noon, while still foggy, the migration of boats leaving the marina started. I held back to let the larger boats go first, waiting as long as possible. Around 12:30, the fog lifted, and with fifteen minutes to spare before being kicked out, I pulled out of the public docks. By 1:30, I was at Starks State Harbor Marina, a brand new facility with floating docks and dock house, complete with a large laundry room. Several other Loopers showed up a couple docks away from me within the hour. I was getting used to being put with the local day use fishing boats, while the other Looper boats were put on the larger transient docks. It was another reunion with the crews of *Summerland, Fruitcakes, Wye Tug,* and *De De,* as we all shared dinner that evening at the picnic tables next to the dock house. My Looper friends planned to visit Mackinac Island the next day by ferry. My plan was to go the 50 nautical miles to Harbor Springs.

Meg from *Sanctuary,* was at the dock waiting for me in Harbor Springs at Ahlstrom Marine, which was on the edge of town, and had 24-hour security. *Estrellita* was anchored out and *Serenity* was at the city dock. Meg took Stel, Kathy, and me to the local butcher shop and grocery store, and we planned for a party that evening at Meg and Jim's summer home. After dropping off Stel and Kathy, Meg told me to get my bag. I'd spend the afternoon at her house, where she figured I could use a bath, enjoying the simple pleasure of relaxing in hot water, a Calgon moment.

Harbor Springs reminded me of Southport, a small community loaded with character. Each day a line forms outside Gurney's, the local liquor store, for lunch. In the back of the shop, they bake the best bread and sell sandwiches. Approaching the counter, I placed my order and asked, "Can I buy a loaf of pumpernickel?"

"No, ma'am. We don't sell loaves, and we don't have any extras."

"Oh, I'm here on my boat and hoped to take a loaf with me when I leave in a couple days."

He must have sensed my disappointment. "Come by at 11:00 tomorrow, and I'll have a loaf set aside for you."

I smiled and looked up at him. I was in luck. I took my lunch bag with a roast beef sandwich, pickle and chips, and filed out of the liquor store with the locals. My next stop was Tom's Mom's Cookies, with another line of loyal customers paying $18.00 per dozen.

Despite the beautiful boating weather, I chose to stay in Harbor Springs four days, which gave me time to provision, have *Annabelle* professionally cleaned, and order a few necessities from Amazon. While in Kagawong, Kat and Kermit from *Good Karma* gave me a list of places to visit along the Michigan Coast, and I prepared to move south. I returned to Gurney's, where I bought lunch, and was charged a mere $2.50 for the loaf of pumpernickel bread, the best I'd ever had.

Malcolm called to welcome me back to the States. We chatted about Canada, the Trent-Severn Canal, and the beauty of Georgian Bay. It had been at least a month since we had talked. As usual with Malcolm, he remarked how I was living his dream, something he hoped to do when he retired in a couple years.

After Harbor Springs, I planned to stop in Charlevoix. When I arrived just after 9:00 a.m., there was a waiting list for the municipal marina. The bridge was 11 feet, much lower than the published height of 16 feet, too low for *Annabelle* to go through. I'd have to wait 20 minutes for an opening. Lake Michigan was smooth as glass, so I decided to make the most of the day and go further south. I called Leland Municipal Marina, and they were also full. Michigan is filled with planners, boaters on a schedule. I looked at my chartplotter and saw an anchorage at South Manitou Island. It was a little further than I wanted to go, but it was a perfect day to leave the shoreline. After nine hours underway, I arrived at the small island in the middle of the afternoon, with five hours of daylight left to spend a peaceful and relaxing night.

At daybreak, I took a picture of the South Manitou Island Lighthouse on my way south to Arcadia, where I saw John and Kathy from *Serenity*. They planned a leisurely trip down the Michigan coast with reservations in Chicago at the end of August. I felt I needed to keep moving, taking advantage of good weather and calm lake conditions. The three of us rode our bikes around the small town, stopping at an old-fashioned ice cream parlor attached to local gift shop and marine supplier. The owners of the combination store also owned the gas station/convenience store next door, basically the entire retail industry in the small town. We stopped at the narrow, steep public beach where the water was icy cold. I only put my feet in, and missed the warm waters near my home on the Atlantic coast.

Early in the morning, I left Arcadia and went to Pentwater where the dockmaster expected all boaters to reserve slips through the Michigan State system, which has a $10 reservation fee. The dockage for the municipal marina is $1 per foot plus $10, making my dockage $35 for the night, more expensive than the local private marina, Snug Harbor. The municipal marina is in the middle of downtown, where shops and restaurants line the streets. I arrived in the early afternoon with plenty of time to walk around.

My fair weather was quickly coming to an end; rainstorms were making their way east across the Midwest. I stopped in Grand Haven for one night, quickly realizing I didn't want to stay there any longer. It was a bad choice of marinas for me since the town was across the river and the bathrooms seemed like they were a mile from my slip. I would've been better off anchored. There wasn't any help in finding my slip, and the teenage dockhands had difficulty finding a key for the restroom, as if they had just started working that day. This might be a good marina for locals who would be familiar with the layout and could park their cars and drive wherever they needed to go, but for transients there had to be better options.

I left at 6:00 a.m for Saugatuck, on Kat's list of favorite towns, 25 miles south and three quarters of the way down the Michigan shoreline. I arrived late in the morning, just ahead of bad weather. A cold front would end the hot August nights.

During the four days I stayed at the Saugatuck Yacht Club, the temperature dropped to 40 degrees at night. The winds howled, and there were reports of 15-foot seas in the lake. Despite the rain, I put on my rain jacket and rode my bike around town where I saw another Looper boat, *Knot so Fast*, an American Tug. When I knocked on the hull, nobody answered. Being ahead of my friends, I felt disappointed the Loopers weren't on their boat.

Mark and Jane called to let me know they too had returned to the States. Jane remarked, "Looping is different than cruising in that we have to keep moving forward." It was approaching the middle of August, and the general rule of Looping is to get through Chicago by Labor Day, before the weather changes. I was on track, not knowing when I'd cross over to Chicago, but also feeling that the omen of the weather change was upon me. As much as I appreciated Saugatuck, I wanted to keep moving; I'd been Looping for four months.

I methodically checked weather reports and wave heights, noting that during the night, when it was cold, waves were lower than during daytime hours. On Wednesday, the wave heights had come down to 6 feet, still much higher than I could handle, but during the night, they were supposed to be less than 3 feet. My opportunity to go south arrived, if I was willing to start in the middle of the night. At 2 a.m., I left the small town, using my chart plotter to help me navigate out the narrow channel into Lake Michigan.

Although 35 miles doesn't seem far, it was one step closer to crossing the southern portion of Lake Michigan and one step closer to Chicago. Through the night, traveling in the dark, I pondered if it was easier not to see the waves crashing against my hull—did I make them out to be bigger or smaller? I struggled to stay awake. I thought back to all the times I had worked night shift, and how difficult 4:30 in the morning had always been for me, getting through the sleepiness, then driving home. I arrived in St. Joseph at 7:45 a.m, dead tired, and ready for a nap. The Looper boat *Francesca* was checking out while I was checking in. They were almost home and willing to cross Lake Michigan with the reports of 6 foot seas. I envied their ability to travel in rougher waters than I could.

Later that afternoon, a 25-foot sailboat came into port beside me. The sailor and his wife had difficulty docking at the fixed docks, and I could see their frustration. They appeared to be in their early-sixties, ready to retire and adventure with their new boat. As much as he may have wanted his beautiful bride to be a part of his plans, his approach was failing by taking her out on a day like this one. Their boat was small, like mine, and despite the differences in the hull, they still would've been tossed around in the lake.

While the wife took a break stepping away from the boat, I helped the gentleman tie up his boat. We rearranged his lines as it was his first time tying up to a fixed dock. They had come from a marina in Hammond, Indiana, that had floating docks. Just before coming into the St. Joseph marina, they'd run aground and onto the rocks when his fuel line got caught in the seat at the stern of his boat. The Coast Guard had pulled their boat off the rocks and troubleshot his fuel problem. He was fortunate it was such a simple fix. Winning over his wife wouldn't be so easy.

Later that evening, I sat with the two of them, while the wife asked me questions about my trip. If there was any knowledge I could impart to them, it was not to rush, be careful with weather, and be willing to change their plans. If this couple was going to get along while sailing, the husband would have to let go of the idea that his plans had precedence over weather. Today he bulldozed his way through the seas, scaring his wife, and luckily neither of them got hurt. I imagined that it didn't turn out as romantically as he had hoped for. A couple weeks later, I got an email from the wife, thanking me for my advice and letting me know that they decided to trailer their sailboat home, as the weather was not cooperating with her husband's plans of sailing back down to Hammond, 35 minutes driving distance from Chicago.

Although reluctant to follow their advice of stopping in Hammond, I wasn't able to make a reservation in Chicago because of the Air and Water Show featuring the Blue Angels. I ended up in Hammond anyway since the docks in Chicago were full.

Not being a person who likes big cities, I contemplated bypassing Chicago. I'd never been there, and it wasn't on the list of places I wanted to see. In Hammond, I also found out that the Lockport Lock, south of Chicago, was closed for repairs until August 19, four days away. One way or another, I wasn't going far. Besides the casino next to the marina, there wasn't much to do in Hammond. I rented a car and decided to drive down to Greenfield, Indiana, where I had buried my father and grandmother. It was only a few hours away by car, just east of Indianapolis. After a couple days, I made a reservation in Chicago, deciding that it would probably be the only time in my life that I'd ever get to this famous city.

For me, Chicago marked the halfway point in this Loop. It is also marked the end of the Great Lakes, and the start of the rivers. There'd be new challenges with bigger locks, barge traffic, and fewer places to stop along the way. I arrived in Chicago on Monday, August 18, two weeks ahead of the Labor Day timeframe. The Chicago Harbor marina was one of the largest I had seen, with 420 slips, and combination locked gates to each of the eight piers. The marina was downtown, at the base of the skyscrapers, next to the Chicago Lock.

After registering at the marina office, I noticed a couple men cleaning and polishing *Knot so Fast*. I called through the secured gate, and they asked the owner to come out. I yelled over to him, "I saw your boat at Saugatuck, I'm doing the Loop too." He walked to the security gate and invited me to come aboard his boat and meet his wife, Lolly. That evening, I took one of the architectural tours on a tourist boat through the Chicago Canals. This city was magnificent. The next day, Lolly gave me a walking tour through Millennium Park, where there is a beautiful amphitheater and massive sculptures. That evening we ordered the famous Chicago pizza, an inch thick, and more filling than any pizza I'd ever eaten. I had leftovers for a couple more meals.

Once the Lockport Lock opened, I had my green light to head south on the rivers. I invited Lolly to go through Chicago with me, as *Knot so Fast* was too tall to go under the bridges. We left at 6:20 in the morning, going first through the Chicago Lock, then under the different bridges until I dropped her off at the circular condos a few miles away, where she could get a cab or walk back to the marina. Once again, I had company on my boat and enjoyed the camaraderie.

21

Illinois River

After dropping off Lolly, I was surprised there was no other traffic on the Chicago River, no barges, no boats, nothing. It was eerily quiet. I knew the Locks were open, because I called the day before and double checked. *Where was everyone?*

About twenty-five miles south of Chicago, in the Chicago Sanitary and Ship Canal, is an electric barrier designed to impede the migration of Asian carp north into Lake Michigan. I had forgotten that they were in the midst of maintenance and had closed the mile-long stretch of water during the daytime hours. A mile north of the warning signs, I was hailed by a Corps of Engineers boat and told I'd have to pull off to the side of the canal until they were finished for the day. It was 11:15 in the morning, and as I looked around, I didn't see any place to tie up. I turned *Annabelle* around, facing upstream, so I could tie onto something, anything protruding from the side of the canal. I could get myself close enough to the side, but I'd have to go out to the back of my boat to grab onto something. I realized quickly that the wall of the canal was made with layers of crumbling shale. I tossed my midship line around a small shrub on the side of the canal, and it seemed to hold.

With my fenders protecting *Annabelle* from the sharp rock walls, I'd be sitting here all day. I shut down my motor, then turned on the generator long enough to heat up a slice of the pizza in the microwave. I may have to wait, but at least I'd be comfortable. It wasn't long before I heard over the VHF radio, "We're taking our lunch break; you can let boaters come through." It was noon, and I was in luck, I wouldn't have to wait for several hours.

I radioed the control boat, "This is *Annabelle*; may I pass through the barrier?"

"You can go through at idle speed."

I knew the rules. I had printed a copy of the warnings, which explained that I needed to wear my life jacket. Nothing was retrievable from the river until a mile south of the electric barrier, which was designed to kill. Ahead of the barrier is a red danger sign, "High Risk of Electric Shock. No Swimming, Diving, Fishing, or Mooring." Having been told that it was not a big deal by Kat and Kermit, I wasn't too worried.

I was more worried that the Asian carp would jump onto the back of my boat after I got through the barrier. They were large, gross, and slimy. Rules stated that you couldn't throw them back into the river alive; once aboard, they had to be killed. They were attracted to the sounds of slower motors, like *Annabelle's*, and would jump out of the water into the cockpits of random vessels. The electric barrier was just a mile long, but the Asian carp would be lurking under the surface until I reached the Gulf.

For the next two days, I continued south with warm weather. Four days after leaving Chicago, I woke up early, and seeing the marina water covered in green algae, I decided to check my strainers for debris. Whether leaves, slime or sludge were the culprits, I knew the green film could clog the water line that cooled my engine. I closed the through hull, the valve that lets the water come from the river into the engine and checked the strainer. It appeared to be clean. I shut the engine hatch, went to the helm, and pulled away from the marina.

Within a couple minutes the engine alarm started screeching, like a car alarm on steroids. I quickly shut down the motor and started drifting down the Illinois River, panicked. My engine was overheated; the temperature gauge was in the red. I couldn't think straight. I called my friend, Ralph, the service manager from Portsmouth, Virginia. He asked if I had done anything different that morning.

Weakly, feeling like an idiot, I confessed, "Yes, I checked my strainer." I should have been checking it daily, as I was taught. I had gotten lazy. He didn't have to say another word; I knew instantly that I had forgotten to open the through hull, which allows the water to cool the motor. With any luck, I didn't do any damage to the engine.

With Ralph on my phone, I went to the stern and opened the through hull. He told me to turn my engine back on. I was fearful that the alarm would sound, the engine wouldn't turn on, or something terrible was going to happen.

Ralph, who so far hadn't chided me, explained that the engine would cool off quicker with it running, than while drifting down the river. Of course. It's not that I didn't understand the idea of a water-cooled diesel engine... I was just having a momentary lapse of common sense... a blonde moment. I did as I was told, and sure enough, it took hardly any time for my engine to cool off to a normal temperature. I was glad that Ralph was there, even if I was embarrassed. He was the voice of reason, a person I trusted with *Annabelle*. He told me to change my impeller at my next stop, as the overheated engine could have been affected it. The impeller is a 2-inch, black, rubber fan blade spinning to bring water into the engine. It works similar to the bilge pump, which helps the water flow out of the boat, or the shower sump pump, both of which I had already changed during this trip. I had two spare impellers aboard; no problem.

A close friend once told me that it is better to have blonde moments in front of other people, because then there is someone to help you. Alone on *Annabelle*, I just had to call people to share these moments. At least I had not drifted into the shore, or gotten in the way of a barge, during my angst.

On that blazingly hot day in late August, the heat was magnified inside the boat cabin. It was a busy Sunday on the river with people hanging out on pontoon boats, picnicking on the shore, fishing, while children splashed about in the shallower waters. With all my windows open, to allow for as much breeze as possible, I slowed down to pass a crowded picnic area, not wanting *Annabelle's* wake to disturb any of the people swimming. After I passed the beach, I pushed my throttle forward to speed up. I didn't hear anything unusual with the engine, but I could have sworn that I saw black smoke behind me. I brought the motor down to an idle and looked back. Nothing. When I sped up, I saw it again. Black smoke was pouring into the cabin. *Shit! What was happening now?*

I pulled off the main channel in the Illinois River and lowered my anchor. While standing on the front of *Annabelle*, I noticed two boats approaching from upriver, which I had seen the day before, one of which was a Looper boat. I hailed the Looper over the VHF radio to let him know I was having engine problems, and we exchanged phone numbers. He explained they were going to Tall Timbers Marina, in Havana, Illinois, for the night, about 15 miles away, and asked if they could be of assistance. I didn't need any help at this point. *I didn't even know what was wrong yet.* If I needed to, I could call for a tow through my TowBoat U.S. insurance. I'd meet them later at Tall Timbers. I'd planned to anchor out tonight, but this was not the scenario I had imagined.

I called Ralph. No answer. He was probably in a meeting. Next, I called my son, Dean. He thought it was a problem with the exhaust from my muffler. He had me open the engine hatch, start the engine, then go back to the door and look for the black smoke. I followed his advice, and sure enough, there was a hole in the elbow of the muffler. I returned to the helm and turned my engine back off. It had been many hours since I had made the mistake with my through-hull, I didn't think it could be related. In reality, the muffler must have weakened under the heat of the engine that morning, but didn't actually melt all the way through until I pushed the throttle forward after passing the swimmers.

My engine compartment was black with soot, and there were traces of the fine black powder in my cabin as well, especially around the engine hatch. It was 90 degrees outside, and over 100 degrees inside the cabin, which felt like an oven. The heat from the engine didn't help. I didn't care what I looked like. I had taken off my bra and underwear, and was wearing shorts and a T-shirt. If I were in the French Riviera, I would have been topless; it was too damn hot for clothes.

The next call I made was to Jon, our Towboat U.S. Captain in Southport, a man who is not fond of towing boats without a good reason. Dean suggested I call him for ideas on a temporary fix to get me to the next marina.

Jon was as practical as anyone I'd ever met. I tried to send him a picture of the hole, which showed it was on the inside of an elbow joint versus a flat surface. Jon never got the picture. I rationalized that he had one of those old flip phones, which explained why the photo didn't go through. I had to describe the problem—harder to do with words. All that mattered to Jon was that I had a hole in the muffler. Everything else I said was just fluff to him.

He asked, "What do you have onboard to patch the hole?"

Confidently, I said, "Duct tape."

Jon shot me down, "It won't hold. Do you have hose clamps? Wire?"

"Both, but I don't think I have a clamp big enough."

"You can put the hose clamps together to make one that will fit. The pressure is going to be pushing out, so you need something strong."

"Okay, I got it. Thanks."

"Call if you need anything else. Good luck."

Under the front V-berth, was a fishing tackle box with all kinds of hardware and several sizes of hose clamps. This was one of those moments I was grateful for being obsessive-compulsive about stocking anything and everything I might need. I took the largest of the hose clamps and started adding on to it to form a clamp large enough to fit the muffler.

I went back to the engine compartment and started wrapping the hard plastic pipe with duct tape. The duct tape wouldn't stick to the wall of the muffler because it was too wet. I tried to dry the area, but to no avail, as water was coming in through the exhaust. I decided that the duct tape only had to stick to itself, not to the muffler. I wrapped it around several times, then took my enlarged hose clamp and tightened it in place. It took me a good hour to patch the hole.

I was filthy, covered in soot from my head to my toes. I called Tall Timbers and the Looper boat to let them know I was on my way. I'd go slow, letting the current do most of the work. I pulled into Tall Timbers just before 5:00 p.m., and stood on line in the marina office which also sold pizza, beer and wings. For the first time that day, I felt embarrassed at how I looked. I was hot, tired, and exhausted. I briefly met the other boaters in the marina office. Three men were sitting at a booth and invited me to join them for a beer. I declined the beer, but sat down with them for a few minutes, to wait for the line to go down before I could check in and get the bathroom code. Their wives were fixing dinner on their boats. I must've smelled really ripe, but none of them seemed to be offended.

As soon as the marina attendant was free, I excused myself, paid for the slip, was given the Internet password, and most importantly, the codes for the restrooms. I hustled back to *Annabelle*, which was in the slip beside the office/restaurant and grabbed my shower bag. In the bathroom mirror, I saw how truly filthy I was, with more soot than skin showing.

When I got back to the boat, I called Ralph, and we talked about the options for fixing the muffler. I texted the pictures I had taken earlier in the day, along with measurements. We both had similar ideas. The simplest of all was to order a new muffler, which I could put in myself. He said he'd call in the morning with the information I needed to order a new one.

If there was one man I wished I could have with me on this trip, it would be Ralph. The following day, he called with the information for the muffler, which could be shipped with next day air. I still needed to change the impeller, clean the air filter, and the boat. I'd go ahead and remove the muffler, in preparation for the new one.

The two boats that came in before me left first thing in the morning. The marina was quiet. The only other transients, Ted and Christena, were from a catamaran. They had a car and offered to help in whatever way they could. I pulled out the old muffler and put it aside. It was fairly simple. Then, I started to work on finding the damn impeller. Prior to my trip, in Southport, a mechanic had changed the impeller. I remembered the difficulties he had getting to it. I laid myself across the blackened engine, reaching under, trying to put my head beside the engine and see with a flashlight. I struggled trying to fit into the small space. Eventually, I removed the generator's muffler, which gave me a few more inches to squeeze myself between the engine and the hull. The impeller plate was under the motor and faced the stern of the boat. If I stretched enough, I could barely see the bottom corner, but not with my arm in the way, or while trying to do anything else. I pulled myself up and out of the engine compartment. The last thing I wanted to do was accidentally pull out bolts for the wrong thing and sink *Annabelle*. Despite my memory, it didn't make sense that the manufacturer would have put the impeller in such a difficult spot.

I walked over to the catamaran and asked Ted for help. He seemed to be mechanically-inclined. We returned to *Annabelle* and looked through the owner's manual. After reaching around with his long arms, and feeling the plate, where I told him I believed it to be, he agreed it was the impeller plate and it was going to be difficult to reach. We tried different ways, including trying to get it through the hatch in the cabin step, to no avail.

Opening the cabin step only allowed more light into the area. I was going to have to suck it up and just squish my body into the space between the engine and hull and unbolt the impeller plate by touch.

It was not quite symmetrical or square, with quarter-inch, skinny bolts in each corner. I planned to remove three of the four bolts, to let the plate swivel around the fourth bolt, to make it easier to replace the plate back.

Crammed into the side of the engine, with my sternum hard up against the corner of the steel, for once I was grateful for my flat chest. As I reached around and under the engine, I felt the impeller plate and started unbolting it, with my small stubby screwdriver. As I pulled out the third bolt, the impeller plate fell into the bilge. Damn! There was no fourth bolt. It infuriated me that the last person to replace the impeller, the same mechanic who assured me my engine mounts were fine, had not replaced the plate with the four necessary bolts, knowing I was heading on a 5,000-mile journey! The bastard! I was one tiny, stainless steel, 20-cent bolt short. The picture of the rookie mechanic flashed through my mind, and then I recalled the moment when I asked him, "Does it really need all four bolts?" I was as infuriated with myself as I was with him.

Ted graciously took me to the local hardware and farm stores to find a replacement bolt. I picked up a few extras, just in case. He had plans for the afternoon, and I thought I was set with replacing the impeller.

Pulling the impeller from its housing was more challenging than pulling out the muffler. Lacking the proper tools, I tried to grab it with a needle nose plier. I couldn't get a good enough grip, and didn't seem to have the strength to pull it out. The owner of the marina, Bob came by, and seeing my struggle, offered to help. I admired Bob for all he had done with the marina. He had bought the land and built the marina, while working full-time, on rotating shifts. How he managed to get so much done amazed me.

Bob climbed down into the engine area, reaching around the engine as I had. Soon, he too was covered with black soot. Even with his strength, pulling the impeller took some time. While he was lying across the engine, I handed him the spare impeller to put in.

Then, it was my turn to lie across the engine to put the plate back on. I needed help with just the first bolt. Bob lay in the cabin, reaching through and around the engine to hold the plate in place. With my left hand reaching under the engine, carefully balancing a bolt on the tip of my screwdriver, I attempted to screw it in. After a couple minutes of silence, Bob said, "Tanya, what are you doing?"

In frustration, since the plate didn't seem to be holding, I responded, "I am screwing as hard as I can! Can't you feel it?"

After another brief moment of silence, Bob started laughing. "I've never had a woman say that to me before."

I realized what I said, blushing, and laughed along with him. I regrouped, stuck my head down the side of the engine, reassessed where the plate was supposed to go, and started again. With Bob's help, I got in the first two bolts. The third and fourth would be simple, as long as they didn't end up in the bilge. Bob left to get ready for work on his evening shift.

The following afternoon, Bob took me to Auto Zone to buy oil while he checked on some parts he had ordered. While there, we saw the UPS driver, who had my muffler in the back of her van. Bob was surprised because overnight shipping usually took an extra day in this remote little town. With fresh oil and my new muffler in hand, I'd have plenty to do.

Christena and Ted were making plans to leave the following morning. They had friends to meet in Alton. We talked about where they'd anchor or stop on the way. Down river was a restaurant with a reputation for exceptional brisket and pies. They offered free docking for boaters eating at their restaurant. If I stopped in Alton, I'd see familiar faces.

In the afternoon, another transient came into Bob's marina, a Great Harbour 37-foot trawler, wide and tall, with the diesel power of *Annabelle*, with a hired delivery captain and younger crew member on board. The gentle, slow, giant boats are known for their spaciousness, and oddly the crew was looking for a hotel. The captain was clearly irritated with his companion, who wore a long sleeve, white, button-down shirt, slacks, and dress shoes, unsuitable for boating. The young man was rude and had a taxi drive him 50 miles away to a big city, where he'd stay the night in a hotel. The captain, in his late fifties, decided to stay on the boat. After I helped with their lines and they had paid for their slip, the younger man left. The captain offered to give me a quick tour of the boat. A nonprofit company used it for wining and dining prospective donors. In addition to the full-size refrigerator was a large wine cooler and snacks with the company logo. Despite the size of the boat, there were no sleeping berths. The captain had brought along a sleeping bag, but said he had spent every night at a hotel. Tonight, he planned to stay on the boat. I declined his offer of wine and returned to my boat. It was approaching dinnertime and I had spent the afternoon socializing instead of working.

As I was started to prepare dinner, the captain of the non-profit yacht came to *Annabelle* and asked if I'd accompany him for dinner. Hesitant, I explained I was making dinner, and he suggested I refrigerate what I was making and have it the next day; he was buying. I'm not one to turn down dinner, so I put everything away and walked into town with him, where we found a pub and ordered burgers.

I had a glass of wine and he had a couple beers. He was delivering the boat, from Lake Michigan, to the Mississippi River. He'd stop in Grafton, where the Mississippi and the Illinois Rivers meet, then he'd go north on the Mississippi to his final destination. His crew was a student of his trying to get his captain's license. He had brought him along to get him some hours and was less than enthusiastic about his skills or progress.

As we returned to our boats, I could sense that this captain had more on his mind than talking about boats. He invited me back to his boat, which I politely declined, sensing he was hoping for more than a simple conversation.

Around 7:00 the following morning, the captain dropped his lines and powered out into the river. His crew had returned on time. As he passed my boat, he yelled out, "Stop in Grafton! I'll see you there!" Later that morning, Christena and Ted left for Alton. I knew where I'd be going.

Grafton is where most Loopers stop for fuel and supplies before heading down the mighty Mississippi. It's a city with many restaurants and services within walking distance from the marina. Alton has a beautiful marina with impeccably clean, private bathrooms. Although the services are not close by, as in Grafton, the owner of the local grocery store in Alton is boater friendly and will pick transient boaters up and deliver them back to their boats.

After Ted and Christena left Bob's marina, I still had to install my muffler. Steve from *Atla* was coming into Tall Timbers that day. He was a short distance behind me and had texted that he was having problems with his chartplotter and was hoping he could find the solution he needed in this small town.

It was a busy day. As Steve pulled up, I was in my engine compartment, once again, covered in black, putting in my muffler. I had it in, but couldn't tighten the clamps without a second set of hands. If Steve could hold it in place, I could get the clamps tightened. I stopped what I was doing and went over to Steve's boat, asking him if he could help me, once he got settled. Once he arrived, I held the muffler in place and he started the clamps, then left me to finish. I was back to having a working boat!

What Steve needed was a memory card reader to reload his charts. He had called the company that made his chartplotter, and they had explained how he could download his charts from the computer, then load them onto his chartplotter. I had a memory card reader aboard, so he was set. He didn't have to buy anything, not that he would have found a memory card reader in Havana anyway.

That evening, Steve and I ate dinner in town. On our way, a man came stumbling toward us, a bit intoxicated. I could see Steve stand up a little taller with his muscles tightening. As the man approached, he said, "Didn't I see you guys heading up to town last night?"

Steve, said, "No. It wasn't us."

"It might have been me, with another gentleman," I said.

The drunken man looked from me to Steve and quizzically asked, "Well, are you coming from the marina?"

Simultaneously, we said, "Yes."

The drunken man then extended his hand, with his truck keys, "It's a hot day. Take my truck."

Steve, now relaxing, said "Thanks, but I think we'll walk." It was a kind gesture from this stranger. I was having dinner with a different man every night and wondered what that looked like to other people, even if I was completely innocent.

That night, I slept like a rock. For the first time in months, I slept in past sunrise and woke up after seven. Steve had already left. Bob had my bill ready for me and was drinking his coffee. I decided to spend the morning cleaning my boat; I was in no hurry to leave. Bob gave me a big hug and wished me well on my journey. He helped with my lines and made sure the exhaust was blowing out the exhaust pipe with my new muffler. I quietly motored out of Tall Timbers Marina, going south on the Illinois River.

That night I anchored out at the spot Bob, Ted, and I had discussed. I motored further south and stopped at the Riverside Restaurant for their famous brisket, mashed potatoes, and green beans. With a to-go box for my leftovers, I also took a couple slices of homemade berry pie.

Passing Grafton, I saw the Great Harbour boat, too wide for a normal slip, at the T dock, closest to the river. I thought about the captain who had taken me to dinner. Meanwhile, the Looper from *Le Hooker* saw me go by and hailed me. I had first encountered him and his wife in Parry Sound. It was frequently easier to remember the boat name, than the crew's names. We changed VHF radio channels and talked freely. We were both a couple weeks ahead of the other Loopers, having headed through Chicago before Labor Day Weekend, when the harbor host in Chicago throws a large Looper barbecue.

I stopped for the night at Alton Marina, where I docked across from Ted and Christena. As soon as I arrived, I called the local grocery store and made arrangements to be picked up the following morning to buy groceries, grateful for their kindness. That evening, I relaxed with Ted and Christena, who were worried about the captain and his intentions. They treated me protectively. They had seen his boat in Grafton and wondered if I'd stop there, but told them I preferred their company over his. A friend of theirs met us at the dock and joined us on their boat. We talked about the recent shooting of a young black man by a white police officer across the river in Ferguson, Missouri, and the racial tensions. I had not seen the news in months and was oblivious of the riots and arrests.

I left Alton after buying my groceries. A woman who owned the store with her siblings picked me up after dropping her kids at school. Her brother brought me back to *Annabelle* and carried my groceries. He said their father had started the tradition of helping transient boaters years before he had died and left them the grocery business. This was one tradition the family planned to keep. I was the first of this season's boaters to call them and I felt honored by their tradition.

Mississippi Barge going into Lock

22

Mississippi, Ohio, Tennessee Rivers

On August 29, I left the Alton Marina and continued south down the mighty Mississippi. The current was swift, adding an extra 3 knots to my speed, so I could travel over 9 knots, with minimal effort. I shared the river with large barges pushed by towboats. Each individual barge can be 30 to 45 feet wide, by 117 to 200 feet long, carrying 1500 tons of cargo. Approaching the barges from the front, all I could see was the platforms, like a football fields of containers. The average towboat pushes fifteen barges and some will push thirty, which are all strapped together. With their impressive size, it's best to stay out of their way; they can't exactly turn on a dime.

The locks are 110 feet wide, by either 600 or 1,200 feet long. Compared to the locks in Canada and the Erie Canal, these locks are enormous. These massive barges can't always fit into a single lock chamber, so the barges will be split between two lockings. The first group of barges is detached and pushed into the lock and released on the other side, then the towboat enters the lock with the second group. With some of the locks having a rise or fall of 50 feet or more, it can take close to an hour each direction. The commercial traffic has priority over the recreational boats, the source of much frustration amongst Loopers, who will compare which locks they had to wait at the longest.

The Mississippi is one of the longest stretches on the Loop without places to pull over to fuel or to stay the night. About 18 miles down the Mississippi from Alton is Hoppie's Marina, owned by Hoppie and Fern, who must be in their late seventies or early eighties. Fern is known far and wide as the broker of knowledge about the river. She knows the nooks and crannies, where it is safe to anchor and where a boater can get into trouble. Hoppie's is the last chance for buying fuel for 228 miles. As one comes down the river, Hoppie's is on the western shore, built of two flat barges tied together, lengthwise, end to end, and tied to the shore. On the shore side edge of the barges are local boats, moored to the barge. On the river side are spaces for transient dockage and fueling.

I was a few hours behind Steve, who had stayed at Hoppie's the night before. He texted, suggesting I anchor instead of staying the night at Hoppie's, because barge traffic had thrown large wakes during the night, slamming his boat into the side of the barge. I pulled to the side of the river, and tied *Annabelle* onto the barge. Hoppie sold me less than two gallons of fuel, since I had filled up at Alton. Knowing that I was pushing my fuel limit for this part of the journey, I'd take every last gallon I could handle. *Annabelle* had a fuel gauge which never worked. Once, I thought it was working, it read three-quarters of a tank. The needle moved and I thought it was miraculous. Only it wasn't working. My tank was emptier than it had ever been, and I had to put 70 gallons into my 75 gallon tank.

Fern is the informational source for the Mississippi, so I asked Hoppie if she was there. It was early afternoon, and I resolved not to stay the night, seeing the barge wakes that Steve had warned me about. Most transients coming down the river stop for the night, if for no other reason than listening to Fern's advice on what to expect and where to anchor.

"You'll find her on the mower up the hill."

"Do you think she'll mind talking to me?"

"She needs to take a break anyhow." Hoppie was one of those quiet men who didn't have much to say and kept his opinions to himself, working hard every day of his life.

I took the small bridge from the barge to the shore and walked up the hill, to several outbuildings and a large house. I didn't see Fern. I asked a man working there if he could point me in the direction of Fern. He told me to go behind the outbuilding and I'd see her on the tractor. As I approached the wrinkled old woman, I couldn't hear a word she said, and I didn't think she could hear me either.

She took one look at me and yelled to meet her at the picnic tables, under a tree. I walked over, and she rode her tractor. Once everything was quiet, I thanked her for taking a break. I felt timid talking to such a legend. I had brought my iPad with me, so I could put the notations into my chart plotter program. I also had a piece of paper and a pen.

After trying to get oriented to the chart plotter, she said, "Just write this down. From here to the Kaskaskia Lock should take you about four hours. You can probably get there before sunset. It's a safe place; ask the lock master if you can stay the night. When you get to mile marker 85, stay to the reds. Before the I-57 bridge, you can anchor on the left side, but stay close to the river. It's shallow in there. Always give yourself an extra four feet of depth for anchoring. The depth of the river can change overnight and you don't want to get stuck. Pass the barges on the inside of a turn if you can. If you have enough fuel, go down the Cumberland instead of the Tennessee River, the Barklay Lock is faster to get through than the Kentucky Dam Lock. Fewer barges go that way."

I wrote as fast as I could, hoping to catch everything Fern said.

I was honored that she took a few minutes in her day to give me the advice she usually gave to transient boaters in the evening. I gave her a quick hug and hustled down the slope to the barge, so I could motor to my next stop, the Kaskaskia Lock off a side channel of the Mississippi River.

As darkness descended, I tied up at the lock wall. The lock master said they'd be there all night watching out for me. Following Fern's advice, I stayed the next night near the I-57 bridge about eight miles from the Ohio River where I'd be going upstream against the current. I realized how close civilization was, with the intermittent thrumming of traffic through the night.

Two nights of staying on *Annabelle* without any place to stretch my legs was making me claustrophobic. I couldn't wait to get to Kentucky Lake. So far, coming down these rivers was pretty easy. I didn't have to wait on any of the locks. I recalled one lock on the Illinois River where I arrived just as a thunderstorm was moving in. I had miscalculated when it would hit and thought I could get to the anchorage on the downstream side of the lock. The lock master offered to let me stay in the lock until the storm passed over us. I accepted his offer and then he asked, "Can we get anything for you?" I think he would have brought me coffee, had I asked. I was lucky compared to other Loopers, some had to wait hours to get through locks.

Steve texted me. "Took five hours to get through Kentucky Dam Lock. Anchored in lake. Rough night. Didn't get any sleep."

"Where are you now?"

"Kentucky Lake State Park."

Wendy was meeting him there, and they planned to look at real estate. She'd drive her car, and he'd meet her along the way in *Atla*.

Going upstream had slowed me down considerably, from 10 knots to 5.6, with my engine running at 2200 RPM instead of 1800. I was burning fuel, and knew I had to make the 230 miles on my one tank of diesel fuel. In an ideal and perfect world, I should be able to make it 300 miles, but with the currents, it was hard to estimate my fuel consumption.

There are two options to navigate into Kentucky Lake and the Tennessee River. Turning right at the Tennessee River is more direct, but more congested with barge traffic and long waits at the Kentucky Lake Lock. The second approach is to go further up the Ohio, then turn south on the Cumberland River and take it to the Barklay Lock and Dam, which doesn't have the barge traffic or long waits. Worried about fuel if I went the Cumberland route, I'd have to anchor somewhere for a third night, and I wouldn't get into Kentucky Lake until the following day. My mind was preoccupied with which direction to pick.

At Lock 52 on the Ohio River, the last lock before heading to either the Cumberland or the Tennessee, I saw massive anchored barges everywhere. Lock 52 has two chambers, one for commercial traffic and the other for overflow commercial traffic or recreational boats. The secondary chamber had been closed all morning. The lock master told me they were about to open the secondary chamber where I could go through. *Annabelle* was the only recreational vessel around. After entering the enormous lock and getting ready to tie up, they asked if I wanted to just float through. I declined and tied up. Locking went smoothly, and I felt incredibly grateful to get through so quickly.

Once past the lock, there was a bridge to pass under. I scanned the water and thought all the barges I saw ahead were anchored. I was already planning ahead to the next lock, deciding if I should go to the Kentucky Dam lock or chance the fuel and go to the Cumberland. I turned the volume of my VHF radio off and called the Kentucky Dam lock master to ask if there was a long line of tugs waiting. He told me things looked good right now, but he couldn't guarantee what it would be like three hours later.

Heading under the bridge, I sensed a profound anger reverberating in my bones. I turned up the volume on my VHF radio just in time to hear the captain of a large tow asking other boats about *Annabelle*. He was furious! We were both heading toward the same bridge, only in opposite directions. I was a few hundred feet from the bridge, and he was just on the other side. SHIT! I spoke into the VHF radio as I steered toward the side of the shipping channel. "This is *Annabelle*. I'm sorry. I'm going to the side of the bridge."

"YOU CAN TAKE THAT BOAT TO THE EDGE OF THE RIVER. I HAVE THE RIGHT OF WAY GOING DOWNSTREAM." He was yelling at me over the VHF, and he had every right to. Every boater within miles could hear us, along with all the lock masters and every tug along the river. I'd pay for this mistake.

"You should have your radio on."

"You're right. I'm sorry."

Our exchange may have put a few extra years on this man's life. He could have had a heart attack worrying that he was going to run me over, unable to stop the barge as we both were heading toward the center of the bridge. Maybe he was worried he'd take out the bridge. I shouldn't have been distracted. I shouldn't have been thinking about which way I was going to turn two miles up the river. I had seen him and thought his barge was anchored. Damn. I had looked right at the barge and hadn't realized the danger. I was not centered in the moment.

I turned *Annabelle* out of the shipping channel. He was right. With my two and a half foot draft, I could be in the shallower side of the river and more importantly, any barge has the right of way, no matter whether upstream or downstream.

That close call affected me to my core. I fucked up and was lucky to come out of it alive. A momentary distraction could have ended my life as quickly as Annie's ended hers with the train; only she knew what she was doing.

Two miles after the bridge, less than fifteen minutes later, I had to make the decision—Cumberland or Tennessee. I swerved my boat right into the Tennessee. Even if I had to wait a few hours, I'd rather be at anchor than burning up the last of my fuel. In just over two hours I'd reach the Kentucky Lake Lock and Dam. Arriving at 5 p.m. a tow, with thirty barges strapped together, was entering the lock. The towboat crew would have to split the barges apart into two lockings: one with twelve barges, the other with eighteen. The larger one would go through first. The second set of barges would go through with the towboat, then they'd strap both parts back together on the other side. The lock master suggested I could tie up to one of the federal mooring cells, which are circular groups of pilings tied together with a diameter of 20 feet. These pilings had places where larger boats could tie off. As I approached, the current tossed *Annabelle* to the side. No matter which direction I approached, even head on, I couldn't slow down enough to tie off. *Was the lock master sitting up there, looking down on me, laughing?*

I remembered that Steve had anchored. I called the lock master. "Is there a good place to anchor?"

"You can go to the side of the river, above the mooring cells. Just don't block the entrance or the river." I wished he would have told me this from the beginning.

I thanked him and did as I was told, going upstream a few hundred yards, and dropping my anchor inside the northern shore. With two hours for each locking, it might be 9 or 10 before I'd lock through.

After I dropped my anchor, two small powerboats, meant for waterskiing, came down to the lock. The heavy steel doors were barely shutting on the first load of barges. They radioed the lock master. "We want to get locked down to the lake."

"You'll have to wait; I have a barge going down."

They seemed to be oblivious how long the wait might be. They zoomed here and there, going upstream and downstream. After half an hour of ripping around the water, they called again, "How long is it going to be?"

The lock master didn't respond.

"Hey! Barklay Dam, we're calling you! How long?"

Were they drunk? They messed up the name of the lock! This was bad. With them as lock companions, it could be forever before we'd be allowed in. They continued with their obnoxious demands. Finally, the lock master told them it would be a few hours.

I didn't trust that I'd be given fair notice to pull my anchor. As offensive as these boaters were, I knew I'd shown up with my own reputation. I'd have to time it, and listen for the horns, which signaled the lock opening and closing. If I could hear the lock close on the other side, after dropping off the second half of the barge, I'd have at least a half hour to pull my anchor. It was getting late, after nine, "Looper's midnight."

I was afraid that if I lay down, I might fall asleep and miss the lock all together, not that it was a bad idea. Maybe I could be in the first lock in the morning. No, that wouldn't work; there'd be barges going through this lock all night long. One way or another, I'd be waiting. My best bet would be to just listen. I lay down in my V-berth and looked up at the stars. Maybe, I could just shut my eyes for a few minutes. I sat up. No, I better not. Well, maybe, if I set an alarm. I set my iPhone for 10:00 then lay back down. It felt like just a moment had passed when my alarm went off. I got up and made myself a cup of coffee in the dark.

Just as it finished brewing, I heard the other boats calling the lock master. "Hey, Lock master! You up there? You awake? How much longer do we have to wait?" Wow, sitting for hours, drinking beer didn't help their attitude. The lock master ignored them.

I started my engine and started pulling up my anchor. As soon as my anchor was free, I heard the lock master tell the other boaters that they could enter the lock when the green light came on. He didn't acknowledge *Annabelle*. I radioed the lock master, "This is *Annabelle*, the small blue tug. I'll be coming in after the other two boats." No response. I was persona non grata.

As the lock opened, I pulled in behind the other two boats. I had *Annabelle* tied up first, and hailed the lock master, "*Annabelle* is secured." The other boaters tied up their waterski boats and then followed my lead, letting the lock master know they were ready.

By the time we got to the bottom of the lock, it was after 11:00 p.m., pitch dark, on a moonless night. Kentucky Lake was choppy, not that I could see much of anything, but the feel of it was bad. The small boats powered out of the lock and headed along the dam, toward the shore. I could see their lights in the distance, but was no match for their speed. I'd need to find the marina by trusting my GPS. If Steve had anchored in this mess, it would've been a horrible night. Unfamiliar with the area, I slowly hobbled my boat toward Kentucky Dam State Park and Marina, afraid I'd hit a buoy. According to my chartplotter, the entrance was between two overlapping seawalls. Once behind the protective barriers, I could anchor near the seawall on the northern side, rather than trying to find a slip.

With my floodlight scanning the horizon, I saw the seawall. It was hard to judge the distance in the dark. How much room was there between the two walls? *Breathe, just a few more minutes, and you'll be safe for the night.* My body was jittery from coffee and adrenalin, like a chemically-induced stress test, but my mind just wanted to crawl into bed and rest.

As I passed the end of the second wall and entered the protected lagoon, I saw the smaller boats at a dock on the far side of the water. I moved *Annabelle* in their direction, and dropped my anchor halfway between the marina and their dock. I hoped this would be a safe location for the night, far enough out of the way for the early morning fishermen.

It was a long day. I had left my anchorage at 6:25 in the morning, and it was close to midnight. I thought I'd pass out the minute my head hit the pillow, but with the caffeine, I had sabotaged my sleep.

In the morning, still feeling dead tired, I pulled up my anchor and motored to the marina to fill my tank with fuel and stop for the day and night, arriving at 8:00 when they opened. Surprisingly, I had only burned 50 gallons since leaving Hoppie's. The attendant docked me beside *Atla*. After a quick trip up the hill to use the restroom, I saw Wendy and Steve come out of their boat. They had not noticed me pulling in beside them. Later, the three of us went to lunch at Patti's and Bill's, two restaurants owned by a couple, sharing the same kitchen, with separate entrances for each. Due to the shorter wait at Bill's, we ate there. I ordered the pork chop special with flowerpot bread. The bread was baked in a clay pot, easily found at any nursery.

The food was tasty. The waitresses dressed like they had just come from the *Little House on the Prairie* with matching gunnysack dresses. I wondered if the dresses were Patti's idea, or Bill's? The male waiters didn't have to wear anything unusual. Did this fall into the same sexist category as Hooters? I couldn't see myself dressing in either attire, ever. On the other hand, if it was the only job I could get, maybe I would. Come to think of it, I've had worse jobs, like when I was pregnant with my daughter and worked in a factory coiling sterile hospital enema bags. Not only did I work all day, but I dreamt about it all night.

From Kentucky Lake State Park, I'd continue down the Tennessee River to the Tombigbee River, at Counce, Tennessee. The Tombigbee would take me the rest of the way to Mobile Bay, Alabama, the entrance to the Gulf of Mexico.

23

Tennessee and Tombigbee Rivers

When I left Steve and Wendy at the Kentucky State Park, I had the feeling I wouldn't be seeing many more Loopers. Steve and I were ahead of my contacts. For the next week, my focus was going south on the rivers. On the way, I stopped at small marinas: Paris State Park, Cuba Landing State Park, and Riverstone Marina.

At Riverstone, I ordered dinner from a local restaurant, Mio Maio's, and had it delivered. The owners of the marina had a small kitchen in their office and offered breakfast. That morning as I ate my bacon and eggs, I met a couple, who were also doing the Loop, but planned to stay at Grand Harbor Marina for a month, before heading south to the Looper Rendezvous in Alabama, which takes place in October.

Over breakfast we talked about how fast we'd be going. If I went just a little slower than them, I'd have to wait for each lock. My best strategy would be to go the same speed. They said they would be doing 7 knots. Great, I could do 7 knots. However, once on the river, they were doing closer to 7.5 or 8, and I was pushing my engine to keep up with them. By the time we arrived at Grand Harbor Marina, where the Tombigbee starts, I was beat. I had planned to stay a couple days at this marina, but was sorely disappointed with their service. Despite calling ahead to reserve the space, they clearly didn't expect my arrival and assigned me the inside of the fuel dock. My Looper friends had been assigned a slip where they didn't fit, because it was covered and their boat was too tall. It was frustrating.

I had run out of bottled water. The manager offered to sell me water at $10 per case, the most expensive bottled water I'd buy on the trip. More than anything else, the cost of the water made me decide to leave the next morning. One of the boaters who came in on his fast boat for fuel told me I should stay at another marina.

"You staying the night?"

"Yeah."

"If you haven't paid yet, go to the marina about a half mile from here. Show up after five, stay on the fuel dock and leave first thing in the morning. Then, you don't have to pay."

I wondered how many people actually did that. Clearly, he would.

"I don't mind paying for my dockage."

Before turning back to his boat he said, "Just trying to save you a few bucks."

There were times on the Loop when I did arrive after a marina was closed and left before they opened. Each time I called and made sure they had my credit card information to charge me, even if it was after I left. I wondered how many boaters took advantage of marinas like this guy who was not the kind of person I wanted to hang out with.

On September 10, I arrived in Demopolis. The Demopolis Lock had been closed for a few days for repairs and I arrived before their scheduled reopening. I called the fuel dock, "This is *Annabelle*, I need a slip for the night and would like to fuel up before going to my slip."

"Do you need help tying up to the fuel dock?"

"No, I've got it. Thank you."

I steered over to the fuel dock, stepped off my boat with my midship and stern line in my hand, but there were no cleats to tie off to. The marina was in the midst of renovations. The dock attendant came out of the office and apologized. Meanwhile, one of the towboat captains came over and helped me tie *Annabelle* to pilings, so I could get fuel. The dock attendant sent me over to the covered slips where there were several boaters waiting for the lock to open, including three Looper boats heading south: *Sea Fever*, *dARfV*, and *Le Hooker*.

I was amazed to run into Looper boats, as we were a month ahead of most other Loopers. At the Rendezvous in Alabama the previous year, I had met Debi and Jim from *Sea Fever*. Debi passed me in the hallway and handed me a book about women cruisers. I stopped by *Sea Fever* later that evening to visit. She was the captain of her boat, and her husband was the first mate. They were on their last year of doing the Loop, taking 14 years from start to finish, with two different boats. They had continued to work and took trips back and forth from home. They hosted a lot of company on their boat, and had given me a guide for entertaining guests. Their boat was 50 feet long, definitely more conducive to company than mine. For the next two days, I hung out with them and a few other boaters.

From Demopolis to Fairhope, Alabama, would be three to four days of travel for me. I could stop at Bobby's Fish Camp, at the halfway point, for fuel, dockage, and a catfish dinner, but then I expected another two days underway. Debi and Jim planned to get to Fairhope in two days. Their boat went faster than mine, so it was more feasible for them to stop overnight at Bobby's. As a rule, they didn't anchor. It surprised me how many people I met along the way, who wouldn't anchor. I enjoyed anchoring, for one night at a time; I'd enjoy it even more if I weren't by myself.

The lock opened on the night of September 11th. Several of us who hoped to lock through the following morning called the lock master to schedule a good time to go through, understanding there was a line of barges that had also been waiting. We were told to be at the lock around 8:30 a.m., and he'd let the pleasure boats go through. One 60-foot yacht, *Black Pearl*, was being delivered. Her crew ignored the time frame, which was planned ahead of time, and they left the marina at 6:30 in the morning. They had decided to get locked through before the rest of us. At 8:00, three of our boats left the marina together to wait at the lock for the 8:30 opening.

Arriving early at the lock, I saw *Black Pearl* circling in front of the lock doors. Over the VHF, the lock master told them to stay away from the doors, as a tow would be coming out, and they needed to stay out of the way. I pictured *Black Pearl* making circles for the last two hours, annoying the shit out of the lock master. I had heard that *Black Pearl* needed the windlass repaired for their anchor. The repairman planned to go down to Fairhope, pick up the part, then meet them on the river, to put the windlass on the boat, while they were underway. Their plan was to take their dinghy to the shore and pick up the repairman at a dock.

Halfway through the morning, a couple hours downstream from the lock and a mile or two ahead of *Black Pearl*, I overheard a conversation between the captain of the yacht and the skipper of the dinghy. The dinghy was traveling much faster than my usual speed of 7 knots. The dinghy skipper hadn't figured out how to spot the mile markers on the riverbanks. He radioed

Black Pearl. "I'm going to ask that girl on the little blue tender, the one we saw earlier today."

Ouch. Little blue tender? *Annabelle* had a name, and she wasn't a tender. Stifling my irritation, I waited for him to come beside me and ask the question he had asked his buddy on the mother ship. I told him where we were and how far he needed to go, without telling him to go to hell and back. A half hour later, I saw him fly by in the opposite direction with the repairman. Later that night, they might get ahead of me. The yacht was huge compared to mine, but their speed was no different. At sunset, after 12 hours behind the helm, we'd both be anchoring.

I found a small creek, which I was able to navigate, with my shallow draft. Peaceful night. I left before the sun came up and made it to Bobby's Fish Camp around 9:30 a.m. Three large trawlers were already on the dock, and when I called Bobby's on the VHF, they told me I would have to wait for one of the transients to leave. I scoped out the dock and decided that if I put my boat in stern first at the downriver end of the dock, perpendicular to the shore, I should have just enough room to step off and fuel up. Pulling up to the dock as I did, was not exactly normal. Nobody from Bobby's actually expected me to be able to dock, as nobody was there to help me with fuel. A nice couple on one of the trawlers suggested I walk up to the restaurant. The fuel is turned on at the street, so I had to hike up the hill a couple times to get fuel. The nozzle didn't seem to fit into my tank, so it was slow going. At the restaurant, the woman suggested I wait around for a couple hours and have lunch. If I left too late, I'd be anchoring two more nights, instead of one. Two nights in a row of anchoring is more than plenty.

After fueling, I looked at my AIS receiver and noticed that a tug was a two miles up the river. He had the right of way, but if I got to the next lock first, I'd be let through first. I called the tow to see if he were small enough to have me tag along in the lock; not that I'd ever been in a lock with a barge before. He told me he'd take up the whole lock. I'd wait for him to go by and get the next lock. When I called the lock master, he estimated when I could go through. The couple on the large trawler beside mine, who planned to leave later that morning, offered me a piece of pie and coffee. We chatted until it was time for me to proceed to the lock at 11:00 a.m. If I wasn't pressed for time, I could've had some catfish at the restaurant which was getting ready to open for the lunch crowd.

That night, I made my way to Three Rivers Lake, just off the Tombigbee, and anchored. It had been another long day behind the helm. It was a winding river, with hairpin turns and beautiful green landscape. As far south as I was, there must be alligators; fortunately, I didn't see any. For the most part, I didn't see many boats other than an occasional fisherman.

One fisherman, with a full white beard, wearing overalls, in a flat bass boat, without any shade, had just caught a carp or a catfish. I don't know much about fish, but this one was so large I was surprised he could hold it up. As I passed, he smiled at me, showing off the fish, with a grin and twinkle in his eye. I slowed down as I passed him, then, after going past him a few hundred feet I turned around and asked if I could take his picture with his catch. I made my loop, and he beamed. I pulled out my camera, and he held up two large fish, each of them being about 3 feet long. They looked so heavy I thought he'd drop them.

These three days of boating down the river were so quiet. I had the minimal amount of human interaction anyone could possibly have. I looked forward to getting to Fairhope where I'd see my Looper friends again.

I made it through the "14 mile bridge" just before their change of shift. Once again, luck was on my side. *Annabelle* could fit under most bridges, if they had a clearance, or air draft, of 13 feet. This was one benefit of a small boat: I only had to wait at a handful of bridges for openings. Bridge clearance is not fixed, as it depends on the water level. For instance, in tidal areas the distance between the bridge and the water changes according to the tide. Markings on the side of the bridge show what the clearance is. I always had my binoculars handy, so I could grab them to look for the water levels.

As I approached Mobile, Alabama, the barge traffic increased. Many barges lined the river. At the final bridge, all I could see were barges; I slowed *Annabelle* down and moved to the side of the river, outside the channel markers. In focusing on the barges, my depth had gotten too shallow. In less than three feet, *Annabelle* was about to run aground. I steered nearer to the channel and stayed on the edge wondering if anyone had been watching. Sometimes in Southport, boaters unfamiliar with our waters try to cut the channel marker close to downtown. If they do, they can easily run aground on an oyster bank. I've warned a boat or two against cutting that corner. If it's high tide, they're lucky, but if it's anywhere close to low tide, the boat will be stuck until the tide comes up or until Towboat Jon comes to rescue them.

Once I passed the shipyards in the city of Mobile, the bay lay ahead of me. I just had to cross over to Fairhope, where a slip was waiting. It was the middle of the afternoon, with clear skies and a forecast of showers and thunderstorms. I had crossed most of the Bay to Fairhope, when I heard Debi and Jim behind me, talking on the radio to Ray and Arlene. They were quickly catching up to me. A mile before the inlet to Fairhope, they caught up and let me enter the narrow channel first. I navigated through the shallow waters, to the fuel dock. No sooner had I finished fueling than the storms arrived with a vengeance, and by the time I got to my slip, literally ten feet from the fuel dock, I was soaked. *Annabelle* and *Sea Fever* had covered slips, with one empty slip between them. For the next couple days, I hung out with Debi and Jim; we rode our bikes to downtown Fairhope. I lined up routine maintenance on *Annabelle*. One day, I took the loaner car into town and found a hairdresser who made room in her busy schedule for me.

As I walked the friendly streets of town, I stopped in various shops. One shopkeeper, a friendly older gentleman, a retired physician was a boater. He told me about his former yacht and the traveling he had done. I asked how he came to be a shopkeeper. After being widowed, he remarried and owning a boutique was his second wife's dream. He was absolutely smitten with his wife, as he talked about how good she was at selecting merchandise and marketing local products. At one point he asked, "What about you? Where's your husband?"

I had been asked this question at least a hundred times. "I'm not married."

"You've been doing this trip by yourself?" I nodded and he continued. "You need to find a partner. I met my wife though eHarmony. It was the best thing I ever did. I never imagined I'd ever meet someone after my wife died, but I did."

I thanked him for his advice and bought a candle from his shop. It was true. This trip was getting more and more lonely, not just because of the isolation of being alone on *Annabelle*, but I was feeling even more sensitive to hanging out with married people, wishing I had the companionship that they had.

One evening Debi, Jim, and I played cards until 10:30, a late night for me. I had a glass of wine around 5 p.m., but after that, I was drinking water. I didn't mind losing every time because the two of them were so competitive with each other that it was fun watching them banter back and forth. Finally, exhausted, I left their boat to go home to *Annabelle*. The narrow finger pier at the fixed dock angled down to the width of the piling, and my foot slipped. I fell eight feet into the shallow waters at low tide. Debi and Jim heard my splash and came running. Embarrassed, I climbed onto my swim platform into the back of my boat. I was grateful they were there. I couldn't believe I had fallen into the water. I didn't even seem to have a good excuse. In the darkness, I dropped my soaking wet clothes onto the deck outside my door. After a quick shower, I went to bed and looked forward to the next stage of my journey, crossing the Panhandle.

In the Bay, after leaving Fairhope, I received a phone call from the marina. When I paid, I had left my credit card on the countertop. The marina owner came out on his center console speed boat to return my credit card.

It was mid-September, I saw my first dolphin since leaving the Atlantic Ocean. I was on my way home. The sea breeze and salty smell enticed me to move forward.

24

Gulf of Mexico

The most common question one Looper asks another is how their Gulf crossing went. Crossing the Gulf of Mexico, even just the northeastern tip, can provoke fear amongst those of us that haven't been far from shore. For safety, most Loopers cross the Gulf in groups. The distance to the Clearwater area from Carabelle, the town where most people launch, is about 185 miles. For *Annabelle* it could be a 24-hour trip. However, as I'm not inclined toward sleep deprivation, and being alone, without any buddy boats or crew, I decided to go to Steinhatchee at the upper corner of the Florida Western Coast, just south of the Panhandle. From there, I'd motor down to Cedar Key, Tarpon Springs, and finally into Clearwater.

Just west of Carabelle is Appalachicola, known for their oysters. I arrived in this quaint little town late on a Saturday afternoon and went straight to Up the Creek Raw Bar, where I filled up on a dozen oysters, a 'gator empanada, salad, and key lime pie. The balcony deck in the open air bar overlooked the water. After my early dinner, I strolled around and window shopped. I looked forward to returning the following day to a shop with boat-themed wares including a wall-sized net of colorful crab buoys. Debi had a picture of the net decorating her salon.

As I was eating breakfast the next morning, I checked the weather. It was a beautiful day, but I didn't know what the weather would be like over the next few days when I was hoping to cross the Gulf. I checked AccuWeather for general storm conditions, then I checked NOAA for wave heights and sea conditions. The following day, Monday, there'd be one or two foot waves with northeast winds at 5 to 10 mph and isolated thunderstorms in the evening. Tuesday, the seas would build up to 5 feet, with winds coming from the west. Even if *Annabelle* could handle the seas, I couldn't. The forecast for the remainder of the week did not look any better. It could be a week before another weather window would allow me to cross.

Before making the crossing, one way or another, I still needed to fill my fuel tank. I cancelled my leisurely plans of walking and biking around Appalachicola. Instead I went straight back to *Annabelle,* and left for Carabelle to prepare for the crossing. In Carabelle, I could get fuel, clean my boat, do laundry, and buy a few groceries. Appalachicola, with its abundance of character, lacked some basic necessities.

I approached Carabelle tracking my course with my iPad, so I could find my way out in the morning darkness. From Carabelle to Steinhatchee is about 85 miles. I'd have to leave before 6 a.m. to get there by 5 p.m., when most marina offices close. I prefer to navigate into an unknown place in the light rather than in the dark. Both the dockmaster and dockhand concurred that this was the best strategy. There weren't any other Loopers or boaters around to talk to, as most cruising boats wait until November 1st before coming this far south, due to hurricane season. Once I made it across to Steinhatchee, I could hug the coastline south toward Clearwater and once in the Gulf, I'd be committed to moving forward. I had no intention of turning around.

I set my iPhone alarm clock for 5:00 a.m., to give me time to eat, have coffee, and drop my lines by 6:00 a.m. When I woke up, I called and emailed my mom and one of my friends, letting them know that today I'd be hitting my GPS locater every two hours while on the Gulf, starting at 8:00, not that they could do anything about it if I were in danger and not that I had ever felt that compelled to call anyone before this. For the worst case scenario of getting lost at sea, I had my GPS locater, a personal locater beacon, and three VHF radios from which I could call the Coast Guard. Have I mentioned that I had nine life jackets aboard? Enough to make a raft. Not that I would need one with my dinghy fully inflated and ready to be dropped into the water at a moment's notice. I pulled my lines at 5:45 a.m. I was in one of the rare marinas with staff available 24 hours a day. As I passed the dockhand, we waved at each other and he wished me a safe crossing.

The red and green lights from the buoys reflected off my windows, throwing light in every direction, making it difficult to figure out which lights were real navigation markers. I was grateful for my cookie crumb trail that I had saved on my iPad, which I relied on to navigate into the Gulf. Slowly and carefully, I made it out of the town limits and into the bay. On the horizon, there was just a sliver of moon as I entered the darkness of the Gulf. Stars lit up the sky. I could feel the chop in the water and wondered if my imagination was making it out to be worse than it really was. By the time I made it to open, deep waters, the sun was creeping up over the horizon. I set my autopilot and let *Annabelle* steer herself.

Despite my fears, my Gulf crossing was uneventful, not much different from crossing Lake Michigan on a calm day, just longer. As the day progressed, seas became calmer until the water was as smooth as glass. The most uncomfortable part of the day was the heat. I opened the front hatch, and periodically climbed out to stand at the bow pulpit, like Kate Winslet in *Titanic*, with the breeze blowing through my hair. As early afternoon approached, I began to see dead fish floating on the water, reminding me of snapper lying on ice at the fish market. There weren't a lot of them, but I wondered where they came from and how they died. There weren't any fishing boats around, so I couldn't ask anyone. The most exciting part of the day was when I saw a small flying fish, maybe six inches long, which flitted across the top of the water like skipping rocks. It stood on its tail fins, with its pectoral fins spread out like butterfly wings. The day went by slowly, lazily.

I arrived in Steinhatchee at 4:30 p.m. A few miles offshore when I finally had cell phone service, I called my first choice marina, and the dockmaster told me they had no room for me. The second marina I called said they could accommodate me, although they were a couple miles further up the river, just past a bridge. As I passed the first marina, I noticed an abundance of empty slips and was angry they didn't welcome me. They must have misunderstood my request with all the static from poor cell phone reception, even if it was the best I could do. I passed through the small town, noting an anchorage filled with sailboats, went further upstream under the bridge and finally arrived at River Haven Marina, filled with small fishing boats.

The current was strong, as the tide was going out. The first slip I was assigned was too narrow for *Annabelle*. Even so, a couple of the fisherman argued that my boat could actually fit; I almost expected them to pull out a tape measure. As I pulled up, and the slip lay along the line of the river, with the current going out, I put my boat hard into reverse to get back out to the river without damaging either my boat, or the boat in the neighboring slip. The second option was on the other side of the dock, perpendicular to the river. Instead of approaching against the current, I made the mistake of turning with the current, which caught my boat and carried it downstream into the outboard motor propellers of fishing boats at the next pier.

Fishermen standing on a patio at the deckhouse yelled, "Turn around, you're gonna run aground. No depth over here."

I yelled back, "I'm trying!" It was all I could do to keep *Annabelle* away from the boats. Finally, the marina owner came down to fend my boat off the other boats and help me turn *Annabelle* around, so she was facing away from the shoreline. As I pulled out toward the river, with the starboard side of my boat being swept into the propellers, I envisioned each of the propellers scraping *Annabelle's* hull. I gunned the engine, pulled away from the fishing boats, and got upstream to the pier to tie off. I'd be staying for a few days, with the forecast of daily storms. Surprisingly, *Annabelle* didn't have any scratches, nor had I damaged any of the fishing boats. The only injury was a small hole in my rubber dinghy.

I shamefully walked to the marina office to register, embarrassed, knowing all these fishermen had witnessed my worst docking of the entire trip. I expected a few sarcastic remarks like, "This is why women shouldn't be driving boats!"

I was wrong though. Instead of jeers, I was greeted with respect. "You handled that well. The current can be strong in here." They wanted to know who I was and welcomed me into their circle, as a fellow boater. One of the men asked, "I see your hailing port is in North Carolina; how'd you get here?"

"The long way."

"Did you trailer her down?"

"No. I came across the Gulf today."

With a furrowed brow and cocking his head to the side, "Did you see the red tide?"

"I saw some dead fish floating in the water." My answer appeared to diminish his skepticism.

"That's from the red tide. It was bad here a few days ago." The tension was broken, and I felt like I had just passed a test.

Now I knew what killed those fish and why other fish in the Gulf weren't eating them. The red tide is caused by an overgrowth of a type of algae in salty waters near a shoreline that kills fish by emitting neurotoxins. The winds and current carried these coastal fish into the deeper waters where I saw them.

For dinner, I walked to a local restaurant close to the marina. On the patio, with my Kindle app in hand, I ordered seafood gumbo. Across the patio was one of the fishermen, Dan, sitting with a few friends. He came over to my table, invited me to join them for dinner and introduced me to everyone. One gentleman, sitting beside me, wanted to do the Loop, but his wife didn't like boating. As Dan's friend and I walked back to the marina, he asked if he could come by the following day, see my boat, and take a picture.

The following day was windy with the threat of rain throughout the day. The clouds looked ominous, but the storms bypassed the marina. I patched my dinghy with the small kit, consisting of a two part adhesive and round rubber patch. I thought the process should be simple, but it was time consuming as I had to take the dinghy off the back of my boat then get help to lift it onto the pier before patching it. First, I thought I could patch it while the dinghy was inflated; however, it continued to leak profusely. For my second attempt I deflated the dinghy, glued the patch on, then put a heavy lead weight on it, hoping to eliminate any air bubbles. My frustration with the leak was that it was on a seam, making it difficult to lay flat. It still had a slow leak, but I used up my patching glue, so it would have to suffice. Even patching takes practice.

In the afternoon, I saw Dan on the patio, and he invited me to join him for dinner. He also offered to let me use his hotel room to take a bath. Across the narrow two lane street was a four-room hotel, owned and operated by the marina. Dan was renting one of the rooms for the fishing season. I decided to make due with the marina showers, but agreed to dine with him that evening.

Dan was a very tall, slender man, fit for his age, about as old as my father would be, if he were still alive. You could tell that Dan was handsome as a young man by the way he carried himself with a cowboyish air. Maybe his skin was leathery from spending too much time in the sun as a young man on waterskis or now fishing in the Gulf of Mexico and its estuaries.

At the picnic table outside the small marina motel, grilling steak, he asked, "How do you protect yourself on your boat?" Mostly men asked me this question, usually retired law enforcement officers. Sometimes it was more of a statement than a question. "Both my daughters have guns, and I made sure they knew how to use them."

"I'd probably shoot a hole through the hull if I had a gun on my boat." If someone really wanted to come aboard, with bad intentions, I doubted I'd even have time to get a gun loaded and ready in time to do anything with it. The most harmful thing I could imagine would be an alligator, which might be too stubborn to leave my swim platform, but as long as my dinghy was leaning against the hull, upright from the swim platform, I didn't think any alligators would bother me. Truth be told, I'd probably be more upset if a cockroach were on my boat. Then I could see myself shooting at it, while it scampered away, too quick for me to hit it. In case I ever changed my stance on gun ownership, I made a quick mental note to never get anything semi-automatic.

Dan looked at me as if I were crazy. "Maybe I should take you to buy a gun tomorrow. Only I don't think you'll be here long enough to learn how to use it."

"Probably not." Then, I added, "I have a dive knife aboard. It's sharp. My son helped me pick it out. I keep it within reach. Besides, I thought you were looking at houses tomorrow?"

Originally from Georgia, Dan had fallen in love with this Florida fishing village and had spent most of the summer here. "I am. In the morning I have an appointment with a Realtor. Want to come with me?"

"Sure, it'll get me off the docks."

He pulled the steaks and foil-wrapped potatoes off the grill, and we had leftover salad from the night before. As he sat drinking his bourbon out of a Big Gulp container, I had a plastic glass of red wine.

As we finished up dinner, Dan pulled a cigarette out of his pack. After lighting it up, he pulled out a pistol and laid it on the table, within both of our reaches. I didn't feel threatened; my impression was that he made himself more vulnerable, by disarming himself. For a moment, I was confused, but then Dan made his desires clear. I suppose, had I not thought of him as a fatherly figure, I might have felt more endangered or intimidated. He clearly had too much to drink.

"I'm figuring it's been a while since you've been with a man. I mean, what man would ever let you do this trip by yourself?" The question was purely rhetorical. "It's been a while since I've been with a woman. So, I'd like to invite you to spend the night with me, so I can make love to you."

I took a quick deep breath to center myself. I wasn't expecting that. This wasn't the first time someone my father's age had made advances toward me, but it still felt as icky as me dating someone my son's age. "Dan, I'll take that as a compliment, but I'm not interested in spending the night with you." The air felt thick, and I wanted to get back to *Annabelle*. The enjoyable evening with a fellow boater had just become awkward.

"I'm sorry, I just thought, well…we were getting along so well."

"I'll get back to my boat now."

"Let me walk you over there."

"You don't need to. It's just across the street."

"Tanya, I'm sorry. I didn't mean to offend you."

I put on my best bland psychiatry face, not that I was ever good at it. "No offense taken, I'll still look for houses with you in the morning."

Despite my protestations, Dan walked me across the street, wished me a good night, and told me he'd meet up with me in the morning.

As I got on my boat, I thought to myself that I'd never been around anyone so forward. Then again, I wondered what nonverbal messages I might be sending, having been on the water so long. However, this was the South, the backwoods of northern Florida, where a twenty—year age difference seemed reasonable to some men, even if it creeped me out. Was it because my father had married someone closer to my age? Dad grew up in Florida and North Carolina. Maybe I was overly sensitive. Considering Dan had been drinking all day, I wondered if he'd even remember his proposition in the morning.

Though I was eager to keep moving down the Florida west coast, the winds kept me dock bound. In the morning, Dan did remember and apologized one more time, chalking it up to drinking too much. However, if I was still game for house hunting, he'd appreciate the company.

The Realtor's office was just a few blocks away from the marina. Dan described what he wanted in a house and the amount of money he was willing to pay. The Realtor quickly narrowed choices to one house he thought would fit the bill: a modest three bedroom home on a wooded lot, two blocks from the city marina, with an outbuilding large enough for Dan's boat. The three of us rode in the Realtor's minivan to the house. It was precisely what Dan had in mind, move-in ready and mostly furnished. On the three-minute ride back to the office, Dan made a verbal offer, which the Realtor relayed to the owners. By the time he typed up the offer on the correct forms, the owners had accepted it, without any counter offers. I don't know that I had ever seen a house sell so quickly. Perhaps it was the bourbon, but Dan wanted to give me the credit for his luck. He felt he had gotten lucky with me, just not the way he'd originally thought.

Within the hour, we were back at the marina, and Dan was like a kid on Christmas morning, telling everyone about his new house. He spent the afternoon on the marina patio emailing friends. I rode my bike around town and made plans to leave the following day. That evening at the restaurant, I ate dinner alone for the first time since stopping in Steinhatchee. I ordered extra smoked fish spread to take with me. After dark, when I returned to the marina, Dan was still typing on his laptop.

"Have you had anything to eat?"

Entranced in the screen, he responded, "I had pizza earlier."

"I'm heading south first thing in the morning."

Dan looked up from his computer screen. "If I'm not up, come get me. I want to be there when you drop your lines."

"I'm not going to wake you up. Take care of yourself and enjoy your new house."

"I will. See you in the morning." Dan was usually up before I was, but tonight, he was glued to the table, long after everyone else had gone home and gone to bed.

Around 10:30 that night, I got up out of my berth, and looked out my window to see if he was still on the patio. He was. I went back to bed and woke at dawn.

As I prepared to leave, the water was still, and the marina was quiet. A couple of the fishermen were out early and waved goodbye as I left. I half expected Dan to be asleep at the table or lying on a bench. He must have finally stumbled back to his room. I had no intentions of rousing the man from his slumber.

A couple hours after leaving Steinhatchee, going south in the Gulf of Mexico toward Cedar Key, I saw a small boat quickly approaching me. With my autopilot on, I went to the back of *Annabelle* and watched the boat come closer and closer. As it came within a hundred feet, I recognized Dan. I went inside and put *Annabelle*'s engine into neutral, virtually coming to a stop. He pulled his boat around the bow of my boat then laid his along my port side, so we were facing in opposite directions.

"When I woke up you were gone. You should have woken me up."

"I figured you needed your sleep after yesterday. You were up pretty late."

"I can't believe I slept in. You're my lucky charm. I couldn't have found that house without you. If you ever come to Steinhatchee, you have a place to stay, whether I'm here or not. I'm going to wish you luck the best way I know how, by circling you with my boat." I looked at him quizzically. Then he added, "Think of a lucky horseshoe." He handed me a card with his number on it and told me to keep in touch.

After our short exchange, Dan circled *Annabelle* with his boat, then sped back toward Steinhatchee across the open Gulf waters.

25

Clearwater, Florida

From Steinhatchee, I went south and anchored at Cedar Key. It was an ideal time to use my dinghy, because there is no dockage, except for small boats able to fit under an 8-foot bridge. Overcast with 15-knot winds and storms brewing every day around suppertime, if I got to the island and the weather worsened, I might not get back to *Annabelle*. Sometimes being by myself was more conducive to worrying than exploring, so I stayed aboard and read a mystery by John D. MacDonald, about Travis McGee on Cedar Key. It was not the kind of book I wanted to fall asleep reading, since it involved murder and bad guys. Many of the books I read on my trip, I picked up along the way at trading libraries in marinas, most of which only had a shelf of paperbacks. Occasionally, someone would recommend a book and I'd download it to the Kindle app on my iPad. This was one of those recommendations.

Before dawn, still dark with the sun threatening to peak above the horizon, I pulled my anchor and started navigating out the narrow, shallow channels surrounding the island of Cedar Key. To my delight, I had lots of company. A school of dolphin joined me as I motored into the Gulf. They swam beside and in front of *Annabelle*, jumping out of the water by my helm. I could have reached out and touched them as they flew past my window, if I only had the right timing. They escorted me for forty-five minutes. While trying to videotape them on my iPad, I was lucky I didn't run aground. Maybe luckier I didn't drop the iPad in the water, as I held it out the window with my right hand, while steering with my left. Omens of good luck, I hoped.

My original plans were to stay two nights at Anclote Cove Marina near Tarpon Springs, but the marina didn't have shower facilities, and I'd have to use the bathroom behind the bar. It was too far to walk or ride my bike to town. Shortly after I arrived, it started pouring down rain; another day of hanging out on my boat. I couldn't imagine spending any time here.

I called Clearwater Municipal Marina, in hopes of leaving the marina as soon as possible, despite my reservations. The marina was booked because of the Super Boat National Offshore Boat Race for the weekend. I planned to stay a week in Clearwater, visit friends, and relax. I was trying to slow down since I was a month ahead of where I thought I'd be at this point on the Loop.

When I woke up in the morning, I called the Clearwater City Marina again, just to see if one of the boats with reservations hadn't shown up. Luck was on my side, the dockmaster asked how quickly I could be there. He said he'd have to meet me at the slip because the current made docking difficult. I explained that I was on a slow boat; it would take a couple hours. I must've been the first person to call when he opened the office that morning, or at least the most persistent. The Clearwater City Marina was in downtown, with easy access to buses that could take a person across the large bridge to the beach. It was a great place to explore.

In Clearwater, I connected with a friends, including Ray and Arlene, from *dARf V,* whom I had met in Demopolis and spent time with in Fairhope. They had finished their Loop in Clearwater, their home waters. Floods in the Mississippi River stranded many Loopers in Grafton and Alton, where they waited for the waters to recede. I was tempted to leave my boat in Clearwater to fly to the mid-October Looper Rendezvous in Rogersville, Alabama. The rendezvous was in 12 days and I really missed my Looper friends. It had been over three months since I had seen Mark and Jane, and almost five months since I had left Southport.

One afternoon, while cleaning *Annabelle* in Clearwater, I got a call from Malcolm, the corporate pilot. It had been a few weeks since I had talked to him. As usual, he started by asking how my trip was going, since he had read my blog.

I asked, "What about you?"

He responded, "Really busy. I'm about to go on vacation."

"Vacation? Where?" I thought to myself that vacation for Malcolm could mean just staying at home for a few days, for a change of pace.

"Italy."

He traveled the world with his job. "Why Italy?"

"Debbie and I got married Friday. She already had this trip planned, so we're going there for our honeymoon."

Wow. I hadn't expected that. I mean, I knew he had a girlfriend, but it was all so fast. "That was quick. It was just a few months ago, you told me about her." I did the math in my head; it was less than a year ago when he and I had met. Ironically, our last trip together was to St. Pete, next door to Clearwater. He had said he wanted to marry someone who enjoyed boating with him, as his first wife had not been a boater, and neither did the woman he dated for several years before me. I added, "So, she's taken up boating then."

"Well, no."

Awkwardly, I said, "Oh. Well, enjoy your honeymoon." I felt as if I had just been sucker punched.

"When you get to Georgia, give me a call; maybe we can meet at Jekyll Island. I'm sure Debbie would love to meet you. I've told her so much about you."

We said our goodbyes, and I sat down thinking this is where a good stiff drink must come into play. He and Debbie were the last people I'd want to see on Jekyll Island, or anywhere. If it felt awkward for me, I imagined it would feel awkward for her too. *Idiot*! *Why'd he even call me?* It wasn't like we were ever in a committed relationship or anything. I wasn't available because I was Looping, and apparently he was between relationships. *What was I to him? The hot sex rebound chick?* Okay... now I could laugh about it, I'd be okay. I was overreacting.

I remembered when we talked about his meeting me along the way, spending a week here and there on my boat. He was always supportive of this trip of mine. His work meant he had to fly when he was told—how high and how far. He wasn't exactly available, either, especially from a long-distance relationship perspective. He and Debbie lived in the same city, meaning he actually could spend more time with her. I was happy for him. I had never met anyone I felt so comfortable with on a boat. From the first time he came to Southport, we had an easy way of being together. I wanted someone to have and share dreams with, not someone who would push me off the shore and wish me well on my journey, sending me off alone.

This wasn't about Malcolm; it was about me. I needed to go home. I had paid for the week, but left a day early. I knew the rest of the trip would be very quiet: anchor, marina, anchor, marina - one town after another.

Maybe I was being overly sensitive; my son was about to turn thirty. Focusing on my career and my kids had always been a good excuse not to be in a relationship, but at some point I had to face up to the fact that my kids had grown up. Heck, my grandkids were growing up: sweet Annabelle, my boat's namesake, just turned ten; Donovan was almost fifteen.

The first night after leaving Clearwater, I anchored out in Roberts Bay. The second night, I stayed in Edgewater. From the marina, I could walk to the beach and restaurants. It was a small marina with fixed docks, and some of the boats were longer than their dock spaces, making it difficult to navigate. The marina owner had me bring *Annabelle* to a small space, tucked into a back corner. He could have let me stay on the T head, at the end of the dock, but he told me he was saving it, just in case a larger boat showed up. I was grateful for my bow and stern thrusters, which deserved the credit for *Annabelle* not hitting any other boats.

After getting settled, I walked into the owner's office to pay the bill. As I turned to leave, he asked if I had any books on my boat.

I turned back and looked up at him, "Well, yeah."

"But do you have THE Book onboard?"

I looked at him quizzically, "THE book?"

"The Bible. Of course."

Not being good at lying, I looked down, and said, "No, I don't have THAT book on my boat." I didn't tell him about the wooden rosary, the Jesus bling bracelet, St. Brendan medallion, a bolo tie, pocket prayer shawl, or any of my other amulets which I carried in my little box on the dashboard. It was a small menagerie of gifts, some of which came from my patients. Maria, my clinic director, called them boundary violations. One way or another, it was my special box, my favorite color of teal, inscribed with: *We can never cross the ocean, until we have the courage to lose sight of the shore.* I had a picture of Teresita, who had died from cancer. She used to think we were her guardian angels, but she was the angel we were all guarding.

I looked back up at him, and he handed me a Gideon Bible, the kind you find in the drawer at a Super 8 Motel. I meekly took the Bible, looked into his eyes, and thanked him. When I got back to *Annabelle*, I put the book in the basket with my navigational charts.

I left the following morning and found my way to Fort Myers, the southernmost point I would travel. I didn't want to go around the outside of Florida; it was hurricane season. From Fort Myers, I'd cut through the state via the Okeechobee waterway to Stuart, Florida.

On the second day, as I approached Lake Okeechobee, I noticed a road which traveled alongside the canal I was in. I noticed an older gentleman on a cruiser bicycle, the kind we have in Southport, with a basket. His bike looked similar to mine, and we were moving at the same speed. I smiled to myself, realizing that I had traveled most of the Loop, over 3,500 miles so far, going the same speed as this geezer on his beach bike.

Early in the afternoon, after crossing the 25-mile lake, I arrived at Indiantown Marina early. I had time to do laundry, and ordered Italian food, which was delivered to my boat. A large decrepit trawler was moored near *Annabelle*, with a couple who seemed like hillbillies. It wasn't just their accent or the way they were dressed; their bodies were as dilapidated as their boat; it seemed like they ate junk food for breakfast, lunch, and dinner, and couldn't figure out why their cholesterol might be skyrocketing. The trawler was covered with tarps to keep it shaded, and they told me that they'd gotten her real cheap. They were taking it across Florida, then to Alabama and Mississippi. They didn't have navigational lights or a generator, and it wasn't clear if they even had a VHF radio aboard.

I was surprised the trawler's engine ran. They'd been stopping along the way at docks alongside the canal and expressed surprise that the people they encountered weren't always friendly and welcoming. After speaking a few minutes, I realized they'd been trying to dock at private piers, attached to beautiful houses with lawns maintained by professional landscapers. Apparently, they didn't understand that private docks are just that—private.

Just after the marina office closed and the couple had finished their dinner, the wife, on the back of their boat was throwing leftovers down to small alligators who were circling and waiting, as if they knew exactly when to show up.

She looked over at me and said, "They's cute, ain't they?"

Appalled, I responded, "I didn't know you could feed alligators like that."

"Not s'posed to. Got in trouble the other day when the office was open. Can't help it. I love animals."

Then she threw in another bone, which an alligator instantaneously snatched up and devoured. I shook my head and wondered if they were completely oblivious to the factors which made them bad boat neighbors. I thought back to when

I had fallen into the water in Fairhope and was grateful I hadn't encountered any alligators there, especially ones that circled around boats waiting for dinner.

26

Home Stretch—Atlantic Ocean

The following day around noon, I finished crossing Florida. On the eastern shore in Stuart, I turned north on the Atlantic Intracoastal Waterway. I felt euphoric looking out over the Atlantic. *My ocean, my waters, where I've made my home.* It was hard to believe I hadn't seen these waters since New York with Mom.

My first stop on the eastern shore was Vero Beach where I stayed on a city mooring ball. I spent a second night in Vero Beach at Loggerhead Marina when my electronics started randomly going out after I left the mooring field. Within five minutes of leaving the mooring ball, my chartplotter turned itself off a couple times. The engine seemed to be running fine. I pulled into Loggerhead at 7:45 that morning before they even opened. When I opened my engine hatch to check the voltage on my batteries, I noticed one of the terminals had corrosion. I cleaned it off, and the simple solution fixed the problem. I stayed in Vero Beach for the day to clean my boat and buy groceries. While there, I met several boaters from Canada who invited me to join them for dinner. They were planning their upcoming trip to the Bahamas.

"You should come with us. Your boat could make it."

"Thanks, but I have to get home and get back to work."

"Is it the crossing you're afraid of? It's only 50 miles, and we go the speed of the slowest boat. We even have a couple sailboats crossing with us."

"I know my boat could make it, and I'm not afraid of making the crossing. When I go to the Bahamas, I want to go with someone, not on a boat by myself."

I could picture my Canadian friends snorkeling and frolicking about in the crystal clear waters, having umbrella drinks, while I'd be slaving away for the basic necessities of living. Their boats had water makers and luxuries I could only dream of. I imagined myself trekking back and forth to shore in my dinghy, carrying a few gallons of water at a time to my boat. Water, fuel, food. If something broke down, I'd have a hard time finding help. And then there'd be the loneliness of being in a foreign country, with limited contact home to the United States. At least in Canada, I saw people I knew, and the Canadians seemed to be the friendliest people on earth.

On the other hand, if I were traveling with friends and had a partner, a best friend, lover, companion, I could sail the world and go to any island and never feel lonely. He'd have to be really good with boats, though, in case we ever broke down.

On October 12th the Looper Rendezvous was starting without me and I was 640 miles from home, a distance I could travel in two weeks. I pushed ahead, going northward, only stopping if I needed to and anchoring more often than I stayed in marinas. I was as antsy to get home as *Bluenoser* Jim had been. I spent three days in Daytona due to rainstorms. I could handle the rain, but didn't like the wind. I arrived just before Biketoberfest, which might be considered good timing for Harley motorcycle owners, but not for me.

A dockhand offered to show me around town. He was a retired gentleman who had moved to Daytona from

Pennsylvania, after spending several years traveling down for Bike Week. His wife chose not to join him in his retirement, preferring to stay closer to her family and friends, so they got divorced. Now he was enjoying a new way of living as a bachelor. He had a show bike, which came out of the garage on special occasions. What he enjoyed most about Biketoberfest was the camaraderie, guys drinking beer, and watching all the people walk by. In the middle of the day, as we walked through the exhibits I found the biker gear for women extremely offensive. For instance, there were T-shirts that said vulgar things like, "Don't just fuck me. Spank me and pull my hair."

My companion for the day suggested, "Look, you could earn some extra money while you're here by putting on your bikini and washing Harleys." Was he being sarcastic? Or, did he think he was funny? I struggled to find any humor in what he was saying. I wondered how a seemingly nice retired man, could even find such things entertaining. Now I understood why his wife didn't move south to Florida with him. As the day progressed, I felt more and more uncomfortable and creeped out. Daytona Beach was feeling downright skanky. I didn't want to be out on these streets after dark. I felt grateful that *Annabelle* was safe behind the locked gates at the marina.

After leaving Daytona, with brisk winds and a strong current, I navigated north to St. Augustine. A few miles from the town, I noticed an old man, appearing to be standing on the water ahead and slightly to the right of me. I wondered what was going on. He was frantically waving both his arms, and it seemed like he was standing on a paddle board, without any paddles, struggling to keep his balance. He was sopping wet, from head to toe. There were a few other boats around, much larger than mine, heading south for the fall migration, when many boaters prepare to cross over to the Bahamas. However, nobody seemed to be stopping. I thought he might be in shallow water.

I took *Annabelle* over to the wet man and realized he was standing on the hull of his boat, which had capsized. He wasn't wearing a life jacket and didn't have a radio to call for help. If he had a cell phone, it would've been dead on impact with the salt water. He was barefoot with khaki shorts and a T-shirt. "Are you okay?" *What a stupid question.*

"My sailboat flipped over."

I envisioned the mast sticking down into the river, and it surprised me that it was still floating and hadn't gotten caught on the bottom. The Matanzas River was 25 feet deep so it could be the kind of sailboat that young people learn on, which don't have large sails.

"What can I do to help? Want a life jacket?"

"No, I have a life jacket, at least I think I do. It could've been swept away. Can you help me right the boat?"

"Sure. Why don't you come aboard, and we can figure out what we need to do." I handed him a line to tie onto the small sailboat. He lay down on the hull, reaching under the bow, to tie the line to the bow handle. He carefully stood up again and climbed into the cockpit of *Annabelle*, leaving a puddle of water, with his clothes dripping wet. I grabbed a towel for him. He was shivering. "Do you want to come into the cabin to get warm?"

"No, ma'am. I wouldn't want to get your things wet. I sure appreciate you stopping. I got this boat as a trade. I've been a fisherman all my life, and been out on all kinds of boats, but never a sailboat. I figured if these young kids could do it, how hard could it be? I'm not used to paying attention to how strong the wind is. I've always been on powerboats."

He went on to tell me of his health problems, including being legally blind. He was one of those old salty men that despite himself would live to be a hundred: smoking, drinking whisky, and taking chances. I imagined he caught fish for dinner and spent his free time tinkering with a dozen unfinished projects. He seemed like one of those characters, well known by all in town for his eccentricities, who'd be sorely missed if he didn't show up for coffee in the morning at the local diner with a good story to tell.

Sunfish sailboats are great for lake sailing with light winds, but on a gusty day like this one, true sailors would know better than to put their sails up. These boats have slightly curved hulls, with a daggerboard keel, which drops into a slot on the topside of the fiberglass hull to aid in stability. His boat could have easily drifted out of the inlet to the ocean with the winds and current, with him holding on for his dear life. When the winds caught his sail, he would've been perpendicular to the force of the winds. I wondered if the sails dragging in the water slowed him down.

At this point, both of our boats were floating downstream, attached. I needed to keep an eye on the depths, and we needed to quickly come up with a plan to get his boat righted and get the Old Salt safely back to land. Marshes lined both sides of the waterway. He pointed inland and said he was living on an old junker trawler tied up in one of the side creeks among the grass. I could vaguely make out the small channels in the marsh across the river.

We swiftly determined that my customized aluminum crane, made specifically to lift my dinghy motor, could be used effectively in this situation. He took the clip on the line as I released it for him to attach to the far side of his hull where he had a cleat on the top deck. Once attached, he clamored back aboard *Annabelle*. We pulled the rope through the pulley on the crane, and the mast popped to the surface. Now, the boat was lying on its side, with the sail spread out across the water. I could see his life jacket, tied onto the boom. "I guess you still have that life jacket!"

"Yeah, but I lost the daggerboard."

He was one of those people that would tie a life jacket to the spreaders to cover himself in case the Coast Guard comes across him—it would be legal, within reach. He could've used the life jacket. "I have plenty of life jackets, if you want to take a dry one with you."

"No thanks. I have a pile of 'em on my boat." He said while unclipping the line from the side cleat and re-attaching it to the rigging.

I could see my crane bending, ever so slightly and hoped the aluminum didn't snap. "You'll want to drop that sail before we try to right her."

He released the sail, so it wouldn't scoop up the heavy water. The sailboat was starting to drift toward the backside of *Annabelle*. I suggested we just pull her, lying on her side, across the river. We were getting into shallower waters on the far edge of the waterway, and I worried about running aground, getting us both stuck.

I put *Annabelle* into gear, and slowly started across the river. The line attached to his boat was taut as I pulled forward.

Suddenly, there was a slam against *Annabelle*, as the sailboat righted itself, and the mast smacked into the eyebrow trim above *Annabelle's* windows. I looked over at the Old Salt and smiled. I put *Annabelle* back into neutral, and the Old Salt jumped onto his boat. We slackened the line and let her drift out behind *Annabelle*. As I approached the inland side of the river, the Old Salt pointed me in the direction of where he could safely be dropped off. Once his sailboat was released, I found myself maneuvering in three feet of water. After a quick farewell, I put *Annabelle* into reverse, and pulled back slowly until comfortably safe in deeper waters. I felt good about helping another boater, as so many had helped me.

I left Florida behind two days later, after spending a night in St. Augustine and a night at Amelia Island. I was one state closer to home. Once in Georgia, I stopped at Jekyll Island, which had rave reviews from Malcolm and many other boater friends. I enjoyed a leisurely afternoon riding my bike around the island, stopping to check out the Rah Bar at the Jekyll Wharf Marina. The bar was full and people were waiting for tables in the hot sun. I opted to eat at Sea Jay's at the Jekyll Harbor Marina where *Annabelle* was tied up.

As I left Jekyll Island, heading north, the winds were light and the water tranquil. I watched a sailboat leaving the St. Simon Sound out to the Atlantic. I was at a fork in the waterway. I could turn right and follow the sailboat out the inlet or turn left to navigate up the Intracoastal Waterway. I turned left. Then, I looked over my shoulder and felt a longing to be in the ocean. I turned around and steered toward the inlet. *No, I should err on the side of caution.* I turned *Annabelle* back toward the waterway. Another minute went by, but I couldn't do it. *I couldn't stay in the waterway on such a beautiful day.* Turning once again, I left the safe waters and motored out the St. Simon Sound into the Atlantic. Once offshore, I turned on my auto pilot, relaxed, heading north 50 miles until St. Catherine's Sound, where *Annabelle* surfed the tide back into the waterway. Dean called as I was doing my best to keep *Annabelle* heading straight on the surf through the breakers. I hung up quickly, aware of the danger if *Annabelle* got turned sideways with the following tide. It seemed like the waves were higher than my boat. After getting through the breakwaters, it was smooth sailing, once again.

That night, I anchored out in a small, calm creek. The following night, I stayed in a marina in Beaufort, South Carolina. On October 21st, exactly six months from the day I left Southport, I went offshore one last time. I passed Folly Beach where I had bought *Annabelle* and took a picture of the Folly Beach Lighthouse. I had come full circle, but I wouldn't celebrate the Loop until I returned to Southport. In Charleston, I saw some friends, sailors I had met when first moving to Southport. I left the following afternoon at slack tide. Storms from the night before had finally dissipated, and Wednesday had turned into a beautiful day.

Ten miles from home, my phone rang. It was Maria, my clinic director from Nogales, "Tanya, enough is enough. You need to get back to work. We need you here, your patients need you."

"I'll be there as soon as I can. I'll fly out next week." I wondered what the rush was. I hadn't planned on returning until January or February, having promised to return before she retired in the springtime. I had formally given a year's notice to our company before leaving on the trip, and our staff and patients had a map with the route so they could follow my progress. I'd be happy to return to work early and looked forward to seeing everyone. I was glad they still needed me.

An hour and a half later, on October 24th, at 2:30 in the afternoon, I crossed my wake in Southport. Dean got a ride from Towboat Jon to meet me in the waterway so he could finish the Loop with me. He boarded *Annabelle* in the same way he had gotten off when I left, hopping from one boat to the other. As I passed my neighborhood pier, Beth and Gus, my future neighbors, who were house and dog sitting for me, took pictures of *Annabelle* making her final approach to the marina next door, Deep Point. As I pulled into the slip, my phone rang. It was Malcolm, with his impeccable timing. "Are you home? Have you crossed your wake?"

"Yes, just docking. I've gotta go."

At the marina, my friend Richard was working and offered me a home-cooked Southern meal after helping Dean and me tie up *Annabelle*. The sun was shining, Gus and Beth came over to the boat, and we took pictures with my new Gold Looper Burgee, signifying the completion of the Loop, crossing my wake.

27

Home

After returning to Southport, I went straight back to Tucson and Nogales, Arizona. I wanted to get back to my life, my people, *mi gente*, my career. I missed my patients and all the people I worked with. For seven months, I had worried about them, hoping they were well and that whoever had replaced me had taken good care of them.

Thursday, October 30, when I arrived in Tucson, I called Christina, my assistant. "I'm here in Arizona. I can't wait to see you and get back to work."

"Maria says you need to head straight to Yuma and talk to our Chief Operating Officer."

"I don't want to talk to her; Yuma isn't exactly on the way. What day works best for Maria?" I wasn't about to change my plans; besides, I needed more info from Maria before I saw the COO.

"Friday or Monday. How long can you stay?"

"I'll be there Monday. I can't wait to see everyone. I'd work the next three weeks if she wanted me to."

Monday morning I stopped at Starbucks and loaded up on pastries to take with me to Nogales, a tradition. For many years, when I worked in the clinic, I'd bring in pastries for special occasions. Then, after I started seeing my patients through telemedicine, I'd bring pastries when I was in town. I was excited about going down to Nogales, the border town, where I had worked for ten years, including the last few seeing my patients online.

As I walked in the office, my co-workers hugged me, asking when I was going to start. "I don't know, I guess we have to figure it out. I'd start today if I could." Recredentialed two weeks before leaving for the Loop, I figured I'd be clear to start anytime.

Maria walked in and asked if I'd be around for lunch. As I walked into her office, it seemed like the tone had changed. She looked worried and said, "We desperately need you back, but I don't think the COO understands. With budget cuts, you might have to take less pay."

"I'll take a cut in pay to work here. We need to figure what exactly she's talking about."

Maria wrote a number down on a piece of paper, but it was just a number, and I didn't know if it meant salary, hourly, or what. "She told me to give you this figure. It's what we're paying the new NPs."

Without parameters, the number was meaningless to me. I was confused. I looked up from the paper. "How are our patients doing?"

"I'm worried about them. We've had one NP after another. Some of our patients have seen three different people since you left. The one we have now doesn't have your experience and half the patients aren't even showing up for their appointments. I've asked to get you back for a couple days per week."

"That works for me. I don't want to work anywhere else and am fine with two days per week."

"The other thing is that the chief operating officer doesn't know when she can have you start. She seems to have other plans. Call her. She says we don't have any openings right now, but maybe in a couple months."

For the remainder of the morning, I visited with my co-workers. A few of us went to lunch, a local restaurant, with the best Mexican food I'd eaten in a year.

As I returned to Tucson, I called the COO on my cell phone. She told me, "We don't have any work for you now. Maria shouldn't even be talking to you about this."

"I'd like to be working in Nogales."

"We want nurse practitioners who are willing to work in any of our clinics at any time, not ones who just work in one clinic or another. We've standardized our pay scale, and you'd have to take a cut in pay. Everyone is paid the same now, no matter what their experience is. Money is tight."

I thought to myself that it was nuts that they were not concerned about either continuity of care or having experienced practitioners; the very reason why Maria was so worried. My clinic needed me.

"I hope we can figure something out."

She responded with, "I'll keep that in mind, I wish you the best."

I felt like the wind had been taken out of my sails. Leaving my job to do the Loop had been risky. However, everyone had told me that I'd be welcomed back, including the COO. I couldn't imagine anyone being able to work long term under the conditions she wanted, switching from one clinic to another to another, seeing patients across southern Arizona, throughout the day, just because it was done through videoconferencing.

I called Maria. "I spoke to the COO."

"Great! When do you start?"

"Maria, she doesn't have a position for me."

"Well, not today, but they will. She's promised me that when we have an opening, we could hire you back. Give it a couple months."

As I hung up the phone, I felt like the ground under my feet was moving, almost like trying to walk on dry land after being on the water for too many days. My head was clear, but everything around me was spinning. I had no idea what direction I was going.

During the three weeks I spent in Tucson, I started working on my back-up plan, meeting with the chief administrative officer of a telepsychiatry company. He'd hire me in a heartbeat if it didn't work out in Nogales. When I had worked part-time in administration a few years before, our company had hired psychiatric providers from them, so he knew me and my reputation. I offered to start at one day per week, but with the paperwork involved it would be a couple months before I started.

My friends and family in Tucson all went to work during the day. I felt lost. I decided to do everything I could to get myself back to having a focus and an idea of where I was going. In addition to seeing my friends, I stopped in to see my acupuncturist, Katie. As I stepped into her peaceful room, with the massage table on one side of the room and her eastern textiles on the wall, I felt the serenity. As she checked my pulses and examined me, she asked how the trip was.

"Wonderful, but now I feel lost."

"What do you mean?"

"The Loop was great because I met so many wonderful people. Everyone was kind, caring and helpful. When I crossed Lake Ontario, there was fog all around, and I couldn't see anything, but I knew my direction. Now, I can see clearly, but have no direction. When I returned to Nogales, the COO told me that they don't have a job for me." I started crying, not something I do in front of people. "I don't feel like I fit in anywhere, not even at home. I am overly sensitive to all the married people around me. Even on the Loop, everyone was married. I never noticed it as much. I feel like the fifth wheel."

I don't know what it is about Katie, but she has a way of making me open up. She looked at me in her gentle way, "Tanya, you've done something extraordinary in your life. The doors have closed because you need to move forward. You can't just go back to your old life."

"But, Katie, I loved my old life. I loved my patients, my co-workers. These are my people."

"The people you met on the Loop are your people too, and so are the people you'll meet in the future. You have love for many people. Think about what people have told you; maybe there is something else you need to focus on right now. Think about your options, something will come to you. Just be open to other ideas. The fog will lift, and you'll see your path."

Katie was so wise for such a sweet young lady, the daughter of my psychopharmacology instructor. When I left her office, my stomach no longer ached and I recalled all the people I had met along the way who had encouraged me to write. I stopped at San Xavier Mission to light a candle. Although I wasn't raised Catholic, the church has always been a quiet place to contemplate. San Xavier is where I've always gone when patients have died, with the heavy wooden doors open to the public. Usually, I lit candles for everyone else, but today, I lit one for myself and asked for grace.

Three months later:

I went back to work, but not in Nogales. I did fly to Arizona for Maria's retirement party to celebrate with her. My co-workers asked when I'd be back, but it had been clear to me that the COO didn't want me back. I felt grateful for the honor of having worked with such a great group of people.

I started working for Southeastern Arizona Behavioral Health Services, where I had worked before, where the CEO had asked if I'd work for him when I returned from my boating trip a few years earlier. It was a strange coincidence that I did exactly that, for one day a week. When it was clear I wouldn't be working in Nogales, I took another part-time telepsychiatry job for another a second company in Southern Arizona. Work felt temporary.

One year later:

It hardly seems feasible that it has been a year since I returned home from the Great Loop. When I came home I was excited about returning to work with all my favorite people in Nogales. After a few months of telecommuting in Arizona, a friend found an advertisement for a part-time psychiatric nurse practitioner in Southport. I started working "in-person," and I love my new job.

Annabelle:

After crossing my wake, without work or income, I sold *Annabelle*. Dock fees, maintenance, and insurance alone would cost at least $500 a month. I shipped her up to Virginia, where she had repairs done at Tidewater Marina, before being sold to a man from Maryland.

I miss her very much! I miss the sunrises and sunsets. I miss the peacefulness of anchoring out. I have looked at other boats, but nothing has fit the bill the way *Annabelle* did. My next boat will be slightly larger, for two people instead of one. I look forward to new adventures, but don't know what they will be. I dream of going through the canals in Europe and sailing in the Caribbean.

Many people have asked how I made it back to Southport so quickly. Tom, from the fast boat *No Compromises*, got home to Southport a couple months after I did, then Mark and Jane arrived three months after Tom. I had to be very careful on *Annabelle*, because she was smaller and slower than the other boats and I was traveling alone. If the weather was good and the seas were calm, I took advantage of it and went as far as I could go. I stopped in places I didn't expect, and sometimes bypassed the places I hoped to stop. I think back to Solomons Island, hearing all my friends planning a party for that evening, while finding myself on the picture-perfect, glassy waters of the Chesapeake Bay. Reluctantly I moved onward toward Annapolis. I anchored at an island in Lake Michigan, when the marina was full in Charlevoix. Yet, it was all perfect, in its own way.

As usual with his impeccable timing, Malcolm called while I was at a psychopharmacology conference in Orlando, to tell me he was in Florida dropping his new boat into the water. Driving through Jacksonville on my way home, I stopped for a couple hours to see his boat. With the mechanic onboard, we took *Burning Daylight* for a spin. She's a fast day cruiser, not at all like the boat that he and I had talked about together.

He put his white Looper burgee on the bow, signifying that he still dreams of finishing the Loop. It felt good seeing him and knowing that there was closure in this relationship. Someday, I'd find a partner, and I was glad it wasn't him.

In this small world of ours, paths will cross. *Bluenoser* Jim came through Southport and we had a party, inviting Mark and Jane, who are building their house a block away from mine. Mark and Jane bought the Southport Inn from Tom. Dean is living on his sailboat, and while anchored in Morehead City, Dean ran into Kat and Kermit from *Good Karma*, who offered him dinner. A patient came into my office, and handed me a picture he had found on the Internet of me crossing my wake.

A friend from Tucson suggested I read the book *Travels with Charley*, by John Steinbeck. I've learned to understand his description: "A journey is a person in itself; no two are alike. And all plans, safeguards, policing, and coercion are fruitless. We find after years of struggle that we do not take a trip; a trip takes us."

For pictures of the actual trip, the blog is still available:

> www.TanyaGreatLoop.blogspot.com

In addition, check out these blogs:

> Average Looper: www.AverageLooper.blogspot.com
>
> Bluenoser Jim: www.Adventuresof Bluenoser.wordpress.com

General information is available at:

> America's Great Loop Cruisers' Association: www.greatloop.org

Acknowledgments:

I would like to thank all the people who made this trip and this book possible. My family and friends have been very supportive throughout the journey. I have had support throughout the boating community, from boat repairmen, dock hands, lock masters, to other boaters and Loopers. There are too many people to name. Strangers, whom I doubt I will ever meet again, showed me kindness along the way.

After returning from doing the Loop, I joined the Writers' Roundtable at St. James, and this group of authors has taught me more about writing than I could have ever imagined. Thank you, Fj Harmon, Flora J Soloman, JoAnn Franklin Klinker, PhD, and Evelyn A. Petros. In addition to these fine writers, I have had editors, Susan Schmidt, PhD and Virginia Jones, PhD, from the Beaufort Writers Group; Susan Warren from Books 'n Stuff in Southport, and Alice Osborn, from Raleigh, North Carolina. Dan Sutkovs, a graphic artist, helped me with the cover design and look at the interior pictures. Tony Alderman painted the picture for the cover. Renee Clement and Jim Fox contributed with pictures. Ron and Eva Stob from Raven Cove Publishing allowed me to reprint America's Great Loop Cruise Route Map.